# MAKING
# SENSE
*of*
# BIBLE
# DIFFICULTIES

# MAKING SENSE

# of

# BIBLE DIFFICULTIES

*Clear and Concise Answers from Genesis to Revelation*

Norman L. Geisler and Thomas Howe

BakerBooks

*a division of Baker Publishing Group*
Grand Rapids, Michigan

Published by Baker Books
a division of Baker Publishing Group
P.O. Box 6287, Grand Rapids, MI 49516-6287
www.bakerbooks.com

Abridged and revised edition published 2009

Paperback edition published in 2008 under the title *The Big Book of Bible Difficulties*

Originally published in 1992 under the title *When Critics Ask*

Printed in the United States of America

Library of Congress Cataloging-in-Publication Data
Geisler, Norman L.
    Making sense of Bible difficulties : clear and concise answers from Genesis to
    Revelation/ Norman L. Geisler & Thomas Howe. —Abridged and rev. ed.
        p.   cm.
    Rev. ed. of: When critics ask.
    Includes bibliographical references. (p.    ).
    ISBN 978-0-8010-7188-1 (pbk.)
    1. Bible—Miscellanea. 2. Bible—Evidences, authority, etc.—Miscellanea. I. Howe,
Thomas A. II. Geisler, Norman L. When critics ask. III. Title.
BS612.G45  2009
220.1′32—dc22                                                           2009021358

# Contents

# Acknowledgments

We wish to thank Bill Roach for his helpful assistance in preparing this manuscript. Also, special thanks is due to Barbara Geisler for the untold hours given in proofreading the manuscript. Without their valuable efforts, this book would be significantly diminished.

# Preface

The Bible is without errors, but the critics are not without criticism. In the face of this, the Bible insists that we "know how you ought to answer each one" (Col. 4:5–6). Peter urged believers, "Sanctify the Lord God in your hearts, and always be ready to give a defense to everyone who asks you of the reason for the hope that is in you, with meekness and fear" (1 Peter 3:15). Indeed, Jesus commanded us to "love the Lord your God with all your heart . . . soul . . . and . . . mind" (Matt. 22:37). Part of this loving duty to Christ is to find answers for those who criticize God's Word. For, as Solomon said, "Answer a fool according to his folly, lest he be wise in his own eyes" (Prov. 26:5).

This book is offered as a guide to fulfill these biblical mandates. Jesus said, "You shall know the truth, and the truth shall make you free" (John 8:32). We have nothing to fear from the truth. Jesus said to the Father, "Your word is truth" (John 17:17). The Bible has withstood the criticisms of the greatest skeptics, agnostics, and atheists down through the centuries, and it is able to withstand the feeble efforts of unbelieving critics today. Unlike many other religions today that appeal to mystical feeling or blind faith, Christianity says, "Look before you leap."

This is a book for those who believe we should *think* about what we believe. God places no premium on ignorance, nor does He reward those who refuse to look at the evidence. On the contrary, He will condemn those who refuse the plain evidence He has revealed (Rom. 1:18–20).

This book grows out of over forty years of attempts to understand the Bible and answer those who would undermine faith in God's eternal Word. It is written as a companion to the Bible, so that one may find the answer to a difficulty in the text at the very place the problem occurs. As you read through the Bible and encounter a difficulty, just look up the verse and study the comment on it. If your question is not answered here, then look in *The Big Book of Bible Difficulties* (Baker, 2008).

In many ways, this book is five books in one. First, it is a book on Bible difficulties that gives answers to many of the major questions raised about the Bible. Second, this is a work in apologetics, since it helps defend the faith once for all delivered to the saints. Third, it functions like a critical commentary, since it treats most of the difficult passages in the Bible. Fourth, it is a book that will help strengthen your spiritual life as you receive answers to your questions and your faith in God's Word is increased. Finally, this book is helpful in pre-evangelism and evangelism. For as you witness for Christ, people will ask you questions to which you may not have an answer. Rather than stop sharing Christ because you fear questions you can't answer, you can continue in confidence because you have a ready guide to help answer the questions of those who sincerely seek to know the truth.

It is our prayer that God will use this book to strengthen your faith and to help bring many others to the faith. Our own confidence in the Sacred Scriptures has increased over the years as we have delved deeper into the marvels of God's truth. We are confident that yours will also.

# Introduction

## How to Approach Bible Difficulties

Critics claim the Bible is filled with errors. Some even speak of thousands of mistakes. The truth is there is not even one demonstrated error in the original text of the Bible.

### The Bible: Errors, No!

This is not to say that there are not *difficulties* in our Bibles. There are, and that is what this book is all about. It is only to point out that there are not actual *errors* in the Scriptures. Why? Because the Bible is the Word of God, and God cannot err. Come, let us reason. Let's put it in logical form and then examine the premises:

> GOD CANNOT ERR.
> THE BIBLE IS THE WORD OF GOD.
> THEREFORE, THE BIBLE CANNOT ERR.

As any student of logic knows, this is a valid syllogism (form of reasoning). So, if the premises are true, the conclusion is also true. As we will show, the Bible clearly declares itself to be the Word of God.[1] It also informs us that God cannot err. The conclusion, then, is inevitable. The Bible cannot err. If the Bible errs in anything it affirms, then God would be mistaken. But God cannot make mistakes.

### God Cannot Err

The Scriptures declare emphatically that "it is impossible for God to lie" (Heb. 6:18). Paul speaks of the "God who cannot lie" (Titus 1:2). He is a God who, even if we are faithless, "remains faithful; He cannot deny Himself" (2 Tim. 2:13). God is truth (John 14:6) and so is His Word. Jesus said to the Father, "Your word is truth" (John 17:17). The psalmist exclaimed, "the entirety of Your word is truth" (Ps. 119:160).

### The Bible Is the Word of God

Jesus referred to the Old Testament (OT) as the "Word of God" that "cannot be broken" (John 10:35). He said, "until heaven and earth disappear, not the smallest letter, not the least stroke of a pen, will by any means disappear from the Law until everything is accomplished" (Matt. 5:18, NIV). Paul added, "All Scripture is God-breathed" (2 Tim. 3:16, NIV). It came "from the mouth of God" (Matt. 4:4). Although human authors recorded the messages, "prophecy never had its origin in the will of man, but men spoke from God as they were carried along by the Holy Spirit" (2 Peter 1:20, NIV).[2]

Jesus said to the religious leaders of His day, "You nullify the word of God by your tradition" (Mark 7:13, NIV). Jesus turned their attention to the written Word of God by affirming over and over again, "It is written . . . It is written . . . It is written" (see Matt. 4:4, 7, 10). This phrase occurs over ninety times in the New Testament (NT). It is a strong indication of the divine authority of the written Word of God. Stressing the unfailing nature of God's truth, the Apostle Paul referred to the Scriptures as "the word of God" (Rom. 9:6). The writer of Hebrews declared that "The word of God is living and active. Sharper than any double-edged sword, it penetrates even to dividing soul and spirit, joints and marrow; it judges the thoughts and attitudes of the heart" (Heb. 4:12, NIV).

### *The Logical Conclusion: The Bible Cannot Err*

Yes, God has spoken, and He has not stuttered. The God of truth has given us the Word of Truth, and it does not contain any untruth in it. The Bible is the unerring Word of God.[3]

### *Can the Bible Be Trusted in Science and History?*

Some have suggested that Scripture can always be trusted on moral matters but it is not always correct on historical matters. They rely on the Word in the spiritual domain, but not in the sphere of science. If true, however, this would render the Bible ineffective as a divine authority for two reasons. First, the whole Bible claims to be the inspired Word of God. Second, the spiritual is often inextricably interwoven with the historical and scientific so that the two cannot be separated.

A close examination of Scripture reveals that the scientific (factual) and the spiritual truths of Scripture are often inseparable. For example, one cannot separate the spiritual truth of Christ's resurrection from the fact that His body permanently vacated the tomb and later physically appeared (Matt. 28:6; 1 Cor. 15:13–19). Likewise, if Jesus was not born of a biological virgin, then He is no different from the rest of the human race on whom the stigma of Adam's sin rests (Rom. 5:12). Likewise, the death of Christ for our sins cannot be detached from His shedding literal blood on the cross, for "without shedding of blood there is no remission" (Heb. 9:22). And Adam's existence and fall cannot be a myth. If there were no literal Adam and no actual fall, then the spiritual teaching about inherited sin and eventual or physical death are wrong (Rom. 5:12). Historical reality and theological doctrine stand or fall together.

Also, the doctrine of the Incarnation is inseparable from the historical truth about Jesus of Nazareth (John 1:1, 14). Further, Jesus's moral teaching about marriage was based on His teaching about God's joining a literal Adam and Eve together in marriage (Matt. 19:4–5). In each of these cases the moral or theological teaching is devoid of its meaning apart from the historical or factual event. If one denies that the literal space-time event occurred, then there is no basis for believing the scriptural doctrine built upon it.

Jesus often directly compared OT events with important spiritual truths, such as His death and resurrection, which were related to Jonah and the great fish (Matt. 12:40). Or His second coming as compared to the days of Noah (Matt. 24:37–39). Both the occasion and the manner of comparison make it clear that Jesus was affirming the historicity of those OT events. Indeed, Jesus asserted to Nicodemus, "If I told you earthly things and you do not believe, how will you believe if I tell you heavenly things?" (John 3:12). In short, if the Bible does not speak truthfully about the physical world, then it cannot be trusted when it speaks about the spiritual world. The two are intimately related.

Inspiration includes not only all that the Bible explicitly *teaches*, but also everything the Bible *touches*. This is true whether the Bible is touching upon history, science, or mathematics. Whatever the Bible declares is true—whether it is a major point or a minor point. The Bible is God's Word, and God does not deviate from the truth in any point. All the parts are as true as the whole that they comprise.

### If It Is Inspired, Then It Is Inerrant

Inerrancy is a logical result of inspiration. Inerrancy means wholly true and without error. And what God breathes out (inspires) must be wholly true (inerrant). However, it is helpful to specify more clearly what is meant by "truth" and what would constitute an "error."[4] By truth we signify that which corresponds to reality. An error, then, is what does not correspond to reality. Truth is telling it like it is. Error is not telling it like it is. Hence, nothing mistaken can be true, even if the author intended his mistake to be true. An error is a mistake, not simply something that is misleading. Otherwise, every sincere utterance ever made is true, even those that were grossly mistaken.[5] Likewise, something is not true simply because it accomplishes its intended purpose, since many lies succeed.

The Bible clearly views truth as that which corresponds to reality. Error is understood as a lack of correspondence to reality, not as intentionally misleading. This is evident from the fact that the word "error" is used of unintentional mistakes (Lev. 4:2). The Bible everywhere implies a correspondence view of truth. For example, when the Ten Commandments declare "You shall not bear false testimony" (Exod. 20:16), it implies that misrepresenting the facts is wrong. Likewise, a correspondence view of truth is used when the Jews said to the governor about Paul, "By examining him yourself you will be able to learn the truth about all these charges we are bringing against him." In so doing, he adds, "You can easily verify the facts" (cf. Acts 24:8).

### *"Has God Said?"*

Of course, wherever God has made the truth clear, Satan's strategy is to cast doubt on it. Whenever God has spoken with authority, the devil desires to undermine it. "Did God really say that?" he sneers (cf. Gen. 3:1). This confusion often takes the following form: the Bible may be the inspired Word of God in some sense, but it is also human words. It had human authors, and "to err is human." Hence we are to expect some errors in the Bible. So goes the argument. In short, the clear, simple truth of God has been confused by the lie of Satan, the master of lies (John 8:44).

Let's analyze what is wrong with this reasoning. A simple analogy will help. Consider some parallel but equally faulty reasoning:

1) Jesus was a human being.
2) Human beings sin.
3) Therefore, Jesus sinned.

Any Bible student can readily see that this conclusion is wrong. Jesus was "without sin" (Heb. 4:15). He "knew no sin" (2 Cor. 5:21). Jesus was "a lamb without blemish or defect" (1 Peter 1:19). As John said of Jesus, "He is pure" and "righteous" (1 John 2:1; 3:3). But, if Jesus never sinned, then what is wrong with the above argument that Jesus is human and humans sin, therefore, Jesus sinned? Where does the logic go astray?

The mistake is to assume that Jesus was like any other human. Sure, mere human beings sin. But, Jesus was not a *mere* human being. He was a perfect human being. Indeed, Jesus was not only human, but He was also God. Likewise, the Bible is not a mere human book. It is also the Word of God. Like Jesus, it is both divine and human. And just as

Jesus was human but did not sin, even so the Bible is a human book but does not err. Both God's living Word (Christ) and His written Word (Scripture) are human but do not err. They are divine and cannot err. There can no more be an error in God's written Word than there was a sin in God's living Word. God cannot err, period.

## The Bible: Difficulties, Yes!

While the Bible is the Word of God and, as such, cannot have any *errors*, nonetheless, this does not mean that there are no *difficulties* in it. However, as St. Augustine wisely noted, "If we are perplexed by any apparent contradiction in Scripture, it is not allowable to say, the author of this book is mistaken; but either the manuscript is faulty, or the translation is wrong, or you have not understood."[6] The mistakes are not in the revelation of God, but are in the misinterpretations of man.

The Bible is without mistake, but the critics are not. All their allegations of error in the Bible are based on some error of their own, and these mistakes fall into the following main categories.

### Mistake 1: Assuming That the Unexplained Is Not Explainable

No informed person would claim to be able to fully explain all Bible difficulties. However, it is a mistake for the critic to assume, therefore, that what has not yet been explained never will be explained. When a scientist comes upon an anomaly in nature, he does not give up further scientific exploration. Rather, he uses the unexplained as a motivation to find an explanation. No real scientist throws up her hands in despair simply because she cannot explain a given phenomenon. She continues to do research with the confident expectation that an answer will be found. And the history of science reveals that such faith has been rewarded over and over again.

Scientists, for example, once had no natural explanation of meteors, eclipses, tornadoes, hurricanes, or earthquakes. Until recently, scientists did not know how the bumblebee could fly. All of these mysteries have yielded their secrets to the relentless patience of science. Neither do scientists know how life can grow on thermo-vents in the depths of the sea. But no scientist throws in the towel and cries "contradiction!"

Likewise, the Christian scholar approaches the Bible with the same presumption that what is thus far unexplained is not therefore unexplainable. He or she does not assume that discrepancies are contradictions. And, when something is encountered for which there is no explanation, he or she simply continues to do research, believing that one will eventually be found. In fact, if he or she assumed the opposite, studying would stop. Why pursue an answer when one assumes there is none? Like their scientific counterparts, Bible students have been rewarded for continued faith and research. For, many difficulties for which scholars once had no answer have yielded to the relentless pursuit of truth through history, archaeology, linguistics, and other disciplines. For example, critics once proposed that Moses could not have written the first five books of the Bible because there was no writing in Moses's day. Now we know that writing was in existence a couple of thousand years or more before Moses. Likewise, critics once believed that the Bible was wrong in speaking of the Hittite people, since they were totally unknown to historians. Now all historians know of their existence by way of their library that was found in Turkey. This gives us confidence to believe that biblical difficulties that have not yet been explained have an explanation and we need not assume there is a mistake in the Bible.

### Mistake 2: Presuming the Bible Guilty until Proven Innocent

Many critics assume the Bible is wrong until something proves it right. However, like an American citizen charged with an offense, the Bible should be presumed "innocent" until proven guilty. This is not asking anything special for the Bible—it is the way we approach all human communication. If we did not, life would not be possible. For example, if we assumed road signs and traffic signals were not telling the truth, then we would probably be dead before we could prove they were telling the truth. Likewise, if we assume food labels are wrong until proven right, we would have to open up all cans and packages before buying. And what if we presumed all the numbers on our currency were wrong? And what if we assumed all restroom signs were wrong? Well, enough is enough.

The Bible, like any other book, should be presumed to be telling us what the authors said and heard. Negative critics of the Bible begin with just the opposite presumption. Little wonder, then, that they conclude the Bible is riddled with error.

### Mistake 3: Confusing Our Fallible Interpretations with God's Infallible Revelation

Jesus affirmed that the "Scripture cannot be broken" (John 10:35). As an infallible book, the Bible is also irrevocable. Jesus declared, "Truly I say to you, until heaven and earth pass away, not the smallest letter or stroke shall pass away from the Law, until all is accomplished" (Matt. 5:18, NIV; cf. Luke 16:17). The Scriptures also have final authority, being the last word on all it discusses. Jesus employed the Bible to resist the tempter (Matt. 4:4, 7, 10), to settle doctrinal disputes (Matt. 21:42), and to vindicate His authority (Mark 11:17). Sometimes a biblical teaching rests on a small historical detail (Heb. 7:4–10), a word or phrase (Acts 15:13–17), or even the difference between the singular and the plural (Gal. 3:16). But, while the Bible is infallible, human interpretations are not. The Bible cannot be mistaken, but we can be mistaken about the Bible. The meaning of the Bible does not change, but our understanding of its meaning does.

Human beings are finite, and finite beings make mistakes. That is why there are erasers on pencils, correcting fluid for typing, and a "delete" key on computers. And even though God's Word is perfect (Ps. 19:7), as long as imperfect human beings exist, there will be misinterpretations of God's Word and false views about His world. In view of this, one should not be hasty in assuming that a currently dominant view in science is the final word on the topic. Prevailing views of science in the past are considered errors by scientists in the present. So, contradictions between popular opinions in science and widely accepted interpretations of the Bible can be expected. But this falls short of proving there is a real contradiction between God's world and God's Word, between God's general revelation and His special revelation. In this basic sense, science and Scripture are not contradictory. Only finite, fallible human opinions about each can be contradictory.

### Mistake 4: Failing to Understand the Context of the Passage

Perhaps the most common mistake of critics is to take a text out of its proper context. As the adage goes, "A text out of context is a pretext." One can prove anything from the Bible by this mistaken procedure. The Bible says, "there is no God" (Ps. 14:1). Of course, the context is that "The fool has said in his heart, 'There is no God'" (Ps. 14:1). One may claim that Jesus admonished us "not to resist an evil" (Matt. 5:39), but the anti-retaliatory context in which He cast this statement must not be ignored. Likewise, many fail to understand the context of Jesus's statement to "Give to him who asks you," as though one had an obligation to give a gun to a small child who asked, or nuclear weapons to a militant dictator just because he asked. Failure to note that meaning is determined by context is perhaps the chief sin of those who find fault with the Bible, as comments on numerous pages in this book will illustrate.

### Mistake 5: Neglecting to Interpret Difficult Passages in the Light of Clear Ones

Some passages of Scripture are hard to understand. Sometimes the difficulty is due to their obscurity. At other times, the difficulty is because passages appear to be teaching something contrary to what some other part of Scripture is clearly teaching. For example, James appears to be saying salvation is by works (James 2:14–26), whereas Paul taught clearly that it was by grace (Rom. 4:5; Titus 3:5–7; Eph. 2:8–9). In this case, James should *not* be construed as contradicting Paul. Paul is speaking about justification *before God* (which is by faith alone), whereas James is referring to justification *before men* (who cannot see our faith, but only our works).

Another example is found in Philippians 2:12 where Paul says, "work out your own salvation with fear and trembling." On the surface this appears to be saying salvation is by works. However, this is flatly contradicted by a host of Scriptures that clearly affirm that we are "saved by grace through faith, and that not of ourselves; it is a gift of God, not of works, lest anyone should boast" (Eph. 2:8–9). And, "to him who does not work but believes on Him who justifies the ungodly, his faith is accounted for righteousness" (Rom. 4:5). Also, it "is not by works of righteousness which we have done, but according to His mercy [that] He saved us" (Titus 3:5–6). When this difficult statement about "working out our salvation" is understood in the light of these clear passages, we can see that, whatever it *does* mean, it *does not* mean that we are saved by works. In fact, what it means is found in the very next verse. We are to work salvation *out* because God's grace has worked it *in* our hearts. In Paul's words, "for it is God who works in you both to will and to do for His good pleasure" (Phil. 2:13).

### Mistake 6: Basing a Teaching on an Obscure Passage

Some passages in the Bible are difficult because their meanings are obscure. This is usually because a key word in the text is used only once (or rarely), and so it is difficult to know what the author is saying, unless it can be inferred from the context. For example, one of the best-known passages in the Bible contains a word that appears nowhere else in all existing Greek literature up to the time the NT was written. This word appears in what is popularly known as the Lord's Prayer (Matt. 6:11). It is usually translated, "Give us this day our daily bread." The word in question is the one translated "daily"—*epiousion*. Experts in Greek still have not come to any agreement either on its origin or its precise meaning. Different commentators try to establish links with Greek words that are well-known, and many suggestions have been proposed as to the resulting meaning. Among these are:

Give us this day our *continuous* bread.

Give us this day our *supersubstantial* (indicating supernatural, from heaven) bread.

Give us this day bread *for our sustenance.*

Give us this day our *daily* (or, what we need for today) bread.

Each one of these proposals has its defenders, each one makes sense in the context, and each one is a possibility based on the limited information that is available. There does not seem to be any compelling reason to depart from what has become the generally accepted translation, but this example does serve to illustrate the point. Some passages of the Bible are difficult to understand because the meaning of some key word appears only once, or very rarely.

At other times, the words may be clear but the meaning is not evident because we are not sure to what they refer. This is true in 1 Corinthians 15:29 where Paul speaks of those who were "baptized for the dead." Is he referring to the baptizing of live representatives to ensure salvation for dead believers who were not baptized (as Mormons claim)? Or, is he referring to others being baptized into the church to fill the ranks of those who have passed on? Or, is he referring to a believer being baptized "for" (i.e., "with a view to") his own death and burial with Christ? Or to something else?

When we are not sure, then several things should be kept in mind. First, we should not build a doctrine on an obscure passage. The rule of thumb in Bible interpretation is "the main things are the plain things, and the plain things are the main things." This is called the perspicuity (clearness) of Scripture. If something is important, it will be clearly taught in Scripture and probably in more than one place. Second, when a given passage is not clear, we should never conclude that it means something that is opposed to another plain teaching of Scripture. God does not make mistakes in His Word; we make mistakes in trying to understand it.

### Mistake 7: Forgetting That the Bible Is a Human Book with Human Characteristics

With the exception of small sections, like the Ten Commandments that were "written with the finger of God" (Exod. 31:18), the Bible was not verbally dictated.[7] The writers were not secretaries of the Holy Spirit. They were human composers employing their own literary styles and idiosyncrasies. These human authors sometimes used *human sources* for their material (Josh. 10:13; Acts 17:28; 1 Cor. 15:33; Titus 1:12). In fact, every book of the Bible is the composition of a *human writer*—about forty of them in all. The Bible also manifests different *human literary* styles, from the mournful meter of Lamentations to the exalted poetry of Isaiah; from the simple grammar of John to the complex Greek of

Hebrews. Scripture also manifests *human perspectives*. David spoke in Psalm 23 from a shepherd's perspective. Kings is written from a prophetic vantage point, and Chronicles from a priestly point of view. Acts manifests a historical interest and 2 Timothy a pastor's heart. Writers speak from an observer's standpoint when they write of the sun rising or setting (Josh. 1:15). They also reveal *human thought patterns*, including memory lapses (1 Cor. 1:14–16), as well as *human emotions* (Gal. 4:14). The Bible discloses specific *human interests*. For example, Hosea possessed a rural interest, Luke a medical concern, and James a love of nature.[8] But like Christ, the Bible is completely human, yet without error. Forgetting the humanity of Scripture can lead to falsely impugning its integrity by expecting a level of expression higher than that which is customary to a human document. This will become more obvious as we discuss the next mistake of the critics.

### Mistake 8: Assuming That a Partial Report Is a False Report

Critics often jump to the conclusion that a partial report is false. However, this is not so. If it were, most of what has ever been said would be false, since seldom does time or space permit an absolutely complete report. Occasionally the Bible expresses the same thing in different ways, or at least from different viewpoints, at different times. Hence, inspiration does not exclude a diversity of expression. The four Gospels relate the same story in different ways to different groups of people, and sometimes even quote the same saying with different words. Compare, for example, Peter's famous confession in the Gospels:

Matthew: "You are the Christ, the Son of the living God" (16:16).
Mark: "You are the Christ" (8:29).
Luke: "The Christ of God" (9:20).

Even the Ten Commandments, which were "written with the finger of God" (Deut. 9:10), are stated with variations the second time God gave them (cf. Exod. 20:8–11 with Deut. 5:12–15). There are many differences between the books of Kings and Chronicles in their description of identical events, yet they harbor no contradiction in the events they narrate. If such important utterances can be stated in different ways, then there is no reason the rest of Scripture cannot speak truth without employing a wooden literalness of expression.

### Mistake 9: Demanding That NT Citations of the OT Always Be Exact Quotations

Critics often point to variations in the NT's use of the OT Scriptures as a proof of error. However, they forget that every *citation* need not be an exact *quotation*. It was then (and still is today) a perfectly acceptable literary style to give the *essence* of a statement without using precisely the *same words*. The same *meaning* can be conveyed without using same *verbal expressions*.

Variations in the NT citations of the OT fall into different categories. Sometimes they vary because there is a change of speaker. For example, Zechariah records the Lord as saying, "they will look on *Me* whom they have pierced" (12:10). When this is cited in the NT, John, not God, is speaking. So it is changed to "They shall look on *Him* whom they pierced" (John 19:37).

At other times, writers cite only part of the OT text. Jesus did this at His home synagogue in Nazareth (Luke 4:18–19, citing Isa. 61:1–2). In fact, He stopped in the middle of a sentence. Had He gone any further, He could not have said as He did, "Today this Scripture is fulfilled in your hearing" (v. 21). For the very next phrase, "And the day of vengeance of our God," is a reference to His second coming.

Sometimes the NT paraphrases or summarizes the OT text (e.g., Matt. 2:6). Others blend two texts into one (Matt. 27:9–10). Occasionally a general truth is mentioned, without citing a specific text. For example, Matthew said Jesus moved to Nazareth "that it might be fulfilled which was spoken by the prophets, 'He shall be called a Nazarene'" (Matt. 2:23). Notice, Matthew quotes no given prophet, but rather "prophets" in general. So it would be futile to insist on a specific OT text where this could be found.

There are also instances where the NT applies a text in a different way than the OT did. For example, Hosea applies "Out of Egypt have I called My son" to the Messianic nation, and Matthew applies it to the product of that nation, the Messiah (Matt. 2:15, from Hos. 11:1). In no case, however, does the NT misinterpret or misapply the OT, nor draw some implication from it that is not validly drawn from it. In short, the NT makes no mistakes in citing the OT, as the critics do in citing the NT.

### Mistake 10: Assuming That Divergent Accounts Are False Ones

Just because two or more accounts of the same event differ, it does not mean they are mutually exclusive. For example, Matthew (28:5) says there was one angel at the tomb after the resurrection, whereas John informs us there were two (20:12). But these are not contradictory reports. In fact, there is an infallible mathematical rule that easily explains this problem: wherever there are two, there is always one—it never fails! Matthew did not say there was *only* one angel. One has to add the word "only" to Matthew's account to make it contradict John's. But if the critic comes to the Bible in order to show it errs, then the error is not in the Bible, but in the critic.

Likewise, Matthew (27:5) informs us that Judas hanged himself. But Luke says that "he burst open in the middle and all his entrails gushed out" (Acts 1:18). Once more, these accounts differ, but they are not mutually exclusive. If Judas hanged himself on a tree over the edge of a cliff and his body fell on sharp rocks below, then his entrails would gush out just as Luke vividly describes.

### Mistake 11: Presuming That the Bible Approves of All It Records

It is a mistake to assume that everything contained in the Bible is commended by the Bible. The whole Bible is *true* (John 17:17), but it records some *lies*, for example, Satan's (Gen. 3:4; cf. John 8:44) and Rahab's (Josh. 2:4). Inspiration encompasses the Bible fully and completely in the sense that it records accurately and truthfully even the lies and errors of sinful beings. The truth of Scripture is found in what the Bible *reveals*, not in everything it *records*. Unless this distinction is held, it may be incorrectly concluded that the Bible teaches immorality because it narrates David's sin (2 Sam. 11:4), that it promotes polygamy because it records Solomon's (1 Kings 11:3), or that it affirms atheism because it quotes the fool as saying "there is no God" (Ps. 14:1).

### Mistake 12: Forgetting That the Bible Uses Nontechnical, Everyday Language

To be true, something does not have to use scholarly, technical, or so-called "scientific" language. The Bible is written for the common person of every generation, and it therefore uses common, everyday language. The use of observational, nonscientific language is not *un*scientific, it is merely *pre*scientific. The Scriptures were written in *ancient* times by ancient standards, and it would be anachronistic to superimpose *modern* scientific standards upon them. However, it is no more unscientific to speak of the sun "standing still" (Josh. 10:12) than to refer to the sun "rising" (Josh. 1:16). Contemporary meteorologists still speak daily of the time of "sunrise" and "sunset."

### Mistake 13: Assuming That Round Numbers Are False

Another mistake sometimes made by Bible critics is claiming that round numbers are false. This is not so. Round numbers are just that—round numbers. Like most ordinary speech, the Bible uses round numbers (1 Chron. 19:18; 21:5). For example, it refers to the diameter as being about one-third of the circumference of something. It may be imprecise from the standpoint of a contemporary technological society to speak of 3.14159265 . . . as the number three, but it is not incorrect for an ancient, nontechnological people. Three and fourteen hundredths can be rounded off to three. That is sufficient for a "Sea of cast metal" (2 Chron. 4:2, NIV) in an ancient Hebrew temple, even though it would not suffice for a computer in a modern rocket. But one should not expect scientific precision in a prescientific age. In fact, it would be as anachronistic as wearing a wristwatch in a Shakespearian play.

### Mistake 14: Neglecting to Note That the Bible Uses Different Literary Devices

An inspired book need not be composed in one, and only one, literary style. Human beings wrote every book in the Bible, and human language is not limited to one mode of expression. There is no reason to suppose that only one style or literary genre was used in a divinely inspired Book. The Bible reveals a number of literary devices. Several whole books are written in poetic style (e.g., Job, Psalms, Proverbs). The Synoptic Gospels are filled with parables. In Galatians 4, Paul utilizes an allegory. The NT abounds with metaphors (e.g., 2 Cor. 3:2–3; James 3:6) and similes (cf. Matt. 20:1; James 1:6); hyperboles may also be found (e.g., Col. 1:23; John 21:25; 2 Cor. 3:2), and possibly even poetic figures (Job 41:1). Jesus employed satire (Matt. 19:24 with 23:24), and figures of speech are common throughout the Bible.

It is not a mistake for a biblical writer to use a figure of speech, but it is a mistake for a reader to take a figure of speech literally. Obviously when the Bible speaks of the believer resting under the shadow of God's "wings" (Ps. 36:7), it does not mean that God is a feathered bird. Likewise, when the Bible says God "awakes" (Ps. 44:23), as though He were sleeping, it is a figure of speech indicating God's inactivity before He is aroused to judgment by man's sin. We must be careful in our reading of figures of speech in Scripture.

### Mistake 15: Forgetting That Only the Original Text, Not Every Copy of Scripture, Is without Error

When critics do come upon a genuine mistake in a manuscript copy, they make another fatal error—they assume it was in the original inspired text of Scripture. They forget that God only uttered the original text of Scripture, not the copies. Therefore, only the original text is without error. Inspiration does not guarantee that every copy of the original is without error. Therefore, we are to expect that minor errors are to be found in manuscript copies. But, again, as St. Augustine wisely noted, when we run into a so-called "error" in the Bible, we must assume one of two things—either the manuscript was not copied correctly, or we have not understood it rightly. What we may not assume is that God made an error in inspiring the original text.

While present copies of Scripture are very good, they are not without error. For example, 2 Kings 8:26 gives the age of King Ahaziah as twenty-two, whereas 2 Chronicles 22:2 says forty-two. The later number cannot be correct, or he would have been older than his father. This is obviously a copyist error, but it does not alter the inerrancy of the original.

Several things should be observed about these copyist errors. First of all, they are errors in the copies, not the original. No one has ever found an original manuscript with an error in it. Second, they are minor errors (often in names or numbers) that do not affect any doctrine of the Christian faith. Third, these copyist errors are relatively few in number, as will be illustrated throughout the rest of this book. Fourth, usually by the context, or by another Scripture, we know which one is in error. For example, Ahaziah (above) must have been twenty-two, not forty-two, since he could not be older than his father. Finally, even though there is a copyist error, the entire message can still come through. In such a case, the validity of the message is not changed. For example, if you received a letter like this, would you understand the whole message? And would you collect your money?

> "#OU HAVE WON THE FIVE MILLION DOLLAR
> READER'S DIGEST SWEEPSTAKES."

Even though there is a mistake in the first word, the entire message comes through—you are five million dollars richer! And if you received another letter the next day that read like this, you would be even more sure:

> "Y#U HAVE WON THE FIVE MILLION DOLLAR
> READER'S DIGEST SWEEPSTAKES."

Actually the more mistakes of this kind there are (each in a different place), the more sure you are of the original message. This is why scribal mistakes in the biblical manuscripts do not affect the basic message of the Bible. So, for all practical purposes, the Bible in our hand, imperfect though the manuscripts are, conveys the complete truth of the original Word of God.

### Mistake 16: Confusing General Statements with Universal Ones

Critics often jump to the conclusion that unqualified statements admit of no exceptions. They seize upon verses that offer general truths and then point with glee to obvious exceptions. In so doing, they forget that such statements are only intended to be generalizations.

The Book of Proverbs is a good example of such an issue. Proverbial sayings by their very nature offer only general guidance, not universal assurance. They are rules for life, but rules that admit of exceptions. Proverbs 16:7 is a case in point. It affirms that "when a man's ways please the Lord, He makes even his enemies to be at peace with him." This obviously was not intended to be a universal truth. Paul was pleasing to the Lord and his enemies stoned him (Acts 14:19). Jesus was pleasing the Lord, and His enemies crucified Him! Nonetheless, it is a general truth that one who acts in a way pleasing to God can minimize his enemies' antagonism.

Another example of a general truth is Proverbs 22:6, "Train up a child in the way he should go, and when he is old he will not depart from it." However, other Scripture passages and experience show that this is not always true. Indeed, some godly persons in the Bible (including Job, Eli, and David) had some very wayward children. This proverb does not contradict experience because it is a general principle that applies in a general way, but allows for individual exceptions. Proverbs are not designed to be absolute guarantees. Rather, they express truths that provide helpful advice and guidance by which an individual should conduct his or her daily life.

It is simply a mistake to assume that proverbial wisdom is always universally true. Proverbs are *wisdom* (general guides), not *law* (universally binding imperatives). When the Bible declares "You shall therefore be holy, for I am holy" (Lev. 11:45), then there are no exceptions. Holiness, goodness, love, truth, and justice are rooted in the very nature of an unchanging God and therefore admit of no exceptions. But wisdom takes God's universal truths and applies them to specific and changing circumstances that, by their very nature as changing, will not always yield the same results. Nonetheless, they are still helpful guides for life, even though they may admit of an occasional exception.

### Mistake 17: Forgetting That Later Revelation Supersedes Previous Revelation

Sometimes critics of Scripture forget the principle of progressive revelation. God does not reveal everything at once, nor does He always lay down the same conditions for every period of time. Therefore, some of His later revelation will supersede His former statements. Bible critics sometimes confuse a *change* of revelation with a *mistake*. The mistake, however, is that of the critic. For example, the fact that a parent allows a very small child to eat with his fingers, only to tell him later to use a spoon, is not a contradiction. Nor is the parent contradicting herself to insist later that the child should use a fork, not a spoon, to eat his vegetables. This is progressive revelation, with each command suited to fit the particular circumstance in which a person is found.

There was a time when God tested the human race by forbidding them to eat of a specific tree in the Garden of Eden (Gen. 2:16–17). This command is no longer in effect, but the later revelation does not contradict this former revelation. Also, there was a period (under the Mosaic law) when God commanded that animals be sacrificed for people's sin. However, since Christ offered the perfect sacrifice for sin (Heb. 10:11–14), this OT command is no longer in effect. Here again, there is no contradiction between the latter and the former commands. Likewise, when God created the human race, He commanded that they eat only fruits and vegetables (Gen. 1:29). But later, when conditions changed after the flood, God commanded that they also eat meat (Gen. 9:3). This change from herbivorous to omnivorous status is progressive revelation, but it is not a contradiction. In fact, all these subsequent revelations were simply different commands for different people at different times in God's overall plan of redemption.

Of course, God cannot change commands that have to do with His unchangeable nature (cf. Mal. 3:6; Heb. 6:18). For example, since God is love (1 John 4:16), He cannot command that we hate Him. Nor can He command what is logically impossible—for example, to both offer and not offer a sacrifice for sin at the same time and in the same sense. But these moral and logical limits notwithstanding, God can and has given noncontradictory, progressive revelation that, if taken out of its proper context and juxtaposed with each other, can be made to look contradictory. This, however, is just as much a mistake as to assume a parent is contradicting herself when she allows a child to stay up later at night as he gets older.

After forty years of continual and careful study of the Bible, one can only conclude that those who think they have discovered a mistake in the Bible do not know too much about the Bible—they know too little about it! This does not mean, of course, that we understand all the difficulties in the Scriptures. But it does lead us to believe that Mark Twain was correct when he concluded that it was not the part of the Bible he did not understand that bothered him the most, but the parts he did understand!

# GENESIS

**How can the universe have a "beginning" when modern science says energy is eternal?**

**Problem:** According to the First Law of Thermodynamics, "Energy can neither be created nor destroyed." If this is so, then the universe must be eternal, since it is made of indestructible energy. However, the Bible indicates that the universe had a "beginning" and did not exist before God "created" it (Gen. 1:1). Is this not a contradiction between the Bible and science?

**Solution:** There is a conflict of opinion here, but no real factual contradiction. The factual evidence indicates that the universe is not eternal, but that it did have a beginning just as the Bible says. Several observations are relevant here.

First of all, the First Law of Thermodynamics is often misstated to the effect that energy "cannot be created." However, science is based on observation, and statements such as "can" or "cannot" are not based on observation, but are dogmatic pronouncements. The First Law should be stated like this: "[So far as we can observe] the amount of *actual* energy in the universe remains constant." That is, as far as we know, the actual amount of energy in the universe is not decreasing or increasing. Stated this way, the First Law makes no pronouncement whatsoever about where energy came from, or how long it has been here. Thus, it does not contradict the Genesis declaration that God created the universe.

Second, another well-established scientific law is the Second Law of Thermodynamics. It states that "the amount of *usable* energy in the universe is decreasing." According to this Law, the universe is running down. Its energy is being transformed into unusable heat. If this is so, then the universe is not eternal, since it would have run out of usable energy, a long time ago. Or, to put it another way: if the universe is unwinding, then it was wound up. If it had an infinite amount of energy it would never run down. Therefore, the universe had a beginning, just as Genesis 1:1 says it did.

## GENESIS 1:14

### How could there be light before the sun was made?

**Problem:** The sun was not created until the fourth day, yet there was light on the first day (1:3).

**Solution:** The sun is not the only source of light in the universe. Further, the sun may have existed from the first day, but only appeared or became visible (as the mist cleared) on the fourth day. We see light on a cloudy day, even when we can't see the sun.

## GENESIS 1:27

### Were Adam and Eve real people or just myths?

**Problem:** Many modern scholars consider the first chapter of Genesis to be myth, not history. But the Bible seems to present Adam and Eve as literal people, who had real children from whom the rest of the human race came (cf. Gen. 5:1ff).

**Solution:** There is good evidence to believe that Adam and Eve were real persons. First, Genesis 1–2 presents them as actual persons and even narrates the important events in their lives (= history). Second, they gave birth to literal children who did the same (Gen. 4:1, 25; 5:1ff). Third, the same phrase ("this is the history of"), used to record later history in Genesis (6:9; 9:12; 10:1, 32; 11:10, 27; 17:7, 9), is used of Adam and Eve (Gen. 5:1). Fourth, later OT chronologies place Adam at the top of the list (1 Chron. 1:1). Fifth, the NT places Adam at the beginning of Jesus's literal ancestors (Luke 3:38). Sixth, Jesus referred to Adam and Eve as the first literal "male and female," making their physical union the basis of marriage (Matt. 19:4). Seventh, Romans declares that literal death was brought into the world by a literal "Adam" (Rom. 5:14). Eighth, the comparison of Adam (the "first Adam") with Christ (the "last Adam") in 1 Corinthians 15:45 manifests that Adam was understood as a literal, historical person. Ninth, Paul's declaration that "Adam was formed first, then Eve" (1 Tim. 2:13–14) reveals that he speaks of a real person. Tenth, logically there had to be a first real set of human beings, male and female, or else the race would have had no way to begin. The Bible calls this literal couple "Adam and Eve," and there is no reason to doubt their real existence.

## GENESIS 2:1

### How could the world be created in six days?

**Problem:** The Bible says that God created the world in six days (Exod. 20:11). But modern science declares that it took billions of years. Both cannot be true.

**Solution:** There are basically two ways to reconcile this difficulty. First, some scholars argue that modern science is wrong. They insist that the universe is only thousands of years old and that God created everything in six literal 24-hour days (144 hours). In favor of this view, they offer the following:

1. The days of Genesis have "evening and the morning" (cf. Gen. 1:5, 8, 13, 19, 23, 31), something unique to 24-hour days in the Bible.
2. The days were numbered (first, second, third, etc.), a feature found only with 24-hour days in the Bible.
3. Exodus 20:11 compares the six days of creation with the six days of a literal workweek of 144 hours.
4. There is scientific evidence to support a young age (of thousands of years) for the earth.

5. There is no way life could survive millions of years from
day three (1:11) to day four (1:14) without light.

Other Bible scholars claim that the universe could be billions of
years old without sacrificing a literal understanding of Genesis 1
and 2. They argue that:

1. The days of Genesis 1 could have a time lapse before the
days began (before Gen. 1:3), or a time gap between days.
There are gaps elsewhere in the Bible (cf. Matt. 1:8, where
three generations are omitted, with 1 Chron. 3:11–14).
2. The same Hebrew word "day" (*yom*) is used in Genesis 1–2
as a period of time longer than 24 hours. For example, Genesis 2:4 uses it of the whole six-day period of creation.
3. Sometimes the Bible uses the word "day" for long periods
of time: "One day is as a thousand years" (2 Peter 3:8; cf.
Ps. 90:4).
4. There are some indications in Genesis 1–2 that days could
be longer than 24 hours:
   a) On the third "day" trees grew from seeds to maturity
   and they bore like seeds (1:11–12). This process normally takes months or years.
   b) On the sixth "day" Adam was created, went to sleep,
   named all the (thousands of) animals, looked for a help-
   meet, went to sleep, and Eve was created from his rib.
   This looks like more than 24 hours worth of activity.
   c) The Bible says God "rested" on the seventh day (2:2),
   and that He is still in His rest from creation (Heb.
   4:4). Thus, the seventh day is thousands of years long
   already. If so, then other days could be thousands of
   years too.
5. Exodus 20:11 could make a unit-for-unit comparison between the days of Genesis and a workweek (of 144 hours),
not a minute-by-minute comparison.

*Conclusion:* There is no demonstrated contradiction of fact between Genesis 1 and science. There is only a conflict of interpre-

tation. Either *most* modern scientists are wrong in insisting the world is billions of years old, or else *some* Bible interpreters are wrong in insisting on only 144 hours of creation some several thousand years before Christ, with no gaps allowing millions of years. But in either case it is not a question of the *inspiration* of Scripture, but of the *interpretation* of Scripture (and of the scientific data).

## GENESIS 2:8

### Was the Garden of Eden a real place or just a myth?

**Problem:** The Bible declares that God "planted the garden eastward in Eden" (Gen. 2:8), but there is no archaeological evidence that any such place existed. Is this just a myth?

**Solution:** First of all, we would not expect any archaeological evidence, since there is no indication that Adam and Eve made pottery or built durable buildings. Second, there is geographical evidence of Eden, since two of the rivers mentioned still exist today—the Tigris (Hiddekel) and the Euphrates (Gen. 2:14). Further, the Bible even locates them in "Assyria" (v. 14), which is present-day Iraq. Finally, whatever evidence there may have been for the Garden of Eden (Gen. 2–3) was probably destroyed by God at the time of the flood (Gen. 6–9).

## GENESIS 2:19

### How can we explain the difference in the order of creation events between Genesis 1 and 2?

**Problem:** Genesis 1 declares that animals were created before humans, but Genesis 2:19 seems to reverse this, saying, "the Lord God formed every beast of the field . . . and brought them to Adam to see what he would call them," implying that Adam was created before they were.

**Solution:** Genesis 1 gives the *order* of events; Genesis 2 provides more *content* about them. Genesis 2 does not contradict chapter 1, since it does not affirm exactly *when* God created the animals. He simply says He brought the animals (that He had previously created) to Adam so that he might name them. The focus in chapter

2 is on the *naming* of the animals, not on *creating* them. Genesis 1 provides the *outline* of events, and chapter 2 gives the *details*. Taken together, the two chapters provide a harmonious and more complete picture of the creation events. The differences, then, can be summarized as follows:

| GENESIS 1 | GENESIS 2 |
|---|---|
| Chronological order | Topical order |
| Outline | Details |
| Creating animals | Naming animals |

## GENESIS 4:17

*Where did Cain get his wife?*

**Problem:** There were no women for Cain to marry. There was only Adam, Eve (4:1), and his dead brother, Abel (4:8). Yet the Bible says Cain married and had children.

**Solution:** Cain married his sister (or possibly a niece). The Bible says Adam "Begot sons and *daughters*" (Gen. 5:4). In fact, since Adam lived 930 years (Gen. 5:5), he had plenty of time for plenty of children! Cain could have married one of his many sisters, or even a niece, if he married after his brothers or sisters had grown daughters. In that case, of course, one of his brothers would have married a sister, which was not forbidden until much later (in Lev. 18:9).

## GENESIS 5:1ff

*How can we reconcile this chronology (which adds up to c. 4,000 years BC) when anthropology has shown humankind is much older?*

**Problem:** If the ages are added in Genesis 5 and 10 with the rest of the OT dates, it comes out to 4,000 plus years BC. But archaeologists and anthropologists date modern man many thousands of years before that (at least 10,000 years ago).

**Solution:** There is good evidence to support the belief that humankind is more than 6,000 years old. But there are also good reasons to believe there are some gaps in the Genesis genealogies. First, we know there is a gap in the genealogy in the Book of Matthew. Matthew's genealogy says, "Joram begot Uzziah" (Matt. 1:8). But when compared to 1 Chronicles 3:11–14, we see that Matthew leaves out three generations—Ahaziah, Joash, and Amaziah, as follows:

| Matthew | 1 Chronicles |
| --- | --- |
| Joram | Joram |
| — | Ahaziah |
| — | Joash |
| — | Amaziah |
| Uzziah | Uzziah (also called Azariah) |

Second, there is at least one generation missing in the Genesis genealogy. Luke 3:36 lists "Cainan" between Arphaxad and Shelah, but the name Cainan does not appear in the Genesis record at this point (see Gen. 10:22–24). It is better to view Genesis 5 and 10 as adequate *genealogies*, not as complete *chronologies*.

Finally, since there are known gaps in the genealogies, we cannot accurately determine the age of the human race by simply adding the numbers in Genesis 5 and 10.

## GENESIS 6:14ff

### *How could Noah's ark hold hundreds of thousands of species of animals?*

**Problem:** The Bible says Noah's ark was only 45 feet high, 75 feet wide, and 450 feet long (Gen. 6:15, NIV). Noah was told to take two of every kind of unclean animal and seven of every kind of clean animal (6:19; 7:2). But scientists inform us that there are between half a billion to over a billion species of animals.

**Solution:** First, the modern concept of "species" is not the same as a "kind" in the Bible. There are probably only several hundred different "kinds" of land animals that would have to be taken into the ark. The sea animals stayed in the sea, and many species could have survived in egg or seed form. Second, the ark was not small; it was a huge structure—the size of a modern ocean liner.

Furthermore, it had three stories (6:16), which tripled its space to a total of over 1.5 million cubic feet!

Third, Noah could have taken younger or smaller varieties of some larger animals. Given all these factors, there was plenty of room for all the animals, food for the trip, and the eight humans aboard.

## GENESIS 6:14ff

### How could a wooden ark survive such a violent flood?

**Problem:** The ark was only made of wood and carried a heavy load of cargo. But a worldwide flood produces violent waters that would have broken it in pieces (cf. Gen. 7:4, 11).

**Solution:** First, the ark was made of a strong and flexible material (gopher wood) that "gives" without breaking. The famous early American ship *Old Ironside* was made of wood—and it was so thick and strong that the British cannon balls bounced off it! Second, the heavy load was an advantage that gave the ark stability. Third, naval architects inform us that a long box-shaped, floating boxcar, such as the ark, is a very stable craft in turbulent waters. Indeed, modern ocean liners follow the same basic dimensions or proportions of Noah's ark.

## GENESIS 8:1

### Did God temporarily forget Noah?

**Problem:** The fact that the text says that "God remembered Noah" seems to imply that He temporarily forgot him. Yet the Bible declares that God knows all things (Ps. 139:2–4; Jer. 17:10; Heb. 4:13) and that He never forgets His saints (Isa. 49:15). How then could He temporarily forget Noah?

**Solution:** In His omniscience, God was always aware of Noah being in the ark. However, after Noah was left in the ark for over a year, *as if* he were forgotten, God gave a token of His remembrance and brought Noah and his family out of it. But, God had never forgotten Noah, since it was He who warned Noah in the very beginning in order to save him and the human race (cf. Gen. 6:8–13). We often use a similar expression when we "remember" someone on their birthday, even though we had never forgotten they existe Like God's remembrance of Noah, it is a *special* remembrance, not just a general awareness.

## GENESIS 8:22

*If seedtime and harvest were never to be interrupted, then why were there famines?*

**Problem:** God promised Noah: "While the earth remains, seedtime and harvest... shall not cease." However, there are many famines recorded, even in Bible times, when there has been no harvest (cf. Gen. 26:1; 41:54).

**Solution:** "Cease" (*shabath*) means to come to an end, to be eliminated, to desist completely. This passage only promises that the *seasons* will not cease, not the *crops*. It refers to "seedtime" and harvesttime, not necessarily to the actual planting and harvesting of a crop. And the seasons have never stopped completely since this promise was made to Noah. Further, this general promise was not intended as a guarantee that there would be no *temporary* interruptions. It was only a statement about the *permanent* cycles of the year until the end of time.

## GENESIS 19:8

*Was the sin of Sodom homosexuality or inhospitality?*

**Problem:** Some have argued that the sin of Sodom and Gomorrah was inhospitality, not homosexuality. They base this claim on the Canaanite custom that guarantees protection for those coming under one's roof. Lot is alleged to have referred to it when he said, "don't do anything to these men, for they have come under the protection of my roof" (Gen. 19:8, NIV). So Lot offered his daughters to satisfy the angry crowd in order to protect the lives of the visitors who had come under his roof. Some also claim that the request of the men of the city to "know" (Gen. 19:5) simply means "to get acquainted," since the Hebrew word "know" (*yada*) generally has no sexual connotations whatsoever (cf. Ps. 139:1).

**Solution:** While it is true that the Hebrew word "know" (*yada*) does not necessarily mean "to have sex with," nonetheless, in the con-

ssage on Sodom and Gomorrah, it clearly has this
is evident for several reasons.

n of the twelve times this word is used in Genesis,
.ɔ sexual intercourse (cf. Gen. 4:1, 25).

Second, it means "to know sexually" in this very chapter. For
Lot refers to his two virgin daughters as not having "known" a
man (19:8), which is an obvious sexual use of the word.

Third, the meaning of a word is discovered by the context in
which it is used. And the context here is definitely sexual, as is
indicated by the reference to the wickedness of the city (18:20),
and the virgins offered to appease their passions (19:8).

Fourth, "know" cannot mean simply "get acquainted with,"
because it is equated with a "wicked thing" (19:7).

Fifth, why offer the virgin daughters to appease them if their
intent was not sexual? If the men had asked to "know" the virgin
daughters, no one would have mistaken their sexual intentions.

Sixth, God had already determined to destroy Sodom and Gomorrah, as Genesis 18:16–33 indicates, even before the incident in
19:8. Consequently, it is much more reasonable to hold that God
had pronounced judgment upon these cities for the sins they had
already committed, namely, homosexuality, than for a sin they
had not yet committed—that of inhospitality.

## GENESIS 22:2

*Why did God tell Abraham to sacrifice his son Isaac when God
condemned human sacrifice in Leviticus 18 and 20?*

**Problem:** In both Leviticus 18:21 and 20:2, God specifically denounced
human sacrifice when He commanded Israel, "Do not give any of
your children to be sacrificed to Molech" (Lev. 18:21, NIV), and "Any
Israelite or any alien living in Israel, who gives any of his children to
Molech, must be put to death; the people of the community are to
stone him" (Lev. 20:2, NIV). Yet in Genesis 22:2, God commanded
Abraham to "Take now your son, your only son Isaac, whom you
love, and go to the land of Moriah, and offer him there as a burnt
offering on one of the mountains of which I shall tell you." This appears to contradict His command not to offer human sacrifices.

**Solution:** First, God did not plan that Abraham should actually kill his son. The fact that the angel of the Lord prevented Abraham from killing Isaac (22:12) demonstrates this. God's purpose was to test Abraham's faith by asking him to completely surrender his only son to God. The angel of the Lord declared that it was Abraham's *willingness* to surrender his son, not the actual killing of him, that satisfied God's expectations for Abraham. God said explicitly, "Do not stretch out your hand against the lad . . . for now I know that you fear God, since you have not withheld your son, your only son, from Me" (Gen. 22:12, NASB).

Second, the prohibitions in both Leviticus 18:21 and 20:2 were specifically against the offering of one's offspring to the pagan god Molech. So it is not strictly a contradiction for God to prohibit offering one's offspring to Molech and yet asking Abraham to offer Isaac to Him, the only true God. After all, offering Isaac to the Lord is not offering one's offspring to Molech, since the Lord is not Molech. God alone is sovereign over life (Deut. 32:39; Job 1:21), and therefore He alone has the right to demand when it should be taken. Indeed, He has appointed the day of everyone's death (Ps. 90:10; Heb. 9:27).

Third, Abraham so trusted in God's love and power that he willingly obeyed because he believed God would raise Isaac from the dead (Heb. 11:17–19). This is implied in the fact that, though Abraham intended to kill Isaac, he told his servants, "I and the lad will go yonder; and *we* will worship and *we* will return to you" (Gen. 22:5, NASB).

Finally, it is not morally wrong for God to order the sacrifice of our sons. He offered His own Son on Calvary (John 3:16). Indeed, even our governments sometimes call upon us to sacrifice our sons for our country. Certainly God has an even greater right to do so.

## GENESIS 23

*How could the sons of Heth have been in Hebron in 2050 BC when their kingdom was in what is now modern Turkey?*

**Problem:** Heth was the progenitor of the Hittites, whose kingdom was located in what is now modern Turkey. But, according to some archaeological evidence, the Hittites did not become a prominent force in the Middle East until the reign of Mursilis I, which began about 1620 BC, and who captured the city of Babylon in 1600 BC.

However, several times in Genesis 23 reference is made to Abraham's encounter with the sons of Heth, who controlled Hebron about 2050 BC. How could the Bible claim the presence of Hittites in control of Hebron so many years before they became a significant force in the area?

**Solution:** More recent archaeological evidence from cuneiform tablets describes conflicts in Anatolia (modern Turkey) among the various Hittite principalities from about 1950 to 1850 BC. Even before this conflict, however, there was a race of non-Indo-Europeans called Hattians. These people were subdued by invaders about 2300 to 2000 BC. These Indo-European invaders adopted the name Hatti. In Semitic languages, like Hebrew, Hatti and Hitti would be written with the same letters, because only the consonants were written, not the vowels.

In the days of Ramses II of Egypt, the Hittite Empire reached as far south as Kadesh on the Orontes River (modern Asi). However, additional evidence indicates that the Hittites actually penetrated farther south into Syria and Palestine. Although the Hittite kingdom did not reach its zenith until the second half of the 14th century, there is sufficient evidence to substantiate a Hittite presence in Hebron at the time of Abraham, which was significant enough to control the area.

## GENESIS 46:8–27

*Why does the Bible speak about the twelve tribes of Israel when actually there were fourteen?*

**Problem:** The Bible often states that there were twelve tribes of Israel. Yet, in three different passages, the lists are different. In fact, there are fourteen different tribes listed as one of the twelve tribes.

| Genesis 46 | Numbers 26 | Revelation 7 |
|---|---|---|
| 1. Reuben | Reuben | Reuben |
| 2. Simeon | Simeon | Simeon |

| 3. Levi | — | Levi |
|---|---|---|
| 4. Judah | Judah | Judah |
| 5. Issachar | Issachar | Issachar |
| 6. Zebulun | Zebulun | Zebulun |
| 7. Joseph | — | Joseph |
| 8. — | Manasseh | Manasseh |
| 9. — | Ephraim | — |
| 10. Benjamin | Benjamin | Benjamin |
| 11. Dan | Dan | — |
| 12. Gad | Gad | Gad |
| 13. Asher | Asher | Asher |
| 14. Napthali | Napthali | Napthali |

Were there twelve tribes of Israel or fourteen?

**Solution:** In response, it must be noted that Jacob had only twelve sons. Their descendants comprised the original twelve tribes. However, for various reasons these same descendants are re-arranged at different times into somewhat different groups of twelve. For example, in Genesis 48:22, Jacob grants to Joseph a double portion of inheritance. In the list in Numbers, Manasseh and Ephraim, the sons of Joseph, are substituted for the tribe of Joseph. Also, Levi was not given a portion of the land as an inheritance because the Levites functioned as priests. Scattered among all the tribes in 48 Levitical cities, they taught the tribes the statutes of the Lord (Deut. 33:10). Consequently, Joseph's double portion is divided between Manasseh and Ephraim, his two sons in order to fill the space left by Levi.

In the Revelation passage, Joseph and Manasseh are counted separately, possibly indicating that Joseph and Ephraim (Joseph's son) are counted as one tribe. Dan is omitted from that list, possibly because the Danites took their own allotment by force in the area north of Asher, effectively separating themselves from their original inheritance in the south. Further, the Danites were the first tribe to go into idolatry. Levi is listed here as a separate tribe, possibly because, after the cross, the Levites no longer functioned in the priestly office for all the tribes, and thus could be given a specific land inheritance of their own. In each case, the biblical author is careful to preserve the original number twelve, with its spiritual significance indicating heavenly perfection (cf. the gates and foundations of the heavenly city, Rev. 21).

# EXODUS

*How could God bless the Hebrew midwives for disobeying the God-ordained governmental authority (Pharaoh) and lying to him?*

**Problem:** The Bible declares that "the authorities that exist are appointed by God" (Rom. 13:1; cf. 1 Peter 2:13). The Scripture also says, "Lying lips are an abomination to the Lord" (Prov. 12:22). But Pharaoh, the king of Egypt, had given a direct order to the Hebrew midwives to murder the newborn Hebrew boys. "But the midwives feared God, and did not do as the king of Egypt commanded them, but saved the male children alive" (Exod. 1:17). Not only did the midwives disobey Pharaoh, but when he questioned them about their actions, they lied, saying, "Because the Hebrew women are not like the Egyptian women; for they are lively and give birth before the midwives come to them" (Exod. 1:19). In spite of this, Exodus 1:20 states that God "dealt well with the midwives . . . He provided households for them" (v. 21). How could God bless the midwives for disobedience and dishonesty?

**Solution:** There is little question that the midwives disobeyed Pharaoh by not murdering the newborn male children and lied to Pharaoh when they said they arrived too late to carry out his orders. Nonetheless, there is moral justification for what they did.

45

First, the moral dilemma in which the midwives found themselves was unavoidable. Either they obeyed God's higher law, or they obeyed the lesser obligation of submitting to Pharaoh. Rather than commit deliberate infanticide against the children of their own people, the midwives chose to disobey Pharaoh's orders. God commands us to obey the governmental powers, but He also commands us not to murder (Exod. 20:13). The saving of innocent lives is a higher obligation than obedience to government. When the government commands us to murder innocent victims, we should not obey. God did not hold the midwives responsible—nor does He hold us responsible—for not following a lower obligation in order to obey a higher law (cf. Acts 4; Rev. 13). In the case of the midwives, the higher law was to the preservation of the lives of the newborn male children.

Second, the text clearly states that God blessed them "because the midwives feared God" (Exod. 1:21). It was their fear of God that led them to do what was necessary to save these innocent lives. Thus, their false statement to Pharaoh was an essential part of their effort to save lives.

Third, their lying is comparable to their having disobeyed Pharaoh in order to save the lives of the innocent newborns. This is a case where the midwives had to choose between lying and being compelled to murder innocent babies. Here again the midwives chose to obey the higher moral law. Obedience to parents is part of the moral law (cf. Eph. 6:1). But if a parent commanded his or her child to kill a neighbor or worship an idol, the child should refuse. Jesus emphasized the need to follow the higher moral law when He said, "He who loves father or mother more than Me is not worthy of Me" (Matt. 10:37).

## EXODUS 5:2

### Who was the pharaoh of the Exodus?

**Problem:** The predominant view of modern scholars is that the pharaoh of the Exodus was Ramses II. If this is right, that would mean the Exodus took place about 1270 to 1260 BC. However, from several references in the Bible (Judg. 11:26; 1 Kings 6:1; Acts

13:19–21), the Exodus is dated from ca. 1447 BC. If this is true, then given the commonly accepted dating system, the pharaoh of the Exodus was Amenhotep II. Who was the pharaoh of the Exodus, and when did the Exodus take place?

**Solution:** Although much of modern scholarship has proposed a late date for the Exodus, about 1270–1260 BC, there is sufficient evidence to say that it is not necessary to accept this date, and alternative explanations provide a better accounting of all the historical data, and place the Exodus at about 1447 BC.

First, the biblical dates for the Exodus place it in the 1400s BC, since 1 Kings 6:1 declares that it was 480 years before the fourth year of Solomon's reign (which was about 967 BC). This would place the Exodus around 1447 BC. This fits also with Judges 11:26, which affirms that Israel spent 300 years in the land up to the time of Jepthah (which was about 1000 BC). Likewise, Acts 13:20 speaks of there being 450 years of judges from Moses to Samuel, who lived around 1000 BC. The same is true of the 430 years mentioned in Galatians 3:17 (see comments) spanning from around 1800 to 1450 BC (from Jacob to Moses). The same figure is used in Exodus 12:40. All of these passages provide a 1400 BC date, not 1200 BC as the critics claim.

Second, John Bimson and David Livingston have proposed a revision of the traditional dating of the end of the Middle Bronze Age and the beginning of the Late Bronze Age from 1550 to shortly after 1400 BC. The Middle Bronze Age was characterized by large fortified cities, a description that fits well with the account that the spies brought back to Moses (Deut. 1:28). This would mean that the conquest of Canaan took place about 1400 BC. Since the Scriptures state that Israel wandered in the wilderness for forty years, that would put the Exodus at about 1440 BC, in complete accord with biblical chronology. If we accept the traditional account of the reigns of the pharaohs, this would mean that the pharaoh of the Exodus was Amenhotep II, who reigned from about 1450 to 1425 BC.

Third, another possible solution, known as the Velikovsky-Courville revision, proposes a redating of the traditional chronology of the reigns of the pharaohs. Velikovsky and Courville assert that there are an extra six hundred years in the chronology of the kings of Egypt. Archaeological evidence can be mustered to substantiate this proposal, which again places the date of Exodus in the 1440s BC. According to this view, the pharaoh at this time was King Thom. This fits the statement in Exodus 1:11 that the Israelites were enslaved to build the city called Pithom ("the abode of Thom"). When the biblical chronology is taken as the pattern, all of the historical and archaeological evidence fits together in a unified picture. (See Geisler and Brooks, *When Skeptics Ask*, chapter 9.)

## EXODUS 13:18

*The Bible says there was a great wall of water but archaeology shows it was a shallow "reed sea," not a deep Red Sea.*

**Problem:** In Exodus 13:18, the sea is called the Red Sea. The Hebrew is *yam suph*, which should be translated "Sea of Reeds." In this case there would be nothing supernatural about crossing it.

**Solution:** There are serious problems with this objection. First of all, the drowning of Pharaoh's troops would be impossible in such a shallow sea (Exod. 14:22). Second, this does not account for the great wall of water of which the text speaks. Finally, there is evidence that the crossing was not at this point (see comments on Exod. 14:21–29).

## EXODUS 14:21-29

*How could two million people cross the Red Sea in such a short time?*

**Problem:** According to the account of the crossing of the Red Sea, the massive group of fleeing Israelites must have had no more than 24 hours to cross through the portion of the Red Sea that God had prepared. However, according to the number given, there were some six hundred thousand soldiers plus women and children, which could be two million of them (see Num. 1:45–46). But for a multitude of this size, a 24-hour period is just not enough time to make such a crossing.

**Solution:** First, although the passage may give the idea that the time the nation of Israel had to make the crossing was short, this is not a necessary conclusion. The text states that God brought an east wind that drove back the waters "all that night" (Exod. 14:21). Verse 22 seems to indicate that it was the next morning when the multitude of Israelites began their journey across the seabed. Verse 24 then states, "Now it came to pass, in the morning watch, that the Lord looked down upon the army of the Egyptians." Finally, according to verse 26, God told Moses to "stretch out your hand over the sea, that the waters may come back upon the Egyptians." There is no time reference to this command, however, and it is not necessary to conclude that Israel completed their crossing that very morning.

Second, some give this order for the Israelites crossing as following. Day one: during the day they are at Nuweiba (14:2) and they are considered to be desperate (14:10–12); at sometime near midday Moses raises his hand and the sea is divided (14:21). Day two: the strong winds blow all night long (14:21) and shortly after they start to cross, which takes 24 hours, and they are crossing on dry ground with no wind (14:22). Day three: everyone is on the eastern coast by morning watch (14:24, 27) and Moses stretches out his hand and the sea returns (14:26–27). The sea is then returned to its normal depth (14:25–28).

Third, even if we assume that the crossing took place in 24 hours, this is not as impossible as it may seem. The passage never states that the people crossed in single file, or that they crossed over on a section of ground the width of a modern superhighway. In fact, current research shows that a possible crossing sight for the Israelites was at Nuweiba at the Gulf of Aqaba. If this be the case, then there is a very detailed underwater land road that could warrant such a feat. The distance across is 14 km (roughly 9 miles); the road is very broad (at least 2 km); there is very limited vegetation, no major corals, no pieces of rock, no mountainous formations, no steep slopes, no organic sediments (like mud); it is extremely flat; and the seabed is covered by sand and gravel.[9] The important points that need to be made are: "1) The unusual character of the seabed making it look like a highway or a very wide (at least 2 km wide) underwater road, 2) There is no natural explanation to how the water (according to the text) was cut apart,

3) If the water was cut apart there would be a dry solid ground and the gradient would be possible to walk or ride across."[10] If this is the case, it is reasonable to assume that 2 million people could cross a distance of 14km (roughly 9 miles) in the span of 24 hours. The normal walking rate is nearly 3 miles per hour.

## EXODUS 20:13

*How could God command people not to kill and then, in Exodus 21:12, command that murderers be put to death?*

**Problem:** In the Ten Commandments, God prohibits killing when He says, "Thou shalt not kill" (KJV). However, in Exodus 21:12 God commands that the man who strikes another man so that he dies should be put to death. Isn't it a contradiction for God to command that we not kill and then command that we do kill?

**Solution:** A great amount of confusion has arisen because of the misleading translation of the sixth commandment. The Hebrew word used in the prohibition of this commandment is not the normal word for killing (*harag*). Rather it is the specific term for murder (*ratsach*). A more proper translation of the command is provided by the NKJV and NIV: "You shall not murder." Exodus 21:12 is not a command to murder, but a command to carry out capital punishment for capital crime. There is no contradiction between the command for men not to commit murder, and the command that the proper authorities should execute capital punishment for capital crimes.

## EXODUS 21:22-23

*Does this text show that unborn babies are of less value than adults?*

**Problem:** According to some translations of the Bible, this text teaches that when fighting men cause a woman to have a "miscarriage" they "shall be fined" (v. 22, RSV). But if the fighting men cause the death of the woman, the penalty was capital punishment (v. 23). Doesn't this prove that the unborn was not considered a human being, as the mother was?

**Solution:** First of all, this is a mistranslation of the verse. The great Hebrew scholar Umberto Cassuto translated the verse correctly as follows:

> When men strive together and they hurt unintentionally a woman with child, and her children come forth but no mischief happens—that is, the woman and the children do not die—the one who hurts her shall surely be punished by a fine. But if any mischief happens, that is, if the woman dies or the children, then you shall give life for life.[11]

This makes the meaning very clear. It is a strong passage against abortion, affirming that the unborn are of equal value to adult human beings.

Second, the Hebrew word (*yatsa*), mistranslated "miscarriage," actually means to "come forth" or to "give birth" (as NKJV, NIV). It is the Hebrew word regularly used for live birth in the OT. In fact, it is never used for a miscarriage, though it is used of a stillbirth. But, in this passage, as in virtually all OT texts, it refers to a live, though premature, birth.

Third, there is another Hebrew word for miscarriage (*shakol*), and it is not used here. Since this word for miscarriage was available and was not used, but the word for live birth was used, there is no reason to suppose it means anything other than a live birth of a fully human being.

Fourth, the word used for the mother's offspring here is *yeled*, which means "child." It is the same word used of babies and young children in the Bible (Gen. 21:8; Exod. 2:3). Hence, the unborn is considered just as human as a young child.

Fifth, if any harm happened to either the mother or the child, the same punishment was given, "life for life" (v. 23). This demonstrates that the unborn was considered of equal value with the mother.

Sixth, other OT passages teach the full humanity of an unborn child (see comments on Pss. 51:5 and 139:13ff). The NT affirms the same view (cf. Matt. 1:20; Luke 1:41, 44).

## EXODUS 24:4

*How could Moses have written this when modern scholars say several different authors (JEPD) are responsible for it?*

**Problem:** Modern critical scholars, following Julius Wellhausen (19th century), claim that the first five books of the OT were written by various persons known as J (Jehovist), E (Elohimist), P (priestly), and D (deuteronomist), depending on which sections reflect the literary characteristics of these supposed authors. However, this verse declares that "Moses wrote all the words of the Lord." Indeed, many other verses in the Bible attribute this book to Moses (see points 6–9 below).

**Solution:** Here is another example where negative criticism of the Bible is wrong. There is very strong evidence that Moses wrote Exodus. First of all, no other person from that period had the time, interest, and ability to compose such a record.

Second, Moses was an eyewitness of the events and as such was qualified to be its author. Indeed, the record is a vivid eyewitness account of spectacular events, such as the crossing of the Red Sea and receiving the Ten Commandments.

Third, the earliest Jewish teaching ascribes this book to Moses. This is true of the Jewish Talmud, as well as Jewish writers like Philo and Josephus.

Fourth, the author reflects a detailed knowledge of the geography of the wilderness (cf. Exod. 14). This is highly unlikely for anyone who did not have many years of experience living in this area, unlike Moses. The same is true of the author's knowledge of the customs and practices of the people described in Exodus.

Fifth, the book explicitly claims that "Moses wrote all the words" (Exod. 24:4). If he did not, then it is a forgery that cannot be trusted, nor could it be the Word of God.

Sixth, Moses's successor, Joshua, claimed that Moses wrote the Law. In fact, when Joshua assumed leadership after Moses, he exhorted the people of Israel that "This Book of the Law" should not depart out of their mouths (Josh. 1:8) and that they should "observe to do according to all the law which Moses . . . commanded" (Josh. 1:7).

Seventh, a long chain of OT figures after Moses attributed this book to him, including Joshua (1:7–8), Josiah (2 Chron. 34:14), Ezra (6:18), Daniel (9:11), and Malachi (4:4).

Eighth, Jesus quoted from Exodus 20:1, using the introduction "for Moses said" (Mark 7:10; cf. Luke 20:37). So either Christ is right or the critics are. Since there is strong evidence that He is the Son of God, the choice is clear.[12]

Ninth, the Apostle Paul declared, "Moses writes about the righteousness which is of the law" (Rom. 10:5, citing Ezek. 20:11). So we have it on apostolic authority, as well as on the authority of Christ, that Moses wrote Exodus.

# LEVITICUS

*How can the Bible say that the hyrax and the rabbit chew the cud when science has proven that they do not?*

**Problem:** In Leviticus 11:5–6, two animals, the rock hyrax and the rabbit, were designated as unclean by Leviticus because, although they chew the cud, they do not divide the hoof. But, science has discovered that these two animals do not chew the cud. Isn't it an error when the Bible says they chew the cud when in fact they do not?

**Solution:** Although they did not chew the cud in the modern technical sense, they did engage in a chewing action that looked the same to an observer. Thus, they are listed with other animals that chew the cud so that the common person could make the distinction from his or her everyday observations.

Animals that chew the cud are identified as ruminants; they regurgitate food into their mouths to be chewed again. Ruminants normally have four stomachs. Neither the rock hyrax (translated "rock badger" in the NASB) nor the rabbit are ruminants and technically do not chew the cud. However, both animals move their jaws in such a manner as to appear to be chewing the cud. This action was so convincing that the great Swedish scientist Linnaeus originally classified them as ruminants.

It is now known that rabbits practice what is called "reflection," in which indigestible vegetable matter absorbs certain bacteria and is passed as droppings and then eaten again. This process enables the rabbit to better digest it. This process is very similar to rumination, and it gives the impression of chewing the cud. So, the Hebrew phrase "chewing the cud" should not be taken in the modern technical sense, but in the ancient sense of a chewing motion that includes both rumination and reflection in the modern sense.

The list of clean and unclean animals was intended as a practical guide for the Israelites in selecting food. The average Israelite would not have been aware of the technical aspects of cud chewing, and may have otherwise considered the hyrax and rabbit as clean animals because of the appearance of cud chewing. Consequently, it was necessary to point out that, although it may appear that these were clean animals because of their chewing movement, they were not clean because they did not divide the hoof. We often follow a similar practice when talking to those who are not familiar with more technical aspects of some point. For example, we use observational language to talk about the sun rising and setting when we talk to little children. To a small child the daily cycle of the sun has the appearance of rising and setting (see comments on Josh. 10:12–14). The description is not technically correct, but it is functionally useful for the level of understanding of the child. This is analogous to the use here in Leviticus. Technically, although the hyrax and the rabbit do not chew the cud, this description was functional at the time in order to make the point that these animals were considered unclean.

# NUMBERS

*How could Moses have written Numbers when critics claim it was written centuries after his death?*

**Problem:** Many modern critics claim that Moses did not write the first five books of the Bible traditionally attributed to him (see comments on Exod. 24:4). But the Bible declares here that "the Lord spoke to Moses" (1:1) and that "Moses wrote down" the events of this book (33:2).

**Solution:** The critics have no real evidence for their claim, either historical or literary. The fact that Moses used different names for God (Elohim, Jehovah, [Yahweh]) is no proof. Each name of God informs us of another characteristic of God that fits the narrative in which it is used.

Furthermore, there is strong evidence that Moses wrote the Book of Numbers. First, there is all the evidence mentioned earlier (in comments on Exod. 24:4) that the book reflects a detailed, firsthand knowledge of the time, places, and customs of the period it describes—all of which Moses possessed.

Second, the book claims to have been written by Moses (1:1; 33:2). This would make the book an outright fraud, unless Moses is really its rightful author.

Third, there are a number of NT citations from the Book of Numbers that are associated with Moses (Acts 7; 13; 1 Cor. 10:2–8; Heb. 3:7–16). If Moses did not write Numbers, then these inspired NT books would be in error too.

Fourth, our Lord quoted from Numbers and verified that it was indeed Moses who lifted up the serpent in the wilderness (John 3:14; cf. Num. 21:9). This places the stamp of Christ's authority on the authenticity of the question.

## NUMBERS 25:9

*Why does this verse say that 24,000 died when 1 Corinthians 10:8 offers a different number?*

**Problem:** The incident at Baal-Peor resulted in God's judgment upon Israel, and, according to Numbers 25:9, 24,000 died in the plague of judgment. However, according to 1 Corinthians 10:8, only 23,000 died. Which is the correct number?

**Solution:** There are two possible explanations here. First, some have suggested that the difference is due to the fact that 1 Corinthians 10:8 is speaking only about those who died "in one day" (23,000), whereas Numbers 25:9 is referring to the complete number (24,000) that died in the plague.

Others believe two different events are in view here. They note that 1 Corinthians 10:7 is a quote of Exodus 32:6 and indicates that the 1 Corinthians passage is actually referring to the judgment of God after the idolatrous worship of the golden calf (Exod. 32). The Exodus passage does not state the number of people who died as a result of the judgment of God, and the actual number is not revealed until 1 Corinthians 10:8. According to 1 Corinthians 10:8, 23,000 died as a result of the judgment of God for their worship of the golden calf. According to Numbers 25:9, 24,000 died as a result of the judgment of God for Israel's worship of Baal at Baal-Peor.

# ─── DEUTERONOMY ───

*How can false prophets be distinguished from true prophets?*

**Problem:** The Bible contains many prophecies that it calls upon us to believe because they come from God. However, the Bible also acknowledges the existence of false prophets (Matt. 7:15). Indeed, many religions and cults claim to have prophets. Hence, the Bible exhorts believers to "test" those who claim to be prophets (1 John 4:1–3). But what is the difference between a false prophet and a true prophet of God?

**Solution:** There are many tests for a false prophet. Several of them are listed in these very passages. Put in question form, the tests are:

1. Do they ever give false prophecies? (Deut. 18:21–22)
2. Do they contact departed spirits? (Deut. 18:11)
3. Do they use means of divination? (Deut. 18:11)
4. Do they involve mediums or witches? (Deut. 18:10)
5. Do they follow false gods or idols? (Exod. 20:3–4; Deut. 13:3)
6. Do they deny the deity of Jesus Christ? (Col. 2:8–9)
7. Do they deny the humanity of Jesus Christ? (1 John 4:1–2)

8. Do their prophecies shift the focus off Jesus Christ? (Rev. 19:10)

9. Do they advocate abstaining from certain foods and meats for spiritual reasons? (1 Tim. 4:3–4)

10. Do they deprecate or deny the need for marriage? (1 Tim. 4:3)

11. Do they promote immorality? (Jude 7)

12. Do they encourage legalistic self-denial? (Col. 2:16–33)[13]

A positive answer to any of these is an indication that the prophet is not speaking for God. God does not speak or encourage anything that is contrary to His character and commands. And most certainly the God of truth does not give false prophecies.

## DEUTERONOMY 18:15–18

### *Is this a prophecy about the prophet Mohammed?*

**Problem:** God promised Moses here, "I will raise up for them [Israel] a Prophet like you from among their brethren, and will put My words in His mouth, and He shall speak to them all that I command Him" (v. 18). Many Muslims believe this prophecy is fulfilled in Mohammed, as the Koran claims when it refers to "The unlettered Prophet [Mohammed], Whom they find mentioned in their own [scriptures], in the Law and the Gospels" (Surah 7:157).

**Solution:** This prophecy could not be a reference to Mohammed for several reasons. First, the term "brethren" refers to Israel, not to their Arabian antagonists. Why would God raise up for Israel a prophet from their enemies?

Second, in this very context, the term "brethren" means fellow Israelites. For the Levites were told "they shall have no inheritance among their brethren" (v. 2).

Third, elsewhere in this book the term "brethren" also means fellow Israelites, not a foreigner. God told them to choose a king "from among your brethren," not a "foreigner." Israel has never chosen a non-Jewish king.

Fourth, Mohammed came from Ishmael, as even Muslims admit, and heirs to the Jewish throne came from Isaac. When

Abraham prayed, "Oh that Ishmael might live before You!" God answered emphatically: "My covenant I will establish with Isaac" (Gen. 17:21). Later God repeated: "In Isaac your seed shall be called" (Gen. 21:12).

Fifth, the Koran itself states that the prophetic line came through Isaac, not Ishmael: "And We bestowed on him Isaac and Jacob, and We established the Prophethood and the Scripture among his seed" (Surah 29:27). The Muslim scholar Yusuf Ali adds the word "Abraham" and changes the meaning as follows, "We gave (Abraham) Isaac and Jacob, and ordained Among his progeny Prophethood and Revelation." By adding Abraham, the father of Ishmael, he can include Mohammed, a descendent of Ishmael, in the prophetic line! But Abraham's name is not found in the original Arabic text.

Sixth, Jesus perfectly fulfilled this verse, since 1) He was from among His Jewish brethren (cf. Gal. 4:4). 2) He fulfilled Deuteronomy 18:18 perfectly: "He shall speak to them all that I [God] command Him." Jesus said, "I do nothing of Myself; but as My Father taught Me, I speak these things" (John 8:28). And, "I have not spoken on My own authority; but the Father who sent Me gave Me a command, what I should say and what I should speak" (John 12:49). 3) He called Himself a "prophet" (Luke 13:33), and the people considered Him a prophet (Matt. 21:11; Luke 7:16; 24:19; John 4:19; 6:14; 7:40; 9:17). As the Son of God, Jesus was prophet (speaking to men for God), priest (Heb. 7–10, speaking to God for men), and king (reigning over men for God, Rev. 19–20).

Finally, there are other characteristics of the "Prophet" to come that fit only Jesus, not Mohammed, such as, He spoke with God "face to face" and He performed "signs and wonders."

# JOSHUA

*How could God bless Rahab for lying?*

**Problem:** When the spies came to Jericho, they sought refuge in the house of Rahab. When the king of Jericho commanded Rahab to bring out the men, she lied, saying that the men had already gone and that she did not know where they went. However, when Israel finally destroyed Jericho, Rahab and all her family were saved. How could God bless Rahab for lying when he condemns it elsewhere in Scripture (cf. Exod. 20:16)?

**Solution:** Some argue that it is not clear that God blessed Rahab for lying. God certainly saved Rahab and blessed her for protecting the spies and assisting in the overthrow of Jericho. However, nowhere does the Bible explicitly say that God blessed Rahab for lying. God could have blessed her in spite of her lie, not because of it. Actually, Rahab's act of protecting the spies was a demonstration of great faith in the God of Israel. She firmly believed that God would destroy Jericho, and she exhibited that belief by siding with Israel against the people of Jericho when she protected the spies from being discovered.

Others insist that Rahab was faced with a real moral conflict. It may have been impossible for her to both save the spies and tell the truth to the soldiers of the king. If so, God would not hold

Rahab responsible for this unavoidable moral conflict. Certainly a person cannot be held responsible for not keeping a lesser law in order to keep a higher obligation. The Bible commands obedience to the government (Rom. 13:1; Titus 3:1; 1 Peter 2:13), but there are many examples of justified civil disobedience when the government attempts to compel unrighteousness (Exod. 5; Dan. 3; 6; Rev. 13). The case of the Hebrew midwives lying to save the lives of the male children is perhaps the clearest example (see comments on Exod. 1:15–21).

## JOSHUA 6:1ff

*Hasn't archaeology shown that the account of the conquest of Jericho is inaccurate?*

**Problem:** Joshua 6 records the conquest and destruction of the city of Jericho. If this account is accurate, it would seem that modern archaeological excavations would have turned up evidence of this monumental event. However, haven't these investigations proven that the account in Joshua is inaccurate?

**Solution:** For many years the prevailing view of critical scholars has been that there was no city of Jericho at the time Joshua was supposed to have entered Canaan. Although earlier investigations by the notable British archaeologist Kathleen Kenyon confirmed the existence of the ancient city of Jericho, and its sudden destruction, her findings led her to conclude that the city could have existed no later than ca. 1550 BC. This date is much too early for Joshua and the children of Israel to have been party to its demise.

However, recent reexamination of these earlier findings and a closer look at current evidence indicate that not only was there a city that fits the biblical chronology, but that its remains coincide with the biblical account of the destruction of this walled fortress. In a paper published in *Biblical Archaeology Review* (March/April 1990), Bryant G. Wood, visiting professor to the Department of Near Eastern Studies at the University of Toronto, has presented evidence that the biblical report is accurate. His detailed investigation has yielded the following conclusions:

1. That the city that once existed on this site was strongly fortified, corresponding to the biblical record in Joshua 2:5, 7, 15; 6:5, 20.
2. That the ruins give evidence that the city was attacked after harvesttime in the spring, corresponding to Joshua 2:6; 3:15; 5:10.
3. That the inhabitants did not have the opportunity to flee with their foodstuffs from the invading army, as reported in Joshua 6:1.
4. That the siege was short, not allowing the inhabitants to consume the food that was stored in the city, as Joshua 6:15 indicates.
5. That the walls were leveled in such a way to provide access into the city for the invaders, as Joshua 6:20 records.
6. That the city was not plundered by the invaders, according to God's instructions in Joshua 6:17–18.
7. That the city was burned after the walls had been destroyed, just as Joshua 6:24 says.

Thus, dating this at another period than that of Joshua is unjustified (see comments on Exod. 5:2).

## JOSHUA 6:21

*How can the total destruction of Jericho, including women and children, be morally justified?*

**Problem:** This passage states that the Israelites "utterly destroyed all that was in the city, both man and woman, young and old, ox and sheep and donkey, with the edge of the sword." But how can such a ruthless destruction of innocent life and property be justified?

**Solution:** First, the Canaanites were far from "innocent." The description of their sins in Leviticus 18 is vivid: "The land is defiled; therefore I visit the punishment of its iniquity upon it, and the land vomits out its inhabitants" (v. 25). They were cancerously immoral, "defiled" with every kind of "abomination," including child sacrifice (vv. 21, 24, 26).

Second, it must be remembered that God had given the people of Palestine over four hundred years to repent of their wickedness. The people of that land had every opportunity to turn from their wickedness. According to Genesis 15:16, God told Abraham that in four hundred years the descendants of Abraham would return to inherit this land, but that the iniquity of the people was not yet full. This prophetic statement indicated that God would not destroy the people of the land, including those who dwelt in Jericho, until their sins were such that their guilt merited their complete destruction in judgment.

Third, as for the killing of the little children, several things should be noted. (1) Given the cancerous state of the society into which they were born, they had no chance to avoid its fatal pollution. (2) Children who die before the age of accountability go to heaven (see comments on 2 Sam. 12:23). This was an act of God's mercy to their souls to take them into His holy presence from such an unholy environment. (3) God is sovereign over life (Deut. 32:39; Job 1:21) and can order its end according to His will and in view of the creature's ultimate good.

Fourth, Joshua and the people of Israel were acting according to the direct command of God, not on their own initiative. The destruction of Jericho was carried out by the army of Israel, but the army of Israel was the instrument of judgment upon the sins of these people by the righteous Judge of all the earth. Consequently, anyone who would question the justification of this act is questioning God's justice.

Fifth, it was necessary to completely exterminate any trace of the city and its people. If anything had remained, except that which was taken into the treasure-house of the Lord, there would have always been the threat of heathen influence to pull the people away from pure worship of the Lord. Sometimes radical surgery is required to completely eliminate a deadly cancer from the body.

## JOSHUA 10:12–14
*How is it possible for the sun to stand still for a whole day?*

**Problem:** During the battle with the kings of the land, God gave Israel the power to overcome their enemies. As the armies of the people of the land fled from before Israel, Joshua sought the Lord to cause the sun to stand still so that they might have sufficient daylight to complete the destruction of their enemies. But how could the sun stand still in the midst of the heaven for a whole day?

**Solution:** First, this does not teach a geocentric view of the solar system; it is simply using observational language that even meteorologists use every day when they say "sunrise" and "sunset" (cf. Josh. 1:15). Further, it is not necessary to conclude that the earth's rotation was totally halted. Verse 13 states that the sun "did not hasten to go down for about a whole day." This could indicate that the earth's rotation was not completely halted, but that it was retarded to such a degree that the sun did not set for about a whole day. Or, it is possible that God caused the light of the sun to refract through some cosmic "mirror" so that it could be seen a day longer.

Finally, even if the earth's rotation was completely stopped, we must remember that God is not only capable of halting the rotation of the earth for a whole day, but He is also able to prevent any possible catastrophic effects that might result from the cessation of the earth's rotation. Although we do not necessarily know *how* God brought about this miraculous event, we know *that* He did it.

# JUDGES

*Does the Bible approve of assassinations?*

**Problem:** The Bible says "the Lord raised up a deliverer" (Judg. 3:15) for Israel over their oppressor, King Eglon of Moab. Then it records how Ehud "took the dagger from his right thigh, and thrust it into his [Eglon's] belly" (v. 21). How can the God who forbids murder (Exod. 20:13) condone a brutal assassination like this?

**Solution:** This incident, and others like it (cf. Judg. 4:21), are a good example of the principle that "Not everything *recorded* in the Bible is *approved* by the Bible" (see introduction). First of all, the text does not say that God approved of this evil act. It simply states that it occurred.

Second, the fact that God had "raised up" Ehud does not justify everything he did. God "raised up" Pharaoh too (cf. Rom. 9:17), but God nevertheless judged Pharaoh for his sins (cf. Exod. 12).

Third, there are many sins *contained* in the Bible that are not *condoned* by it. These include Abraham's lie (Gen. 20), David's sin with Bathsheba (2 Sam. 11), and Solomon's polygamy (1 Kings 11).

Fourth, while assassinations as such are wrong, God reserves the right to life (Deut. 32:39; Job 1:21). Should He desire to take a life He gives, He has the right to do so through any instrument He may desire, natural or artificial (see comments on Josh. 6:21).

# RUTH

*Doesn't this verse imply that Ruth had intercourse with Boaz after he was drunk, in order to obligate him to redeem her?*

**Problem:** After Boaz had eaten and drunk, he went to lie down. After he lay down, Ruth came up softly, uncovered Boaz's feet, and lay with him. Doesn't this imply that Ruth had intercourse with Boaz to obligate him to redeem her?

**Solution:** No! There is nothing in the text of Ruth that indicates any moral impropriety on the part of either Boaz or Ruth. First, Ruth did not come at night to hide an immoral relationship with Boaz. Rather, she came in the night so that Boaz would not feel the pressure of public scrutiny. Boaz would have the opportunity to decline the proposal to redeem Naomi and marry Ruth without facing any public embarrassment.

Second, the uncovering of the feet is not a euphemism indicating that Ruth had intercourse with Boaz. Rather, it is a literal description of a customary practice to demonstrate subjection and submission. Ruth merely pulled back the covering from over the feet of Boaz as a symbol of her submission to Boaz and her willingness to become his wife.

Third, the passage states that after uncovering the feet of Boaz, Ruth lay down (v. 7). However, this is not the normal way to indicate sexual intercourse. Sexual intercourse is usually indicated by the phrase "he lay with her." Without the accompanying indication of laying "with" someone, the word normally indicates merely that someone reclines.

Fourth, it was also a symbolic act for Boaz to spread the corner of his garment over Ruth. This refers to the practice of a man spreading a covering over his wife as well as himself. Ruth reminds Boaz of his responsibility according to the law of levirate marriage (Deut. 25:5–10). The word translated "wing" in the NKJV recalls the earlier blessing that Boaz pronounced upon Ruth at their first encounter (2:12). Ruth had sought refuge under the wings of the God of Israel, now she seeks refuge under the wing of Boaz.

# 1 SAMUEL

*How could God condemn Israel's request for a king when the rules for selecting a king were given by God in Deuteronomy 17?*

**Problem:** The Scriptures testify to the fact that God had planned for Israel to have a king. Deuteronomy 17:14–20 specifically lays down the rules for selecting a king in Israel. However, when the people of Israel requested that Samuel appoint a king, the Lord told Samuel that the people "have not rejected you, but they have rejected Me, that I should not reign over them" (1 Sam. 8:7). How could God condemn Israel's request for a king when He had already given them the guidelines for selecting a king? Indeed, God had promised a "king" (Gen. 17:6).

**Solution:** The context of 1 Samuel 8 indicates that the people were not condemned for seeking a king as such. Rather, it was because they had the wrong motive and employed the wrong method in seeking a king for themselves. First of all, the people had the wrong *motive* for seeking a king. In the first verse of chapter 8, we read that Samuel was old when he appointed his sons to be judges in Israel. However, Samuel's sons did not do right in the eyes of God. When the people came to Samuel and requested that he appoint a king, it was not because they wanted to have God's man rule over them. Rather, they wanted to have a man rule over them. The people had mistaken God's administration through Samuel for Samuel's acts. At Saul's inauguration, Samuel reminded the people that it was "your God, who Himself saved you out of all your adversities and your tribulations" (1 Sam. 10:19). They completely ignored the fact that it was God who protected them and led them—not Samuel or any human king whom Samuel would appoint. Consequently, they were not rejecting Samuel. They were rejecting God.

Second, they *failed to seek the Lord* concerning a king to rule over them. They did not bother to ask for God's guidance. They simply requested that Samuel appoint a king. When the elders of Israel came to Samuel, they said, "Now make for us a king to judge us like all the nations" (8:5). However, in Deuteronomy 17:15 God specifically stated that the people would set a king over them "whom the Lord your God chooses." The request of the people in 1 Samuel betrays their lack of consideration for God's part in the process. They had truly rejected God from ruling over them. The Lord was displeased with the people because they did not seek God's man, and they did not employ God's method.

Finally, they sought a king from the wrong tribe. According to Scripture, the king was to come from the tribe of Judah (Gen. 49:10) and Saul was from Benjamin.

## 1 Samuel 15:11

*How can God say that He regretted setting up Saul to be king in Israel?*

**Problem:** After Saul had failed to carry out God's command to utterly destroy the Amalekites, God said to Samuel, "I greatly regret that I have set up Saul as king" (1 Sam. 15:11). However, in 1 Samuel 15:29, Samuel states that God is not a man that He should repent. How can God say that He regretted setting up Saul as king when other passages assert that God does not repent or change His mind?

**Solution:** The statement God made to Samuel does not mean that God relented or changed His mind, but that God was expressing deep emotional sorrow over Saul's failure and the trouble it would bring upon Israel. God selected Saul to be king in Israel to accomplish certain tasks for which Saul was well suited. To regret some course of action that had to be taken is an experience we have all had. God does not actually change His mind, but He does experience deep emotional sorrow over the things that people do.

## 1 Samuel 18:1-4

### *Were David and Jonathan homosexuals?*

**Problem:** This Scripture records the intense love David and Jonathan had for each other. Some see this as an indication that they were homosexual. They infer this from the facts that Jonathan "loved" David (18:3), Jonathan stripped in David's presence (18:4), and they "kissed" each other with great emotion (1 Sam. 20:41). They point also to David's lack of successful relations with women as an indication of his homosexual tendencies. Is this a valid conclusion to draw from these texts?

**Solution:** There is no indication in Scripture that David and Jonathan were homosexual. On the contrary, there is strong evidence that they were not. First of all, David's attraction to Bathsheba (2 Sam. 11) reveals that his sexual orientation was heterosexual, not homosexual. In fact, judging by the number of wives he had, David seemed to have too much heterosexuality.

Second, David's "love" for Jonathan was not sexual (*erotic*) but a friendship (*philic*) love. It is common in Eastern cultures for heterosexual men to express love and affection toward one another.

Third, Jonathan did not strip himself of all his clothes in David's presence. He only stripped himself of his armor and royal robe (1 Sam. 18:4) as a symbol of his deep respect for David and commitment to him.

Fourth, the "kiss" was a common cultural greeting for men in that day. Furthermore, it did not occur until two and a half chapters after Jonathan gave David his clothes (1 Sam. 20:41).

Finally, their emotional expression was weeping, not orgasm. The text says, "they kissed each other and wept together—but David wept the most" (1 Sam. 20:41, NIV).

## 1 Samuel 28:7ff

*How could God allow the witch of Endor to raise Samuel from the dead when God had condemned witchcraft?*

**Problem:** The Bible severely condemns witchcraft and communication with the dead (Exod. 22:18; Lev. 20:6, 27; Deut. 18:9–12; Isa. 8:19). In the OT, those who practiced it were to receive capital punishment. King Saul knew this and even put all witches out of the land (1 Sam. 28:3). Nevertheless, in disobedience to God, he went to the witch of Endor for her to contact the dead prophet Samuel (1 Sam. 28:8ff). The problem here is that she appears to be successful in contacting Samuel, which lends validity to the powers of witchcraft that the Bible so severely condemns.

**Solution:** Several possible solutions have been offered to this episode at Endor. Three will be summarized here.

First, some believe that the witch worked a miracle by demonic powers and actually brought Samuel back from the dead. In support of this they cite passages that indicate demons have the power to perform miracles (Matt. 7:22; 2 Cor. 11:14; 2 Thess. 2:9–10; Rev. 16:14). The objections to this view include the fact that death is final (Heb. 9:27), the dead cannot return (2 Sam. 12:23) because there is a great gulf fixed by God (Luke 16:24–27), and demons cannot usurp God's authority over life and death (Job 1:10–12).

Second, others have suggested that the witch did not really bring up Samuel from the dead, but simply faked doing so. They support this by referencing demons who deceive people trying to contact the dead (Lev. 19:31; Deut. 18:11; 1 Chron. 10:13) and by the contention that demons sometimes utter what is true (cf. Acts 16:17). The objections to this view include the fact that the passage seems to say Samuel did return from the dead, that he provided a prophecy that actually came to pass, and that it is unlikely that demons would have uttered truth of God, since the devil is the father of lies (John 8:44).

A third view is that the witch did not bring up Samuel from the dead, but God Himself intervened in the witch's tent to rebuke Saul for his sin. In support of this view is the following: (a) Samuel seemed to actually return from the dead (v. 14), but (b) neither humans nor demons have the power to bring people back from the dead (Luke 16:24–27; Heb. 9:27). (c) The witch herself seemed to be surprised by the appearance of Samuel from the dead (v. 12). (d) There is a direct condemnation of witchcraft in this passage (v. 9), and thus it is highly unlikely that it would give credence to witchcraft by claiming that witches can actually bring people back from the dead. (e) God sometimes speaks in unsuspecting places through unusual means (cf. Baalam's donkey, Num. 22). (f) The miracle was not performed through the witch, but *in spite of* her. (g) Samuel seems to really appear from the dead, rebukes Saul, and utters a true prophecy (v. 19). (h) God explicitly and repeatedly condemned contacting the dead (see above) and would not contradict this by giving credence to witchcraft. The major objections to this view are that the text does not explicitly say that God performed the miracle, and that a witch's tent is a strange place to perform this miracle.

# 2 SAMUEL

*Should we pray for the dead?*

**Problem:** Based on a verse in 2 Maccabees 12:46 (Douay), Roman Catholics believe it is a holy and wholesome thought to pray for the dead that they may be loosed from their sins. However, David refused to pray for his dead son. Does the Bible teach that we should pray for the dead?

**Solution:** There is nothing in inspired Scripture that supports the Roman Catholic doctrine of praying for the dead that they may be released from their sins. This conclusion is based on strong evidence from many passages. First, the only verse supporting prayers for the dead comes from the 2nd century BC apocryphal book of 2 Maccabees (see comments on 1 Cor. 3:13–15), which the Roman Catholic Church added to the Bible in AD 1546 in response to the Reformation that condemned such practices.

Second, the doctrine of prayers for the dead is connected with the unbiblical doctrine of purgatory. The prayers are for the purpose of releasing the dead from purgatory. But there is no basis for the belief in purgatory (see comments on 1 Cor. 3:13–15).

Third, nowhere in all of inspired Scripture is there a single example of any saint who prayed for the dead to be saved. Surely as passionately as many saints wished for their loved ones to be saved (cf. Rom. 9:1–3), there would be at least one example of a divinely approved prayer on behalf of the dead.

Fourth, the Bible makes it unmistakably clear that death is final and there is no hope beyond the grave. Hebrews declared, "it is appointed for men to die once, but after this the judgment" (Heb. 9:27). Jesus spoke of those who rejected Him as dying "in their sins" (John 8:21, 24), which implies that there is no hope for sins beyond the grave.

Fifth, Jesus set the example in John 11 by weeping for the dead and praying for the living. Upon coming to His friend Lazarus's grave, "Jesus wept" (v. 35). Then He prayed for "the people who are standing by . . . that they may believe" (v. 42).

Sixth, the dead pray for the living (cf. Rev. 6:10), but there are no instances in the inspired Word of God where the living pray for the dead. The martyred saints in glory were praying for vengeance on the wicked (Rev. 6:9). And since there is rejoicing in heaven over one soul saved on earth (Luke 15:10), there is no doubt that there is prayer in heaven for the lost. But the Bible does not hold out even the slightest hope for anyone who dies in their sins (see comments on 2 Thess. 1:9).

## 2 Samuel 12:23

### Do those who die in infancy go to heaven?

**Problem:** The Scriptures teach that we are born in sin (Ps. 51:5) because we "all sinned [in Adam]" (Rom. 5:12). Yet David implies here that his baby, who died, will be in heaven, saying, "I shall go to him" (v. 23).

**Solution:** There are three basic views regarding children who die before the age of accountability—that is, before they are old enough to be morally responsible for their own actions.

*Only elect infants go to heaven.* Some strong Calvinists believe that only those babies who are predestined go to heaven (Eph. 1:4; Rom. 8:29). Those who are not elect go to hell. They see no greater problem with infant predestination than with adult predestination, insisting that everyone is deserving of hell and that it is only by God's mercy that any are saved (Titus 3:5–6).

*Only infants who would have believed go to heaven.* Others claim that God knows the end from the beginning (Isa. 46:10) and the potential as well as the actual. Thus, God knows those infants and little children who would have believed in Christ had they lived long enough. Otherwise, they contend, there would be people in heaven who would not have believed in Christ, which is contrary to Scripture (John 3:36). All infants whom God knows would not have believed, had they lived long enough, will go to hell.

*All infants go to heaven.* Still others believe that all who die before the age of accountability will go to heaven. They base this on the following Scriptures. First, Isaiah 7:16 speaks of an age before a child is morally accountable, namely, "before the child shall know to refuse the evil and choose the good." Second, David believed in life after death and the resurrection (Ps. 16:10–11), so when he spoke of going to be with his son who died after birth (2 Sam. 12:23), he implied that those who die in infancy go to heaven. Third, Psalm 139 speaks of an unborn baby as a creation of God whose name is written down in God's "book" in heaven (vv. 14–16). Fourth, Jesus said, "Let the little children come to Me, and do not forbid them; for of such is the kingdom of God" (Mark 10:14), thus indicating that even little children will be in heaven. Fifth, some see support in Jesus's affirmation that even "little ones" (i.e., children) have a guardian angel "in heaven" who watches over them (Matt. 18:10). Sixth, Christ's death for all made little children savable, even before they believed (Rom. 5:18–19). Finally, Jesus's indication that those who did not know were not morally responsible (John 9:41) is used to support the belief that there is heaven for those who cannot yet believe, even though there is no heaven for those who are old enough and refuse to believe (John 3:36).

## 2 Samuel 24:1

*How can this passage claim that God moved David to number Israel when 1 Chronicles 21:1 claims that it was Satan?*

**Problem:** This passage reports the sin of David in numbering the people of Israel and Judah. Verse 1 affirms that God moved David to number the people. However, according to 1 Chronicles 21:1, it was Satan who moved David to number the people. Who was responsible for prompting David to act?

**Solution:** Both statements are true. Although it was Satan who immediately incited David, ultimately it was God who sovereignly willed to permit Satan to carry out this provocation. Although it was Satan's design to destroy David and the people of God, it was God's purpose to humble David and the people and teach them a valuable spiritual lesson. This situation is quite similar to the first two chapters of Job in which both God and Satan are involved in the suffering of Job. Similarly, both God and Satan are involved in the crucifixion. Satan's purpose was to destroy the Son of God (John 13:2; 1 Cor. 2:8). God's purpose was to redeem humankind by the death of His Son (Acts 2:14–39). The same act by a creature can be meant for evil (by the creature) and for good by God. As Joseph said to his brothers who betrayed him, "You meant it for evil, but God meant it for good" (Gen. 50:20).

# 1 KINGS

***How can this verse say Solomon had forty thousand stalls when 2 Chronicles 9:25 says he had only four thousand stalls?***

**Problem:** In recording the prosperity of Solomon, this passage states that he had forty thousand stalls of horses for his chariots. However, 1 Chronicles 9:25 affirms that Solomon had only four thousand stalls for horses. Which one is right?

**Solution:** This is undoubtedly a copyist error. The ratio of four thousand horses to fourteen hundred chariots, as found in the 2 Chronicles passage, is much more reasonable than the ratio of forty thousand to fourteen hundred found in the 1 Kings text. In the Hebrew language, the visual difference between the two numbers is very slight. The consonants for the number forty are *rbym*,[14] while the consonants for the number four are *rbh* (the vowels were not written in the original text). The manuscripts from which the scribe worked may have been smudged or damaged and have given the appearance of being forty thousand rather than four thousand.

## 1 Kings 6:1

*How can this be an accurate calculation if Ramses the Great was the pharaoh of the Exodus?*

**Problem:** The predominant view of modern scholarship is that the pharaoh of the Exodus was Ramses II. If this is right, it would mean that the Exodus took place about 1270 to 1260 BC. However, since the fourth year of Solomon's reign was 967 BC, adding 480 years to that date would put the Exodus at about 1447 BC, which is in the reign of Amenhotep II. How can this calculation be correct if Ramses the Great was the pharaoh of the Exodus?

**Solution:** If the present chronology of the kings of Egypt is accepted, the pharaoh of the Exodus was not Ramses the Great, but Amenhotep II. If Egyptian chronology is revised, then Ramses lived two hundred years earlier and could be the pharaoh of the Exodus. Although modern scholarship has proposed a late date for the Exodus, ca. 1270–1260 BC, there is no longer any reason to accept this date, and alternative explanations provide a better account of all the historical data and place the Exodus at about 1447 BC. (See comments under Exod. 5:2.)

## 1 Kings 11:1

*How could God allow Solomon to have so many wives when He condemns polygamy?*

**Problem:** First Kings 11:3 says Solomon had seven hundred wives and three hundred concubines. And yet the Scriptures repeatedly warn against having multiple wives (Deut. 17:17) and violating the principle of monogamy—one man for one wife (cf. 1 Cor. 7:2).

**Solution:** Monogamy is God's standard for the human race. This is clear from the following facts: (1) From the very beginning God set the pattern by creating a monogamous marriage relationship with one man and one woman, Adam and Eve (Gen. 1:27; 2:21–25). (2) Following from this God-established example of one woman for one man, this was the general practice of the human race (Gen. 4:1) until interrupted by sin (Gen. 4:23). (3) The Law of Moses clearly commands, "You shall not multiply wives" (Deut. 17:17). (4) The warning against polygamy is repeated in the very passage where it numbers Solomon's many wives (1 Kings 11:2), warning "You shall not intermarry with them, nor they with you." (5) Our Lord reaffirmed God's original intention by citing this passage (Matt. 19:4) and noting that God created one "male and [one] female" and joined them in marriage. (6) The NT stresses that "Each man [should] have his own wife, and let each woman have her own husband" (1 Cor. 7:2). (7) Likewise, Paul insisted that a church leader should be "the husband of one wife" (1 Tim. 3:2, 12). (8) Indeed, monogamous marriage is a prefiguration of the relation between Christ and His bride, the church (Eph. 5:31–32).

Polygamy was never established by God for any people under any circumstances. In fact, the Bible reveals that God severely punished those who practiced it, as is evidenced by the following: (1) Polygamy is first mentioned in the context of a sinful society in rebellion against God where the murderer "Lamech took for himself two wives" (Gen. 4:19, 23). (2) God repeatedly warned polygamists of the consequences of their actions "lest his heart turn away" from God (Deut. 17:17; cf. 1 Kings 11:2). (3) God never *commanded* polygamy—like divorce, He only permitted it because of the hardness of their hearts (Deut. 24:1; Matt. 19:8). (4) Every polygamist in the Bible, including David and Solomon (1 Chron. 14:3), paid dearly for his sins. (5) God hates polygamy, as He hates divorce, since it destroys His ideal for the family (cf. Mal. 2:16).

In brief, monogamy is taught in the Bible in several ways: (1) by *precedent*, since God gave the first man only one wife; (2) by *proportion*, since the amount of males and females God brings into the world are about equal; (3) by *precept*, since both OT and NT command it (see verses above); (4) by *punishment*, since God punished those who violated His standard (1 Kings 11:2); and (5) by *prefiguration*, since marriage is a typology of Christ and His bride, the church (Eph. 5:31–32). Simply because the Bible records Solomon's sin of polygamy does not mean that God approved of it.

# 2 KINGS

*How could a man of God curse these 42 young men so that they were mauled by she-bears?*

**Problem:** As Elisha was going up to Bethel, he was confronted by some young people who mocked him, saying, "Go up, you bald-head!" When Elisha heard this, he turned and pronounced a curse on them, and two she-bears came out of the wood and mauled 42 of the young men. How could a man of God curse these young men for such a minor offense?

**Solution:** First of all, this was no minor offense, for these young men held God's prophet in contempt. Since the prophet was God's mouthpiece to His people, God Himself was being most wickedly insulted in the person of His prophet.

Second, these were not small, innocent children. They were wicked young men, comparable to a modern street gang. Hence, the life of the prophet was endangered by their number, the nature of their sin, and their obvious disrespect for authority.

Third, Elisha's action was designed to strike fear in the hearts of any other such gang members. If these young gang members were not afraid to mock a venerable man of God such as Elisha, then they would have been a threat to the lives of all God's people.

Fourth, some commentators note that their statements were designed to challenge Elisha's claim to be a prophet. They were essentially saying, "If you are a man of God, why don't you go on up to heaven like Elijah did?" The term "baldhead" might be a reference to the fact that lepers shaved their heads. Such a comment would indicate that these young men looked upon Elisha as a detestable outcast.

Fifth, it was not Elisha who took their lives, but God. He alone could have providentially directed the bears to attack them. It is evident that by mocking this man of God, these young men were revealing their true attitudes toward God Himself. Such contempt for the Lord was punishable by death. The Scriptures do not say that Elisha prayed for this kind of punishment. It was clearly an act of God in judgment upon this impious gang.

## 2 Kings 8:26

*Was Ahaziah 22 years old when he began to reign in Judah, or was he 42 years old?*

**Problem:** According to the statement in 2 Kings 8:26, Ahaziah was 22 years old when he began to reign in Judah. However, in 2 Chronicles 22:2 (KJV) we find the claim that Ahaziah was age 42 when he took the throne in Judah. Which is correct?

**Solution:** This is clearly a copyist error, and there is sufficient evidence to demonstrate that Ahaziah was 22 years old when he began to reign in Judah. In 2 Kings 8:17, we find that Joram, father of Ahaziah and son of Ahab, was 32 years old when be became king. Joram died at age 40, eight years after becoming king. Consequently, his son Ahaziah could not have been 42 when he took the throne after his father's death, otherwise he would have been older than his father.

## 2 Kings 17:4

*How can this verse mention a king of Egypt named "So" when there are no records of such a king?*

**Problem:** When Shalmaneser king of Assyria came to do battle with Hoshea king of Israel, Shalmaneser discovered a conspiracy that

Hoshea had begun when he "sent messengers to So, king of Egypt" (2 Kings 17:4). However, besides this statement in the Bible, there are no records of a king of Egypt named So. Is this an error?

**Solution:** The name translated "So" can also be translated "Sais," which was the name of the capital city of Tefnakht, the king of Egypt at the time Hoshea ruled in Israel. Thus the passage should read, "He [Hoshea] sent to Sais, to the king of Egypt." The word "So" in the NKJV is not the name of the king of Egypt, but of the capital city of the kingdom of Egypt. There is no error here.

# 1 CHRONICLES

*What is the correct genealogical relationship of Pedaiah, Shealtiel, and Zerubbabel?*

**Problem:** According to the statement in 1 Chronicles 3:19, Zerubbabel was the son of Pedaiah. However, according to Ezra 3:2, Zerubbabel was the son of Shealtiel. What is the correct genealogical relationship?

**Solution:** In 1 Chronicles 3:16–19 we find the following genealogy.

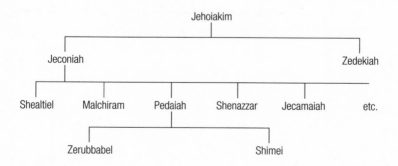

This record shows that Zerubbabel was the son of Pedaiah and the nephew of Shealtiel, Pedaiah's older brother. Although the Bible does not record the death of Pedaiah, it is reasonable to assume that he died shortly after Shimei was born, and Shealtiel, the oldest of the sons of Jeconiah, adopted Zerubbabel as his own son.

## 1 Chronicles 9:1

### *What happened to the missing "Book of Kings"?*

**Problem:** The Books of Chronicles often refer to other missing books on which the inspired record in Chronicles is partially based (cf. 1 Chron. 9:1; 27:24; 29:29; 2 Chron. 9:29; 13:22; 16:11; 25:26; 27:7; 28:26; 32:32; 33:19; 35:27; 36:8). Some of these books were written by prophets (1 Chron. 29:29). How could books that were written by prophets of God, or were the basis of prophetic books, perish? Why did God not preserve His Word?

**Solution:** Prophets as a class were usually an educated group able to read and write. Samuel even led a "group of prophets" (1 Sam. 19:20, NIV). It was only natural that as moral educators in Israel, they would keep a record of events in addition to whatever prophecies God may have given them. Thus, the records of Iddo the Seer may have been normal (uninspired) records that he kept (1 Chron. 29:29). It is noteworthy that they are not referred to as "visions" or "prophecies."

Further, it is not unusual for inspired books of the Bible to cite uninspired ones. The Apostle Paul even cited pagan poets (Acts 17:28; 1 Cor. 15:33; Titus 1:12). This does not mean they were inspired, but simply that they uttered a truth, which a prophet or apostle then incorporated into his inspired book.

# 2 CHRONICLES

*How could Elijah have sent a letter long after his departure into heaven?*

**Problem:** When Jehoram became king in Judah, "he made high places in the mountains of Judah, and caused the inhabitants of Jerusalem to commit harlotry, and led Judah astray" (2 Chron. 21:11). In 2 Chronicles 21:12, we find that, in response to Jehoram's sin, Elijah sent a letter to Jehoram. However, if Elijah was translated prior to the reign of Jehoram the son of Jehoshaphat, then how could he have sent a letter to Jehoram?

**Solution:** Elijah was not translated until sometime during the reign of Jehoram son of Ahab. Jehoram son of Ahab reigned in Israel from about 852 to 841 BC. Jehoram son of Jehoshaphat reigned in Judah from 848 to 841 BC. Therefore, since Elijah was not translated until sometime in the reign of Jehoram of Israel, it is perfectly reasonable that he could have sent this letter to Jehoram of Judah.

# EZRA

*How could the rebuilding have begun during the reign of Cyrus when Ezra 4:24 says it was in the reign of Darius I?*

**Problem:** According to Ezra 3:8–13, the rebuilding of the temple began under the reign of Cyrus the Great (cf. Ezra 5:16), who reigned in Persia from about 559 to 530 BC. However, Ezra 4:24 says the rebuilding of the temple took place during the reign of Darius, king of Persia, about 520 BC. Also, Haggai 1:15 implies that the building of the temple did not begin until 520 BC. How can these statements be reconciled?

**Solution:** The statements in Ezra 3:10 and 5:16 are references to *laying the foundation*, while Ezra 4:24 and Haggai 1:15 concern *resuming the rebuilding project* after a long period of delay. Ezra 4:4 points out that as soon as the people of the land heard about the rebuilding project, they discouraged the people and frustrated their efforts throughout the reign of Cyrus. The project was abandoned for sixteen years. At this point, God directed Haggai to prophesy to the people of Jerusalem to motivate them to begin the project again. This is referred to in Ezra 4:24. The rebuilding of the temple was resumed about 520 BC during the time of Darius and was completed in 516 BC.

# — NEHEMIAH —

*If Ai was destroyed earlier, why is it still inhabited here?*

**Problem:** After an earlier embarrassing defeat because of disobedience to God, Joshua's forces completely destroyed the city of Ai (Josh. 8:28). But it is still flourishing many years later (Neh. 7:32).

**Solution:** This is many centuries later, and the city was rebuilt by survivors or others. Phrases like "utterly destroyed" (Josh. 8:26) refer to all who got caught. It does not say that some did not escape. Nor does it eliminate the possibility that others moved in later to occupy the site.

This same explanation applies to the Amalekites who were completely destroyed (1 Sam. 15:7–8), yet survived to be overthrown at a later date (1 Sam. 30:1, 17). Likewise, Bethel and Gezer were conquered by Joshua (Josh. 12:12, 16) and later under the judges (Judg. 1:22–29). However, Genesis 32:3 may refer to the settlement of Edom by anticipation (cf. Gen. 36:6, 8).

*Was this feast not celebrated since Joshua's time or was it celebrated later by Zerubbabel?*

**Problem:** According to this passage, the Feast of Tabernacles had not been celebrated by Israel "since the days of Joshua the son

of Nun." Yet, Ezra 3:4 declares that Zerubbabel and the Israelites "kept the Feast of Tabernacles" after they returned from the
Babylonian captivity.

**Solution:** The Nehemiah passage means there had been *nothing like
this celebration* since Joshua's day. It does not mean no one had
ever celebrated this feast since Joshua's day. Nehemiah's celebration
was unique in many ways. First, it was commemorated by "the
whole congregation" (Neh. 8:17). Second, it was celebrated with
"great gladness" (v. 17). Third, it was celebrated with a Biblethon—
that is, with continual Bible reading for one week. Fourth, they
celebrated it exactly as Moses had commanded, with a restored
priesthood and temple (8:18; cf. 12:1ff). Nothing like this had
occurred since Joshua's day.

# ESTHER

## ESTHER

*How could this book be part of the Holy Scriptures when God is not even mentioned?*

**Problem:** Although the rabbis at Jamnia, in about AD 90, debated whether the book should continue to be counted among the inspired Scriptures, the Book of Esther has enjoyed a long history of acceptance among the books of the Hebrew canon. However, the Book of Esther is the only book in the entire Bible in which the name of God is not mentioned. How can it be part of the Word of God?

**Solution:** Even though there is an absence of the *name* of God, it is evident that there is no absence of the *hand* of God. The entire book overflows with the providence of God in human affairs. God so directed the lives of those involved that He had the right person at precisely the right place at precisely the right point in time. As Mordecai observed, "Yet who knows whether you have come to the kingdom for such a time as this?" (Esther 4:14).

Further, the name of God is found in the Book of Esther in acrostic form. At four crucial points in the story (1:20; 5:4, 13; 7:7), twice forward and twice backward, God's name (YHWH) is present in acrostic form. The devout Jew would have recognized this, while the Persians would not. This may have been God's

91

way of preserving His sacred name from pagan perversion. Even apart from any explicit use of God's name, the hand of God in directing the affairs of men is glaringly obvious throughout the narrative. Yet the free moral agency of each participant is perfectly preserved. Although He can, God does not need to invade the normal process of daily affairs to accomplish His will. His providence delicately intertwines into the acts and decisions of people so that He accomplishes all His will with divine perfection and precision without violating human free choice. The Book of Esther, like no other book, reveals the hidden, supernatural providence of God in directing all of His creation according to the good purpose of His will. Even in the explicit absence of God's name, Esther reminds us that He is always present and always in control.

## ESTHER 4:16
### *Didn't Esther disobey human government that God had ordained?*

**Problem:** Romans 13:1 informs us that even pagan governments are "appointed by God," and Peter adds, "submit yourselves to every ordinance of man for the Lord's sake" (1 Peter 2:13; cf. Titus 3:1). But it says that what she did was "against the law" (4:16). So, didn't Esther violate the God-ordained laws of Persia by going before the king?

**Solution:** Sometimes it is necessary to disobey human government, namely, when it commands us to sin. For example, if the government says we cannot pray to God (Dan. 6) or we must worship idols (Dan. 3) or we must kill innocent babies (see comments on Exod. 1:15–21), then we must disobey. In Esther's case, however, there was no such law compelling her to sin. But neither did she disobey the law of the land, since the law allowed for someone to come before the king unannounced at his or her own risk (Esther 4:11). Knowing of this provision of the law and accepting the risk of her life, Esther went before the king to save the lives of her people. In this case there was no need to disobey the law, since it was not compelling her to kill anyone or to commit any other sinful act.

# JOB

*Was Job a real historical person?*

**Problem:** The first verse of the Book of Job introduces the main character as a historical figure who actually existed in the land of Uz. However, modern scholars have questioned the historicity of the man Job. Was Job a real historical person?

**Solution:** Job was a person in human history. First of all, verse 1 of the book plainly asserts that Job actually existed. There are no literary indications that this statement should be understood any other way than as a statement of historical fact. There is every reason to accept it with the same assurance one would accept the historicity of any such statement in the Bible.

Second, the historicity of Job is attested by references in other parts of the Scripture. In Ezekiel 14:14 and 20, God names Job along with Daniel and Noah as examples of righteousness. To question the historicity of Job, one would have to question the historicity of Daniel and Noah. Additionally, this would call into question the veracity of God, for He makes reference to these men (through Ezekiel) as real historical figures.

Finally, in James 5:11 we find a reference to Job in which Job is held to be an example of patience in the midst of tribulation. James makes a matter-of-fact reference to Job that assumes the historicity of both the man and the events recorded in the book that bears his name. There would have been no real force to James's appeal if Job were merely a fictional character. For in that case, what actual comfort would his life be to real people?

## JOB 1:6

*How can Satan come before God when he was dismissed from heaven?*

**Problem:** Job 1:6 states that the sons of God came to present themselves to God, and "Satan also came among them." However, this implies that Satan has access to the throne of God when elsewhere it is declared that he has been banished from God's presence (Rev. 12:7–12).

**Solution:** Satan has been *officially* expelled from heaven, but he still *actually* has access there. He was defrocked of his position as an archangel of God when he fell (1 Tim. 3:6), but since God sovereignly overrules the universe, Satan and the rest of the angels report to Him regularly (Job 1:6; 2:1). Several places in Scripture present the idea that Satan has access to the presence of God in order to accuse the saints. In Zechariah 3:1 we find a vision of Joshua standing before the angel of the Lord with Satan on his right hand accusing him. Revelation 12:10 identifies Satan as the accuser of the brethren "who accused them before our God day and night." Apparently, as the prince of the power of the air (Eph. 2:2), Satan appears regularly before God for the purpose of accusing God's people of sin.

## JOB 19:26

*Does this verse indicate that the resurrection body will be a body of flesh?*

**Problem:** Satan had afflicted Job's body, and his flesh was rotting away. However, Job expressed his faith in God by saying, "in my flesh I shall see God" (Job 19:26). Does this mean that the resurrection body will be a body of flesh?

**Solution:** Yes. Although the preposition "from" (*min*) may be translated "without," it is a characteristic of this preposition that when it is used with the verb "to see," it has the meaning "from the vantage point of." This idea is strengthened by the use of contrasting parallelism employed in this verse. Hebrew poetry often employs two parallel lines of poetic expression that sometimes express contrasting words or ideas (called antithetic parallelism). Here the loosing of Job's flesh is contrasted by his trust in God to restore the body that is decaying before his eyes, and that in his very flesh, he would see God. This is a most sublime expression of Job's faith in a literal, physical resurrection (see also Pss. 2:7; 16:10; Isa. 26:19; Dan. 12:2; Luke 24:39; John 5:28–29; Acts 2:31–32).

## JOB 37:18

*Does the Bible err in speaking of a solid dome above the earth?*

**Problem:** Job speaks of God who "spread out the skies" like "a cast metal mirror" (37:18). Indeed, the Hebrew word for the "firmament" (*raqia*) that God created (cf. Gen. 1:6) is defined in the Hebrew lexicon as a solid object. But this is in clear conflict with the modern scientific understanding of space as nonsolid and largely empty.

**Solution:** It is true that the origin of the Hebrew word *raqia* meant a solid object. However, meaning is not determined by *origin* (etymology), but by *usage*. Originally, the English word "board" referred to a wooden plank. But when we speak of a church board member, the word no longer has that meaning. When used of the atmosphere above the earth, "firmament" clearly does not mean something solid. This is evident for several reasons. First, the related word *raqa* (beat out, spread out) is correctly rendered "expanse" by many recent translations. Just as metal spreads out when beaten (cf. Exod. 39:3; Isa. 40:19), so the firmament is a thinned out area.

Second, the root meaning "spread out" can be used independently of "beat out," as it is in several passages (cf. Ps. 136:6; Isa. 42:5; 44:24). Isaiah wrote, "So says Jehovah God, He who created the heavens and *stretched them out*, spreading out the earth and its offspring" (Isa. 42:5, MKJV). This same verb is used of extending curtains or tents in which to dwell, which would make no sense if there was no empty space there in which to live. Isaiah, for example, spoke of the Lord "who sits on the circle of the earth, and its people are like grasshoppers; who *stretches out the heavens like a curtain, and spreads them out like a tent to dwell in*" (Isa. 40:22, MKJV).

Third, the Bible speaks of rain falling through the sky (Job 36:27–28). But this makes no sense if the sky is a metal dome. Nowhere does the Bible refer to little holes in a metal dome through which the drops fall. It does speak figuratively of the "windows of heaven" opening for the flood (Gen. 7:11). But this should probably not be taken any more literally than our idiom "It's raining cats and dogs."

Fourth, the Genesis creation account speaks of birds that "fly above the earth across the face of the firmament" (Gen. 1:20). But this would be impossible if the sky was solid. Thus, it is more appropriate to translate *raqia* by the word "expanse" (as the NASB and NIV do). And in this sense there is no conflict with the concept of space in modern science.

Fifth, even taken literally, Job's statement (37:18) does not affirm that the "skies" *are* a "metal mirror," but simply that they are "*as* [like]" a mirror. In other words, it is a comparison that need not be taken literally, any more than God is really a "strong tower" (cf. Prov. 18:10). Further, the point of comparison in Job is not the solidity of the "skies" and a mirror, but their durability (cf. word "strong" [*chazaq*], v. 18). So when all is considered, there is no evidence that the Bible affirms that the firmament of the sky is a metallic dome. And thus there is no conflict with modern science.

# PSALMS

*How could David have written this psalm when critics insist that most psalms were not completed until much later?*

**Problem:** The inscription on this psalm, as on many others, says, "A Psalm of David." However, biblical critics argue that the form and style of the psalm reflects a much later period than David's time.

**Solution:** Most scholars do not believe these inscriptions are part of the inspired text, but were added later. However, there is a strong evidence that David did write this psalm, as well as some seventy others attributed to him. Consider the following.

First, these inscriptions are very old and reflect the most ancient documentary evidence about the authors of these psalms.

Second, David, being a true poet (cf. 2 Sam. 1:17–27), was certainly capable of writing these psalms.

Third, there is evidence that David possessed the rich imagination needed to write Hebrew poetry (cf. 2 Sam. 1:19–27).

Fourth, David was also a good musician (cf. 1 Sam. 16:18–23), which would greatly aid him in composing these psalms that comprised the ancient hymnal of Judaism.

Fifth, David probably composed the music used in Solomon's temple (1 Chron. 6:31–32) in which these psalms were later sung.

Sixth, the Bible declares that David was endued with the Spirit of God (1 Sam. 16:13), thus enabling him to write such inspired poems.

Seventh, David was deeply spiritual in both character and heart (cf. 2 Sam. 7), something obviously true of the author of the psalms attributed to him.

Eighth, Psalm 18, for example, is also recorded in 2 Samuel 22, where it is directly attributed to King David.

Ninth, David swore on his deathbed that God spoke through his mouth as the "sweet psalmist" of Israel (2 Sam. 23:1).

Finally, both our Lord and NT writers verified by name that David wrote specific psalms attributed to him in these OT inscriptions. For example:

Psalm 2 is cited in Acts 4:25–26 as by David.
Psalm 32 is cited in Romans 4:7–8 as by David.
Psalm 95 is cited in Hebrews 4:7 as by David.
Psalm 110 is cited in Matthew 22:44 as by David.

In brief, there is an ancient and unbroken teaching extending to modern times, which includes our Lord and His apostles, that King David is indeed the author of the psalms attributed to him. No one has provided any solid evidence to the contrary, but have offered instead mere speculations about literary form that generally either beg the question or are based on the fallacious argument from ignorance.

## PSALM 37:9, 34

*When the wicked are cut off, are they annihilated?*

**Problem:** The psalmist affirms that "evildoers shall be cut off." Elsewhere (Ps. 73:27; Prov. 21:28), it says they will perish (see comments on 2 Thess. 1:9). But does being cut off forever mean they will be annihilated?

**Solution:** Being "cut off" does not mean to be annihilated. If it did, then the Messiah would have been annihilated when He died, since the same word (*karath*) is used of the Messiah's death (in Dan. 9:26). However, we know that Christ was not annihilated but lives on forever after His death (cf. Rev. 1:18; also see comments on 2 Thess. 1:9).

## PSALM 109:1ff

*How can the God of love in the NT be reconciled with the vengeful God of these cursing psalms?*

**Problem:** This psalm, like many others in the OT (e.g., Pss. 35; 69), pronounces curses on one's enemies. Thus they are called imprecatory (cursing) psalms. David says, "Let his children be fatherless, and his wife a widow" (109:9). By contrast, Jesus said, "Love your enemies . . . and pray for those who . . . persecute you" (Matt. 5:44). How can the God of vengeance of the OT be the same as the God of love of the NT (1 John 4:16)?

**Solution:** Several important factors must be kept in mind in understanding these imprecatory or so-called cursing psalms.

First, the judgment called for is based on *divine justice* and not on *human grudges*. David said clearly of his enemies in this psalm, "they have rewarded me evil for good, and hatred for my love" (v. 5). While David did pray this imprecation (curse) on his enemies, he nonetheless loved them and committed them to the justice of God for a due reward for their wicked deeds. David's action in sparing Saul's life is vivid proof that revenge was not a motivation behind this psalm. In spite of the fact that Saul stalked David's life, David forgave Saul and even spared his life (cf. 1 Sam. 25; 26). Further, they can't be grudges, since there are self-imprecations that call for judgment on one's self if the author drifts from God (cf. Ps. 7:4–5).

Second, judgment in these psalms is expressed in terms of the culture of the day. Since being fatherless or a widow was considered a tragedy, the curse is expressed in these commonly understood categories.

Third, since the Hebrew culture made no sharp distinction between the sinner and his sin, the judgment is expressed in personal terms rather than abstractly. Furthermore, since the Hebrew family was a solidarity, the whole family was saved (cf. Noah, Gen. 7–8) or judged together (cf. Achan, Josh. 7:24).

Fourth, the phenomenon of imprecation is not unique to the OT. Jesus urged His disciples to curse cities that did not receive the gospel (Matt. 10:14). Jesus Himself called down judgment on Bethsaida and Capernaum in Matthew 11:21–24. Paul declared anathema any who did not love the Lord Jesus (1 Cor. 16:22). Even the saints in heaven cried out to God for vengeance on those who martyred believers (Rev. 6:9–10).

Fifth, imprecations are not a primitive or a purely OT phenomenon. Justice executed on evil is just as much a part of God as is blessing on the righteous. Both are true of God in the OT as well as in the NT. In fact, God is mentioned as being loving more often in the OT than in the NT.

Sixth, because the OT emphasis was on earthly reward, connected with family, prosperity, and the land, OT curses were expressed in these terms. With the NT revelation expressed more in terms of eternal destiny, there was less need to express imprecations in earthly terms.

Even in these OT imprecations, one can see an anticipation of Christ. God has committed all judgment to the Son (John 5:22). So those who long for justice are not only aspiring to His righteous kingdom, but can wait patiently for Him who comes quickly to execute it justly (Rev. 22:12).

## PSALM 139:13–16

*Can it be inferred from this verse that the Bible considers abortion to be murder?*

**Problem:** According to this passage, God looks upon the unborn as a human being. However, if the unborn is fully human, then abortion would be the willful killing of the innocent—murder. Does this passage indicate that God considers abortion to be murder?

**Solution:** Yes. Several other passages reinforce this position. First, the unborn are known intimately and are called out by God. In

Jeremiah 1:5, God says, "Before I formed you in the womb I knew you; before you were born I sanctified you; and I ordained you a prophet to the nations."

Second, the unborn are said to possess personal characteristics—sin, as in Psalm 51:5; or joy, as in Luke 1:44.

Third, anyone who harms the unborn receives the same punishment for harm done to an adult. Elsewhere (see comments on Exod. 21:22–23), equal punishment is given for harm done to a woman or to the child she carries. God looks upon the unborn as fully human. And the willful taking of an innocent human life is murder.

# PROVERBS

*Who is referred to as "wisdom" in these verses?*

**Problem:** Some commentators have claimed that the person identified as wisdom in Proverbs 8:22–31 is Jesus, because 1 Corinthians
1:30 states that Jesus is the wisdom of God. However, though the
NKJV translates 8:22 as "The Lord *possessed* me," the Hebrew
uses the word *qanah*, which is usually translated "to create." If this
passage is a reference to Jesus, then why does 8:22 affirm that the
Lord created wisdom? If "wisdom" in Proverbs is not a reference
to Jesus, then who is it?

**Solution:** This passage is not a direct reference to any person. Poetic
expression often takes an abstract idea and talks about it as if it
were a person. This is called personification. The wisdom referred
to here is not a reference to Jesus since He was not created but is the
eternal Son of God (John 1:1; 8:58). Rather, it is a personification
of the virtue or character of wisdom for the purpose of emphasis
and impact. However, since Jesus is the perfect wisdom of God,
He is the only one who perfectly personified and exemplified the
wisdom spoken of in Proverbs—for "in Whom are hidden all the
treasures of wisdom and knowledge" (Col. 2:3).

## PROVERBS 22:6

*How can this verse be true when experience teaches us that children often abandon the principles of their training?*

**Problem:** According to Proverbs 22:6, if a child is trained in the correct way to live, he or she will not depart from this training even when older. However, experience shows that this is not always true. Isn't this proverb contradicted by experience?

**Solution:** This proverb does not contradict experience because it is only a general principle that allows for individual exceptions. For example, Proverbs 16:7 affirms that a godly man's enemies are at peace with him. But Paul was godly, and his enemies stoned him (Acts 14). Jesus was godly, and His enemies crucified Him! Proverbs are not designed to be absolute guarantees. Rather, they express truths that provide helpful advice and guidance for wise living by which individuals should conduct their daily lives. It is generally true that the diligent training of godly parents will influence children to follow that training in later years. However, circumstances and individual personalities and problems might work against the training a child has received. The proverb encourages parents to diligently fulfill their responsibilities and to trust the future to the grace and sovereignty of God.

## PROVERBS 25:1

*How can Solomon be the author of Proverbs when Hezekiah's men copied them?*

**Problem:** The Book of Proverbs claims to be written by Solomon (1:1; 10:1). Conservative Jewish and Christian scholars have long attributed this book to King Solomon. However, Proverbs 25:1 speaks of King Hezekiah's men "copying" these proverbs long after Solomon's death. Further, the last two chapters claim to be written by Agur (30:1) and King Lemuel (31:1), not by Solomon.

**Solution:** Since Solomon wrote some three thousand proverbs (1 Kings 4:32)—many more than are in this book—it is possible that the Book of Proverbs was not put together from Solomon's many proverbs until after his death. If so, then God would have guided His servants who compiled it so that they selected the ones He wanted in His authoritative Word.

It is also possible that Solomon himself wrote the Book of Proverbs and that the reference to "copying" by Hezekiah's men simply refers to their later transcribing what Solomon wrote on another manuscript. The last two chapters could have been included by Solomon himself or added later since they too were inspired wisdom like that of Solomon's, even though they were written by other men of God named Agur (30:1) and Lemuel (31:1).

# ECCLESIASTES

## ECCLESIASTES 1:1
*If this book is inspired, why isn't it quoted in the NT?*

**Problem:** The NT writers quote the vast majority of the OT from Genesis to Malachi. There are literally hundreds of citations from every major section of the OT. Yet the Book of Ecclesiastes is not quoted once. If it was inspired, then why isn't it cited at least one time?

**Solution:** There are several OT books that are not directly quoted in the NT, including Ruth, 1 and 2 Chronicles, Esther, Song of Solomon, and Ecclesiastes, although persons or events from some are alluded to in the NT. However, all these books were considered inspired by both Judaism and Christianity. Several points should be kept in mind.

First, being quoted in the NT was not a test for the inspiration of an OT book. Rather, the question was whether it was written by a spokesperson accredited by God and accepted by His people. Ecclesiastes meets this test.

Second, while no *text* of Ecclesiastes is cited as such in the NT, many of its *truths* are. For example:

| | |
|---|---|
| What we sow we reap. | Eccles. 11:1; cf. Gal. 6:7 |
| Avoid the lust of youth. | Eccles. 11:10; cf. 2 Tim. 2:22 |
| Death is divinely appointed. | Eccles. 3:2; cf. Heb. 9:2 |
| Love of money is evil. | Eccles. 5:10; cf. 1 Tim. 6:10 |
| Don't be wordy in prayer. | Eccles. 5:2; cf. Matt. 6:7 |

Third, the NT writers had no occasion to quote from every book in the OT. Few Christians have quoted recently from 1 Kings, yet the NT did (Rom. 11:4). Indeed, few believers ever cite 2 or 3 John, and yet they are part of the inspired Word of God. Whether, or even how often, a book is quoted does not determine whether it is inspired but whether it was breathed-out by God (2 Tim. 3:16; 2 Peter 1:20–21).

## ECCLESIASTES 1:2

*How can this book be a part of the Scriptures, since it contains such skepticism?*

**Problem:** Several statements that Solomon makes throughout this book indicate a skepticism that seems contrary to the Bible as a whole. In Ecclesiastes 9:5 Solomon says, "For the living know that they will die; *but the dead know nothing.*" However, the Book of Ecclesiastes is included in the canon of Holy Scriptures as an inspired book. How can such a skeptical book be inspired Scripture?

**Solution:** Although Ecclesiastes does contain statements that, when taken in isolation, appear to be contrary to the teaching of the Bible, the book is not a book of skepticism. Once these statements are understood in their contexts, their meaning is compatible with other Scriptures. Such statements as found in Ecclesiastes 1:2 are not designed to produce or to promote skepticism. Rather, Solomon is recording his search for happiness and meaning in life by pursuing everything that this world offers. Each of these seemingly skeptical observations is aimed at demonstrating that, apart from God, everything "under the sun" is only vanity, and that the only source of true happiness and lasting peace is the Lord our God. Solomon's investigations led eventually to the conclusion that the whole duty of man is to "fear God and keep His commandments" (Eccles. 12:13).

## ECCLESIASTES 3:19

*Is man's fate the same as that of animals?*

**Problem:** Solomon seems to claim here that there is no difference between the death of humans and animals. "One thing befalls them: as one dies, so dies the other." Yet Solomon asserts later that, unlike animals, when a human dies, "the spirit will return to God who gave it" (Eccles. 12:7). How can this conflict be explained?

**Solution:** There are both similarities and differences between the death of animals and humans. In both cases, their bodies die and return to dust. Likewise, their death is certain, and both are powerless to prevent it. In these respects, the *physical* phenomena are the same for both humans and animals.

On the other hand, humans have immortal souls (spirits), and animals do not (Eccles. 12:7; cf. 3:21). Of no beasts does the Bible say, "to be absent from the body . . . [is] to be present with the Lord" (2 Cor. 5:8). Likewise, nowhere does the Bible speak of the resurrection of animals, as it does of all human beings (cf. John 5:28–29; Rev. 20:4–6). So there is a big difference in the *spiritual* realm between the death of humans and animals. Consider the following summary:

### HUMAN AND ANIMAL DEATHS

| SIMILARITIES | DIFFERENCES |
|---|---|
| Physically | Spiritually |
| In the body | In the soul |
| Life before death | Life after death |
| Mortality of the body | Immortality of the person |
| How the body decays | That the body is raised |
| No control over death | Experience of a resurrection |

## ECCLESIASTES 3:20

*If all return to dust, how can there be a resurrection?*

**Problem:** Some have argued against a physical resurrection on the grounds that the scattered fragments of decomposed corpses cannot be reassembled, since some become plants, or others are eaten by animals or even cannibals. Yet, the Bible declares that all bodies will "come forth" from the "graves" (John 5:28–29).

**Solution:** Several things must be noted in this connection. First, as many scholars have pointed out, if necessary it would be no problem for an omnipotent God to bring all of the exact particles of one's body together again at the resurrection. Certainly He who created every particle in the universe could reconstitute the relatively few particles (by comparison) in the human body. The God who created the world out of *nothing* is surely able to fashion a resurrection body out of *something*.

Second, it is not necessary to believe that the *same particles* will be restored in the resurrection body. Even common sense dictates that a body can be the *same physical body* without having the *same physical particles*. The observable fact that bodies eat food and give off waste products, as well as get fatter and skinnier, is sufficient evidence of this. Certainly, we do not say that someone's body is no longer material or no longer his or her body simply because it gains or loses weight.

Third, in the light of modern science, it is unnecessary to believe that God will reconstitute the exact particles one had in his preresurrection body. The physical body remains physical even though, according to science, the exact physical molecules in it change every seven years or so. So, the resurrection body can be just as material as our present bodies and still have new molecules in it.

# — SONG OF SOLOMON —

*How did a sensual book like this get in the Bible?*

**Problem 1:** The Bible condemns the lust of the flesh and sensuality (Rom. 6:6; Gal. 6:16–21; 1 John 2:16). Yet this love song is filled with sensual expressions and sexual overtures (cf. 1:2; 2:5; 3:1; 4:5).

**Solution 1:** The Bible does not condemn sex, but only perverted sex. God created sex (Gen. 1:27), and He ordained that it should be enjoyed within the bonds of a monogamous marriage and in a relationship of love. The Scriptures declare, "Rejoice with the wife of your youth. As a loving deer and a graceful doe, let her breasts satisfy you at all times; and always be enraptured with her love" (Prov. 5:18–19).

After warning against those who forbid marriage (1 Tim. 4:3), the apostle declares that "every creature of God is good" (v. 4), and he goes on to speak of the God "who gives us richly all things to enjoy" (6:17). Hebrews insists that "marriage is honorable among all, and the bed undefiled; but fornicators and adulterers God will judge" (Heb. 13:4).

God realizes that normal people will have sexual desires, but He adds, "Nevertheless, because of sexual immorality, let each man have his own wife, and let each woman have her own husband"

(1 Cor. 7:2). So, sex itself is not sinful, nor are sexual desires. God created them and intends that they be enjoyed within the loving bonds of a monogamous marriage. The Song of Solomon is a divinely authoritative example of how sensual love should be expressed in marriage.

# ISAIAH

*Hasn't it been shown that Isaiah is actually two or more books, and that it was not all written by one Isaiah in the 8th century BC?*

**Problem:** The traditional view of the Book of Isaiah is that it was written by Isaiah, son of Amoz, sometime between 739 and 681 BC. However, modern critics have argued that Isaiah is actually composed of at least two individual books called Proto-Isaiah (1–39) and Deutero-Isaiah (40–66). Is the Book of Isaiah actually several books put together, or is it one book written by the one prophet Isaiah who lives in the 8th century BC?

**Solution:** The traditional view that the Book of Isaiah is a single work written by the prophet Isaiah is supported by several arguments. First, the critical view that separates Isaiah into two or more books is based on the assumption that there is no such thing as predictive prophecy. Modern scholars claim that the prophecies in chapters 40–55 concerning Cyrus must have been written after Cyrus ruled in Persia. This view is anti-supernatural and tries to explain these sections of Isaiah as history rather than predictive prophecy. However, since God knows the end from the beginning (Isa. 46:10), it is not at all necessary to deny the supernatural element in Isaiah's prophecies.

Second, the differences between the two halves of the book can be explained in other ways than the two-author approach. Chapters 1 through 39 prepare the reader for the prophecies contained in chapters 40 through 66. Without these preparatory chapters, the last section of the book would make little sense. Chapters 1 through 35 warn of the Assyrian menace that threatens to destroy God's people. Chapters 36–39 form a transition from the previous section to chapters 40–66 by looking forward to the invasion of Sennacherib (chapters 36–37), and looking back to the spiritual decline that has caused the downfall of Jerusalem (chapters 38–39). These four intervening chapters (36–39) are not in chronological order because the author is using them to prepare the reader for what is to follow.

Third, the difference in words and style of writing between the two sections of the book has been used by critical scholars to substantiate their claim that there are at least two different books. However, these differences are not as great as has been claimed, and the differences that do exist can be explained as a difference in subject matter and emphasis. No author writes in exactly the same style using precisely the same vocabulary when writing about different subject matter. Nevertheless, there are a number of phrases that are found in both sections that attest to the unity of the book. For example, the title "the Holy one of Israel" is found twelve times in chapters 1–39 and fourteen times in chapters 40–66. The following list illustrates these kinds of similarities.

| Chapters 1–39 | Chapters 40–66 |
| --- | --- |
| 1:15—"Your hands are full of blood." | 59:3—"For your hands are defiled with blood." |
| 28:5—"The Lord of hosts will be for a crown of glory and a diadem of beauty to the remnant of His people." | 62:3—"You shall also be a crown of glory in the hand of the Lord, and a royal diadem in the hand of your God." |
| 35:6—"For waters shall burst forth in the wilderness, and streams in the desert." | 41:18—"I will make the wilderness a pool of water, and the dry land springs of water." |

Fourth, in Luke 4:17 we find that when our Lord rose to read in the synagogue, "He was handed the book of the prophet Isaiah." The people in the synagogue and Jesus Himself assumed that this book was from the prophet Isaiah. Other NT writers accepted Isaiah as the author of the entire book. John 12:38 states that Isaiah was the one who made the statement that is found in Isaiah 53:1. Other instances where the NT ascribes portions of chapters in 40–66 to Isaiah include Matthew 3:3 (Isa. 40:3), Mark 1:2–3 (Isa. 40:3), John 1:23 (Isa. 40:3), Matthew 12:17–21 (Isa. 42:1–4), Acts 8:32–33 (Isa. 53:7–8), and Romans 10:16 (Isa. 53:1).

Fifth, the Dead Sea Scrolls include a complete copy of the Book of Isaiah (Isaiah A or IQIs[a]) and an incomplete copy (Isaiah B or IQIs[b]), and there is no gap in the scroll between chapters 39 and 40. This indicates that the Qumran community accepted the prophecy of Isaiah as one book in the 2nd century BC. The Greek version of the Hebrew Bible, which dates from the 2nd century BC, treats the Book of Isaiah as a single book by the single author, Isaiah the prophet.

## ISAIAH 7:14
### *Is this verse a prophecy about the virgin birth of Jesus Christ?*

**Problem:** The prophecy of Isaiah 7:14 concerns the conception of a virgin and the bringing forth of a son whose name would be Immanuel. However, verse 16 seems to place the birth of the child before the invasion of the Assyrian armies and the fall of Samaria in 722 BC, and Isaiah 8:3 seems to be a fulfillment of this prophecy. How can this be a prophecy about the virgin birth of Jesus?

**Solution:** The fulfillment of this prophecy may be twofold. Because of the desperate situation the people of Israel faced, God promised to give them a sign that would assure them He would ultimately deliver His people out of bondage. Many scholars believe this sign came in two ways. First, it came as a sign of the physical deliverance of Israel from bondage to which they were going under the invading Assyrians. Second, it came as a sign of the spiritual deliverance of all of God's people from spiritual bondage to Satan. The first aspect of the sign was fulfilled in the birth of Maher-Shalal-Hash-Baz as recorded in Isaiah 8:3. The second aspect of the sign was fulfilled in the birth of Jesus Christ at Bethlehem as recorded in the Gospels.

The word translated "virgin" (*almah*) refers to a young maiden who has never had sexual relations with a man. The wife of Isaiah who bore the son in fulfillment of the first aspect of the prophecy was a virgin until she conceived by Isaiah. However, according to Matthew 1:23–25, Mary, the mother of Jesus, was a virgin even when she conceived and gave birth to Jesus. The physical conception and birth of the son of Isaiah was a sign to Israel that God would deliver them from physical bondage to the Assyrians. But the supernatural conception and birth of the Son of God was a sign to all of God's people that He would deliver them from spiritual bondage to sin and death.

Others claim that the passage refers only to Jesus since 1) the mother of Maher-Shalal-Hash-Baz was not a virgin; 2) only Jesus was called "Immanuel" (Matt. 1:23); 3) *almah* always means virgin; 4) it was a "sign" (miracle), which only Jesus's virgin birth was. A problem with this view is that the child was to grow up before the Assyrians invaded Israel (Isa. 7:16–17). But proponents retort that this refers to the boy (Jesus) growing up in Isaiah's vision, not Jesus's actual life many centuries later. Both views solve the problem and are within orthodoxy.

## ISAIAH 9:6

### Why is Jesus called "the everlasting Father" if He is the Son of God?

**Problem:** The orthodox Christian doctrine of the Trinity holds that God is one essence in three persons—Father, Son, and Holy Spirit. However, Isaiah 9:6 calls the Messiah "the everlasting Father." How can Jesus be both the Father and the Son?

**Solution:** This verse is not a Trinitarian formula that calls Jesus Christ the Father. Actually, it is easier to grasp the idea when the phrase is rendered literally into English, "Father of eternity." The first part of verse 6 makes reference to the incarnation of Jesus. The part that lists the names by which He is called expresses His relationship to His people. He is to us the Wonderful Counselor, the Mighty God, the Father of Eternity, the Prince of Peace. Considered in this way, we see that Jesus is the One who gives us eternal life.

By His death, burial, and resurrection, He has brought life and immortality to light. Truly, He is the Father of eternity for His people. The name "Father of eternity" indicates that, as a loving father provides for his children, so Jesus loves us and has provided for us by giving us everlasting life.

## ISAIAH 44:28

*How could Isaiah talk in such specific terms about a king who would not exist for some two hundred years?*

**Problem:** In Isaiah 44:28 and 45:1, Isaiah specifically names Cyrus in connection with the future restoration of Israel and the laying of the foundations of the temple. However, Isaiah conducted his ministry sometime between 739 and 681 BC, while Cyrus would not even become king of Persia until 539 BC. That is a period of at least 150 years. How could Isaiah specifically name Cyrus before he even lived?

**Solution:** This is an instance of supernatural prophecy. Although it was not in the power of Isaiah to look into the future, it is certainly in the power of God who declares "the end from the beginning" (Isa. 46:10). Not only does God know who will come to power, but "the Most High rules in the kingdom of men, and gives it to whomever He chooses" (Dan. 4:32). It is God who sets up kingdoms, and it is God who brings them down. It is no small wonder, then, that God is able to name a king almost two hundred years before he takes the throne. (See comments on Dan. 1:1.)

## ISAIAH 45:7

*Is God the author of evil?*

**Problem:** According to this verse, God "creates good and evil" (KJV, cf. Jer. 18:11 and Lam. 3:38; Amos 3:6). But many other Scriptures inform us that God is not evil (1 John 1:5), cannot even look approvingly on evil (Hab. 1:13), and cannot even be tempted by evil (James 1:13).

**Solution:** The Bible is clear that God is morally perfect (cf. Deut. 32:4; Matt. 5:48), and it is impossible for Him to sin (Heb. 6:18). At the same time, His absolute justice demands that He punish sin. This judgment takes both temporal and eternal forms (Matt. 25:41; Rev. 20:11–15). In its temporal form, the execution of God's justice is sometimes called "evil" because it seems to be evil to those undergoing it (cf. Heb. 12:11). However, the Hebrew word for evil (rā) used here does not always mean moral evil. Indeed, the context indicates that it should be translated, as the NKJV and other modern translations do, as "calamity." Thus, God is properly said to be the author of "evil" in this sense, but not in the moral sense—at least not directly.

Further, there is an indirect sense in which God is the author of moral evil. God created moral beings with free choice, and free choice is the origin of moral evil in the universe. So, ultimately God is responsible for making moral creatures who, in turn, are responsible for moral evil. God made evil *possible* by creating free creatures, but the free creatures made evil *actual*. Of course, the possibility of evil (i.e., free choice) is itself a good thing. So, God created only good things, one of which was the power of free choice, and moral creatures produced the evil. However, God is the author of a moral universe and in this indirect and ultimate sense is the author of the possibility of evil. Of course, God only *permitted* evil and does not *promote* it, and He will ultimately *produce* a greater good through it (cf. Gen. 50:20; Rev. 21–22).

The relation of God and evil can be summarized this way:

| GOD IS *NOT* THE AUTHOR OF EVIL | GOD IS THE AUTHOR OF EVIL |
|---|---|
| In the sense of sin | In the sense of calamity |
| Moral evil | Nonmoral evil |
| Perversity | Plagues |
| Moral evil directly | Moral evil indirectly |
| Actuality of moral evil | Possibility of moral evil |

# JEREMIAH

*Can God repent?*

**Problem:** The prophet speaks of God repenting so many times that He is "weary of relenting." Yet in other places the Bible affirms that "He is not a man that He should relent" (1 Sam. 15:29; cf. Mal. 3:6).

**Solution:** God does not actually change, but only appears to change as we change, just as the wind appears to change when we turn and go in another direction. God cannot change His character nor His unconditional promises (Heb. 6:17–18), because they are based in His unchangeable nature (cf. 2 Tim. 2:13). In fact, it is because God is unchangeable in Himself that He appears to change in relation to humans who vary in their character and conduct. God's immutability demands that His feelings and actions toward different human beings be different. He always feels the same revulsion toward sin (Hab. 1:13), but God cannot feel the same toward a person who has just fallen in sin as toward that same person when he confesses his sin and calls upon God's mercy for salvation. In this case, it is not God who changes, but the person who changes in relation to God. When a person moves in relation to the pillar, the pillar does not move in relation to the person.

## JEREMIAH 36:28

*How can this book be inspired if the original manuscript of Jeremiah perished?*

**Problem:** According to evangelical scholars, only the original manuscripts (autographs) were inspired and inerrant, not the copies, since there are minor errors in the copies. But according to this passage, the king destroyed the original manuscript in the fire.

**Solution:** When evangelicals refer to the "original manuscripts" alone being inspired (autographs), they do not exclude the fact that a biblical author may have had a "second edition" in original manuscripts too. Nor do they exclude the fact that, if the original is destroyed, God can inspire another one just like it. Indeed, Jeremiah was told, "Take yet another scroll, and write on it all the former words that were in the first scroll" (v. 28). So both manuscripts were inspired, only the first one perished without a copy. So the second one is now the "original" one.

Technically, we should not claim that only the original *manuscripts* are inspired, but the original *text*. For example, a perfect copy (e.g., a photocopy) of an original manuscript is as inspired as is the original manuscript itself. Likewise, all existing manuscript copies of the original are inspired insofar as they have accurately reproduced the original manuscript. God in His wisdom has not deemed fit to preserve the original manuscripts of Scripture. Some believe this is so men would not make an idol of it (cf. 2 Kings 18:4). Others claim it was His way of keeping Scripture from human distortion by diffusing so many copies that it would be impossible to distort all of them. Whatever the case, the copies we do have are earlier, more numerous, and more accurate than those of any other book from the ancient world. They bring us all the truth of the original text and the minor differences do not affect any doctrine of the Christian faith.

# —— LAMENTATIONS ——

## LAMENTATIONS 3:22
*Is God compassionate or ferocious?*

**Problem:** This and many other verses in Scripture describe God as merciful and compassionate, slow to wrath and plentiful in kindness (cf. Ps. 94:9; James 5:11; 1 John 4:16). By contrast, there are numerous passages in the Bible that reveal God as wrathful and vengeful. God told Moses, "You shall destroy all the peoples whom the Lord your God delivers over to you; your eye shall have no pity on them" (Deut. 7:16; cf. 1 Sam. 6:19; 15:2–3; Jer. 13:14; Heb. 12:29).

**Solution:** In each case, the object is different. God executes His wrath on the wicked, as His justice demands, and He bestows His kindness on the righteous, as His love constrains Him. These are consistent acts of God in accordance with His own unchangeable essence (Mal. 3:6; James 1:17). But since the objects are different, it only appears that God is acting contradictorily, when in fact these actions are eminently compatible in a holy, loving God.

# EZEKIEL

*Does God ever punish one person for another's sin?*

**Problem:** Ezekiel says clearly God does not punish the sons for their fathers' sins, but that "the soul who sins shall die [for its own sins]." However, in Exodus 20:5 we are informed that God visits "the iniquity of the fathers on the children to the third and fourth generations." These seem flatly contradictory.

**Solution:** Ezekiel is speaking of the actual *guilt* of the fathers' sins never being held against the sons, but Moses was referring to the *consequences* of the fathers' sins being passed on to their children. Unfortunately, if a father is a drunk, his children can suffer abuse and even poverty. Likewise, if a mother has contracted AIDS from drug use, then her baby may be born with AIDS. But this does not mean that innocent children are guilty of the sins of their parents.

Additionally, even if the Exodus passage implied that moral guilt was somehow also visited on the children, it would only be because they too, like their fathers, had sinned against God. Noteworthy is the fact that God only visits the iniquities of "those who hate" Him (Exod. 20:5), not those who do not.

Of course, Christ was punished for our sins (Isa. 53:5–6; 2 Cor. 5:21; 1 Peter 3:18), but Jesus only took on our *judicial* guilt, not our

120

*actual* guilt, since He was never actually guilty of sin (Heb. 4:15). Further, Jesus took it on Himself voluntarily (John 1:18), not against His will. Sin indebted us to God, and Jesus voluntarily paid the debt and ransomed us from the marketplace of sin (Mark 10:45).

## EZEKIEL 40–48

*How can these prophecies be understood literally when the NT declares that the sacrificial system has been abolished by Christ's death?*

**Problem:** Ezekiel seems to predict that, in the messianic period, the sacrificial system used by the Jews before the time of Jesus will be reinstituted (chapters 40–48). However, the NT in general and the Book of Hebrews in particular is emphatic in declaring that Christ has by one sacrifice forever done away with the need for animal sacrifices (10:1–9).

**Solution:** There are two basic interpretations of this passage of Scripture. Some take it spiritually and others view it literally. Either view solves the problem.

First, some argue for a *spiritual* interpretation that these sacrifices are not to be understood literally, but only as symbols or foreshadows of what was fulfilled in Christ's all-sufficient sacrifice on the cross (Heb. 1:1–2). They give the following reasons for their view.

1. The NT teaches that Christ fulfilled and abolished the OT sacrificial system and priesthood (Heb. 8:8–10).
2. The Book of Revelation describes the Heavenly City of the future with no temple or sacrifices, only Christ the Lamb (21:22–27).
3. Ezekiel portrays the Gentiles as excluded from Israel's temple, which is contrary to the NT teaching that Jew and Gentile are one in Christ (Gal. 3:28; Eph. 2:12–22).
4. The NT speaks of the church as a spiritual Israel in which OT predictions are fulfilled (Gal. 6:16; Heb. 8:8–10).

Those who object to this view point out, first, that this violates the normal, historical-grammatical way to interpret the text. Further, it illegitimately reads NT meaning back into the OT text, rather than understanding the OT text as it is written. They also argue that the sacrifices predicted by Ezekiel could be pointing back to the cross, just as the OT ones pointed forward to it.

The *literal* interpretation looks to an actual restoration of the temple and sacrificial system, just as Ezekiel predicted it to be fulfilled during Christ's millennial reign on earth (Rev. 20). They support their position with the following points:

1. Ezekiel presents a highly detailed description, with numerous measurements, and historical scenes that do not fit with a spiritual interpretation.
2. If this passage is spiritualized, then on similar grounds most of the OT prophecies could be spiritualized away, including the obviously literal ones about Christ's first coming, which we know from their fulfillment was literal. The same, then, applies to His second coming.
3. The Bible distinguishes between Israel and the church (1 Cor. 10:32; Rom. 9:3–4). Promises unique to Abraham and his literal descendants, such as the Promised Land (Gen. 12:1–3), are not fulfilled in the church, but remain yet to be fulfilled in the future (Rom. 11; Rev. 20).
4. The picture in Revelation 21 is not that of the millennium (Rev. 20), but of the eternal state that follows it. Ezekiel's prediction (40–48) will be fulfilled in the millennium. Later, in the new heaven and the new earth, there will be no temple or sacrifices.
5. The sacrifices mentioned by Ezekiel have no atoning significance. They are merely *memorial* in nature, looking back to the accomplished work of Christ on the cross, much as the Lord's Supper does for believers today.
6. The rest of Ezekiel's prophecy will be fulfilled in a literal thousand-year reign of Christ (Rev. 20:1–7) as He sits on a literal throne with His twelve apostles sitting on twelve literal thrones in Jerusalem (Matt. 19:28). If so, then there is no reason not to take the prophecy about the sacrifices as literal also.

7. The OT did not foresee *how* Jew and Gentile would be joined together (cf. Eph. 3:4–6), but it did envision *that* the Gentiles would be blessed (Isa. 11:10–16). Ezekiel's presentation does not exclude this later revelation (cf. Col. 1:26).

8. The Book of Hebrews speaks only of abolishing animal sacrifices in an *atoning* sense, not in a *memorial* sense.

# DANIEL

*Wasn't the Book of Daniel actually written after about 170 BC?*

**Problem:** Daniel contains an incredible amount of detail concerning the kingdoms of the Gentiles from the reign of Nebuchadnezzar, from about 605 BC, down to the Roman Empire that began to exercise dominance as early as 241 BC and, under the Roman general Pompey, took over the Promised Land in 63 BC. However, conservative scholars have maintained that Daniel wrote in the 6th century BC. How could Daniel have given such historically accurate details of events in the future?

**Solution:** The Book of Daniel contains supernatural prophecies that, from Daniel's time, extended hundreds of years into the future (Dan. 2:7). Daniel 11 presents a sweeping display of detailed prophecy that stretches from the reign of Cyrus the Great, to the reign of antichrist, to the millennial kingdom, to the end of the age and into eternity. The record of the movement of nations and events is so accurate it reads as the historical account of an eyewitness. However, conservative scholarship places the date of the Book of Daniel at a time before any of these events took place. The book itself claims to be predictive prophecy (cf. 9:24ff). To avoid the conclusion that Daniel's prophecy was a supernatural act of God, modern scholars have proposed a number of explanations, including a late date of writing. However, the historical accuracy of Daniel's record confirms a 6th century composition, and the best conclusion is that the Book of Daniel is a revelation from God about historical events that were future to Daniel, and many that are still future to us today.

## DANIEL 5:31

*How can the Book of Daniel be inspired if it makes reference to a man that modern scholarship says never existed?*

**Problem:** According to Daniel 5:31, the kingdom of Belshazzar fell to the invading armies and Darius the Mede took over as king. However, modern scholars have rejected the historical accuracy of the Book of Daniel. They argue that there never was a Darius the Mede, since there is no mention of such a person in ancient documents. Is this an error in Daniel's historical account?

**Solution:** Like the historical record of Belshazzar, which modern scholars questioned until archaeological evidence vindicated Daniel's accuracy, Daniel has again recorded the existence of a man whom other ancient historical documents omit.

Some modern scholars claim that the author of Daniel mistakenly thought that the Medes conquered Babylon instead of the Persians. They claim that this author then confused Darius I, king of Persia (521–486 BC), with the conqueror of Babylon and identified this figure as Darius the Mede. However, there is no reason to assume that the Book of Daniel is in error. Darius the Mede is a different person from Darius I of Persia. Darius the Mede was a subordinate to Cyrus the Great. Cuneiform texts refer to Darius the Mede as Gubaru, who was appointed by Cyrus to be governor over all of Babylonia. The tendency to deny the historical accuracy of Daniel simply because there is currently no corroborating historical information stems from the anti-supernatural bias of modern scholarship. Daniel's historical record has proven to be a reliable source of information.

# HOSEA

*How could a holy God who condemns harlotry command Hosea to marry a harlot?*

**Problem:** God commanded Hosea to "take yourself a wife of harlotry." However, according to Exodus 20:14, adultery is a sin; and according to 1 Corinthians 6:15–18, to have sexual relations with a harlot is immoral (cf. Lev. 19:29). How could a holy God command Hosea to take a harlot as his wife?

**Solution:** Some scholars have attempted to avoid the difficulty by claiming this is an *allegory*. However, while God obviously intended this as a dramatic illustration to Israel of their unfaithfulness to Him (cf. 1:2), there is no indication in the text that it is anything but a literal event. How else could it have been such a forceful example to the wayward people of Israel?

Taken *literally*, there is no real contradiction with any other Scripture for several reasons. First of all, when God commanded Hosea to take Gomer, the daughter of Diblaim, to be his wife, Gomer may not yet have actually committed adultery. However, God knew what was in her heart, and He knew that she would ultimately be unfaithful to Hosea. This is similar to the angel of the Lord calling Gideon a "mighty man of valor" before he had fought a single battle (Judg. 6:11–12). God knew that Gideon

126

would become a great leader in Israel even though he was not yet. God commanded Hosea to take a woman whom He knew would become a harlot. God commanded this as a picture of how Israel had committed spiritual adultery against Him. When God brought Israel out of Egypt, she was a brand-new nation. She had not yet broken the covenant that God would establish with her in the wilderness. Just like Israel had committed spiritual adultery by worshiping other gods, so Gomer would commit physical adultery by having relations with other men. The relationship between Hosea and Gomer was an object lesson for all Israel.

Second, the passage does not condone harlotry. In fact it is a strong condemnation of harlotry, of both the physical and spiritual (idolatry) kind (cf. 4:11–19). The fact that the grave sin of idolatry is depicted as spiritual harlotry reveals God's disapproval of harlotry.

Third, Hosea was commanded to *marry* a harlot, not to commit adultery with her. God said, "Go, take yourself a *wife*." God did not say go and commit fornication with her. Rather, He said marry her and be faithful to her, even though she will be unfaithful to you. Not only does this not violate the commitment of marriage, it actually intensifies it. Hosea was to be faithful to his marriage vows even though his wife would become unfaithful to hers.

Fourth, the command in Leviticus 21:14 to not marry a harlot was given to Levitical priests, not to everyone. Salmon apparently married Rahab the harlot (Matt. 1:5), from whose legal genealogy Christ eventually came. At any rate, Hosea was a prophet, not a Levitical priest; hence, the prohibition to not marry a harlot did not apply to him.

Finally, the command in 1 Corinthians 6:16 not to be joined to a harlot is not a command never to marry a woman who was a harlot. Rather, the command is directed against those who were having sexual relations outside of the marriage relationship. But Hosea did not have sexual relations outside of marriage. God commanded Hosea to marry Gomer and always be faithful to her.

# JOEL

*How could Joel mention the Greeks if his book was written before the 4th century BC?*

**Problem:** According to many scholars, Joel was written in the 9th century BC. However, the Greek reference in Joel 3:6 indicates that the earliest the book could have been written is the late 4th century BC.

**Solution:** It is not necessary to suppose that the mention of Greeks places the composition of the book in the late 4th century BC. The context of chapter 3 is the judgment of the nations. God promises punishment specifically upon the Phoenicians and the Philistines because they had plundered His people and sold them into slavery to the Greeks. Verse 6 states that these nations had sold His people to the Greeks: "That you may remove them far from their borders." If Joel had been written after the expansion of the empire of Greece by Alexander the Great in the middle of the 4th century BC, then God could not have accused the Phoenicians and the Philistines of selling the Jews to the Greeks who were "far from their borders." The Greeks are referred to in ancient Neo-Babylonian inscriptions as early as the 7th century BC, and the Cretan Linear B tablets indicate the beginning of the Greek civilization and language from about 1500 BC. So, it is not possible to use this reference to date Joel's prophecy in the 4th century BC.

# AMOS

*What does Amos mean when he says there will be a famine of hearing the words of the Lord?*

**Problem:** Because of the sin of Israel, God pronounced through His prophet Amos that He would bring judgment upon the people. One aspect of that judgment was that there would be a famine of hearing the words of the Lord. However, there is no indication from history that the Hebrew Scriptures were destroyed or removed from Israel at this time. To what does the "famine" in hearing the words of the Lord refer?

**Solution:** This verse addresses the lack of messengers from God, such as His prophets. Israel had not only despised the messengers of God, but had put many of them to death for their words. In God's judgment upon Israel, there would come a time when Israel would seek for help and guidance, but God would be silent (compare Ezek. 7:26 and Mic. 3:7). He would not send any messengers to them. Although they would still have the written Hebrew Scriptures, there would be a famine of the words of the Lord through His prophets.

# OBADIAH

*Is the prophecy of Obadiah simply an expression of Jewish nationalism?*

**Problem:** The prophecy of Obadiah is essentially a message of divine moral judgment upon the nations. Of the twenty-one verses that comprise this book, sixteen are directed as pronouncements of coming judgment against Edom, and five verses are dedicated to the prophecies of the future triumph of Israel over Edom. But, isn't this simply an example of Jewish nationalism rather than a revelation of God?

**Solution:** The Book of Obadiah is a revelation of the sovereignty of God presented in the midst of national disgrace and defeat. The impotence of God's people against their enemies was a reflection upon the power of the God of Israel. Wasn't Yahweh a defeated God? Wasn't He powerless to resist the enemies of His people? "No!" is Obadiah's resounding reply. The God of Israel will keep His promises even though the future looks black. The nations have not understood that their temporary victory over God's people was the very work of God. The message of Obadiah is that the God of Israel is always in complete control, and He will accomplish His purpose. It is a message of faith and hope, and triumph against the enemies of God. But the triumph of Israel will be a blessing to all nations. Israel's apostasy brought judgment. But, "if their being cast away is the reconciling of the world, what will their acceptance be but life from the dead?" (Rom. 11:15). This book is not simply an expression of Jewish nationalism. It is a declaration of the faithfulness of God, and a testimony to His moral justice, by which He will ultimately establish justice in the earth.

# JONAH

### Is the Book of Jonah fact or fiction?

**Problem:** Traditional Bible scholarship holds that the Book of Jonah records events that actually took place in history. However, because of the literary style of the book and the amazing adventures that are said to have befallen the prophet Jonah, many modern scholars propose that it is not a book of actual historical events, but a fictional story designed to communicate a message. Did the events of Jonah actually happen or not?

**Solution:** There is good evidence that the events recorded in the Book of Jonah are literal, historical events that took place in the life of the prophet Jonah.

First, the tendency to deny the historicity of Jonah stems from an anti-supernatural bias. If miracles are possible, there is no real reason to deny that Jonah is historical.

Second, Jonah and his prophetic ministry is mentioned in the historical book of 2 Kings (14:25). If his supernatural prediction is mentioned in a historical book, why should the historical nature of his prophetical book be rejected?

Third, the most devastating argument against the denial of the historical accuracy of Jonah is found in Matthew 12:40. In this passage Jesus predicts His own burial and resurrection, and provides the doubting scribes and Pharisees the sign that they demanded. The sign is the experience of Jonah. Jesus says, "For as Jonah was three days and three nights in the belly of the great fish, so will the Son of Man be three days and three nights in the heart of the earth." If the tale of Jonah's experience in the belly of the great fish was only fiction, then this would have provided no prophetic support for Jesus's claim. The point of making reference to Jonah is that if they did not believe the story of Jonah being in the belly of the fish, then they would not believe the death, burial, and resurrection of Jesus. As far as Jesus was concerned, the historical fact of His own death, burial, and resurrection was on the same historical ground as Jonah in the belly of the fish. To reject one was to cast doubt on the other (cf. John 3:12). Likewise, if they believed one, they should believe the other.

Fourth, Jesus went on to mention the significant historical detail. His own death, burial, and resurrection was the supreme sign that verified His claims. When Jonah preached to the unbelieving Gentiles, they repented. But here was Jesus in the presence of His own people, the very people of God, and yet they refused to believe. Therefore, the men of Nineveh would stand up in judgment against them, "because they [the men of Nineveh] repented at the preaching of Jonah" (Matt. 12:41). If the events of the Book of Jonah were merely parable or fiction, and not literal history, then the men of Nineveh did not really repent, and any judgment upon the unrepentant Pharisees would be unjust and unfair. Because of the testimony of Jesus, we can be sure that Jonah records literal history.

Finally, there is archaeological confirmation of a prophet named Jonah whose grave is found in northern Israel. In addition, some ancient coins have been unearthed with an inscription of a man coming out of a fish's mouth.

# MICAH

*Does God ever withhold His blessing from those who cry out for it?*

**Problem:** This text and other passages of Scripture (cf. Isa. 1:15; James 4:3) speak of God withholding His blessing from those who cry unto Him. But on the other hand, the Bible contends that God "gives to all liberally" who ask (James 1:5), "for everyone who asks, receives" (Luke 11:10).

**Solution:** These diverse texts are speaking about different kinds of people. God never withholds His promised blessing from those who call with a sincere and repentant heart. But He does withhold it from those who do not call in "faith with no doubting" (James 1:6) or who "ask amiss" to spend it on their own pleasures (James 4:3). In brief, God always grants His promised blessings on the faithful, but He does not always promise the same blessings to the unfaithful.

Second, not all of God's promised blessings are unconditional, as was His unilateral land promise to Abraham and his descendants (Gen. 12; 14–15; 17). Many of His blessings are conditioned on His people's obedience, such as the bilateral covenant with Israel ("If you will indeed obey My voice," Exod. 19:5).

Likewise, God never promises that He will heal everyone in this life of all diseases. In fact, God refused to heal Paul, though he pleaded three times with Him to be relieved of his burden (2 Cor. 12:8–9). Nor does God promise that He will make all believers rich in this life. Even Jesus became poor for us (2 Cor. 8:9), and He declared that there would always be poor (Matt. 26:11), spiritually blessed though they may be (Matt. 5:3). In these cases, no matter how much faith one musters, God will not necessarily bestow the blessing in this life, since He never unconditionally promises to do so.

# NAHUM

*Does God get angry?*

**Problem:** Nahum declares that God "avenges and is furious." Indeed, God is often represented as being angry in the Bible (cf. Isa. 26:20; Jer. 4:8). At the same time, the Bible urges believers not to be angry, since it is a sin (cf. Gal. 5:20). But if it is a sin, then how can God do it?

**Solution:** Anger as such is not sinful. It depends on the purpose, nature, and/or object of anger. Even Jesus, our perfect moral example, was angry at sin (cf. Matt. 23:15–36). Paul exhorted us, "Be angry, and do not sin" (Eph. 4:26). In short, we should be angry at sin, but we should not sin in being angry. The problem with human anger, even in the good sense of anger at sin, is that it is easy to carry it too far so that we sin in our anger. Unlike God, who is "slow to anger" (Neh. 9:17), we are often quick to anger. In short, there is good and bad anger for humans.

| GOOD ANGER | BAD ANGER |
|---|---|
| Over sin | Over being sinned against |
| Against sin | Against sinners |
| Expressed righteously | Expressed unrighteously |
| Being slow to anger | Being quick to anger |
| Done in justice | Done in retaliation |

# HABAKKUK

### Is this a prediction of the prophet Mohammed?

**Problem:** Many Muslim scholars believe this refers to the prophet Mohammed coming from Paran (Arabia), and use it in connection with a similar text in Deuteronomy 33:2.

**Solution:** As already noted, Paran is not near Mecca, where Mohammed came, but is hundreds of miles away. Furthermore, the verse is speaking of "God" coming, not Mohammed. Finally, the "praise" could not refer to Mohammed (whose name means "the praised one"), since the subject of both "praise" and "glory" is God ("His"), and Mohammed is not God.

# ZEPHANIAH

***Hasn't it been demonstrated that Zephaniah is actually composed
of two books with different messages?***

**Problem:** Conservative scholars maintain that the Book of Zephaniah
is a single work composed by the prophet Zephaniah. However,
modern scholarship claims that the book is actually two books with
different messages put together as if they were one. The very beginning of this book is a message of dread and coming judgment. The
overriding theme is the devastation and destruction that is about
to fall in the swiftly approaching Day of the Lord. However, verses
8–13 of chapter 3 present a message of hope that seems completely
out of keeping with the theme of the book as a whole. How can this
book be considered the sole work of one person, Zephaniah?

**Solution:** There is no reason to suppose that the messages of judgment and hope are incompatible. In fact, it is the message of the
Book of Zephaniah that the coming judgment of the Day of the
Lord is the very means by which God would bring about the ultimate restoration of His people. The Day of the Lord is a day of
purification from sin and the salvation of the remnant. The hope
of salvation in the midst of judgment is found as early as 2:1–3 and
3:8–9, clearly pointing out that it is this purifying judgment that
will prepare the way for the restoration of God's people. Zephaniah
is a single unified work by the prophet Zephaniah.

# —— HAGGAI ——

*Why does this verse imply that the building of the temple began in 520 BC?*

**Problem:** Haggai 2:15 implies that the building of the temple did not begin until 520 BC. Ezra 3:8–13 claims that the rebuilding of the temple began in about 536 BC, while Ezra 4:24 says the rebuilding of the temple took place during the reign of Darius, king of Persia. Which one of these is correct?

**Solution:** All of them are correct. They are simply referring to different aspects of the work. For a discussion of these passages, see comments under Ezra 3:10.

# ───── ZECHARIAH ─────

*How can these verses be part of Zechariah when Matthew 27:9 says they belong to the Book of Jeremiah?*

**Problem:** When Matthew presents the prophetic prediction that related to the death of Judas, he quoted from Jeremiah 32:6–9. However, he also quoted from Zechariah 11:12–13 but asserts that these quotes are from the prophet Jeremiah. Does the Zephaniah passage actually belong in Jeremiah?

**Solution:** It is not exactly accurate to say that Matthew quoted exclusively from Zechariah 11 or Jeremiah 32. There are other passages in Jeremiah that refer to the potter's field (Jer. 18:2; 19:2, 11), and Matthew's rendering is not an exact quote from any of the passages. Matthew is combining the various elements of these prophecies to make his point. Because Jeremiah is the more prominent prophetic book, Matthew simply mentions Jeremiah's name as the source of the prophetic message that he is bringing out. Matthew did this earlier (Matt. 5:2) where he cites from two passages (Mic. 5:2 and 2 Sam. 5:2). It was a common practice of the day to cite the more popular prophet.

# MALACHI

## MALACHI 1:3

*If God is love, how could He hate any person?*

**Problem:** In the latter part of verse 2 and the first part of verse 3, God says, "Yet Jacob I have loved; But Esau I have hated." But John says, "God is love" (1 John 4:16). How can a God of love hate any one person?

**Solution:** First of all, God is not speaking about the *person* Esau, but of the *nation* that came from him, namely, Edom. So God is not expressing hate toward any person here.

What is more, "hate" in Hebrew means "to love less." In Genesis 29:30–31, "loved Rachel more" than Leah is equated with "Leah was hated." The same is true in Luke 14:26 where Jesus uses "hate" of one's relatives to mean "love them less" than Him.

Further, the nation Edom was deserving of God's indignation for their "violence against your brother Jacob [Israel]" (Obad. 10). They sided with Israel's enemies, blocked the way of their escape, and even delivered up those who remained (vv. 12–14).

Finally, like the Nicolaitans, God hates the *works* of the sinner, not the sinner himself. John commends the believers who "hate the *deeds* of the Nicolaitans, which I also hate" (Rev. 2:6; also see comments on Ps. 5:5).

# MATTHEW

*Is Joram the father of Uzziah or of Ahaziah?*

**Problem:** Matthew says "Joram begot Uzziah." However, 1 Chronicles 3:11 lists "Joram [and then] his son, Ahaziah." Which one is correct?

**Solution:** Ahaziah was apparently the immediate son of Joram, and Uzziah was a distant "son" (descendant). Just as the word "son" in the Bible also means grandson, even so the term "begot" can be used of a father or grandfather. In other words, "begot" means "became the ancestor of," and the one "begotten" is the "descendant of."

Matthew, therefore, is not giving a *complete chronology*, but an *abbreviated genealogy* of Christ's ancestry. A comparison of Matthew 1:8 and 1 Chronicles 3:11–12 reveals the three generations between Joram and Uzziah (Azariah):

| Matthew 1:18 | 1 Chronicles 3:11–12 |
|:---:|:---:|
| Joram | Joram |
| . . . . . | Ahaziah |
| . . . . . | Joash |
| . . . . . | Amaziah |
| Uzziah | Uzziah (also called Azariah) |

## MATTHEW 1:17

*How many generations were listed between the captivity and Christ,*
*fourteen or thirteen?*

**Problem:** Matthew say the generations "from the captivity in Babylon
until the Christ are fourteen generations" (1:17). However, he lists
only thirteen names after the captivity is counted. So, which is
correct, thirteen or fourteen?

**Solution:** Both are correct. Jeconiah is counted in both lists, since
he lived both before and after the captivity. So, there are literally
fourteen names listed "from the captivity in Babylon until the
Christ," just as Matthew says. There are also literally fourteen
names listed between David and the captivity, just as Matthew
claims (Matt. 1:6–12). There is no error in the text at all.

## MATTHEW 2:6

*How can we explain Matthew's apparent misquotation of Micah*
*5:2?*

**Problem:** Matthew 2:6 quotes Micah 5:2. However, the words Matthew uses are different than those used by Micah.

**Solution:** Although Matthew seems to have changed some of the
words from the passage in Micah, there is no real deviation in
the meaning of the text. Matthew, in some instances, seems to
have paraphrased.

First, Matthew inserts the phrase "land of Judah" for the word
"Ephrathah." This does not really change the meaning of the verse.
There is no difference between the land of Judah and Ephrathah,
except one is more specific than the other. In fact, Ephrathah
refers to Bethlehem in the Micah passage, and Bethlehem is located in the land of Judah. However, this does not change the
basic meaning of this verse. He is speaking of the same area of
land. Interestingly, when Herod asked the chief priests and the
scribes where the child was to be born, they said, "in Bethlehem
of Judea" (Matt. 2:5, NASB).

Second, Matthew describes the land of Judah as "not the least"
but Micah states that it is "little." Here, Matthew may be saying that
since the Messiah is to come from this region, it is by no means least

among the other areas of land in Judah. The phrase in Micah only says that Bethlehem is too little or small, as compared to the other areas of land in Judah. The verse does not say it is the least among them, only very little. Matthew is saying the same thing in different words, namely, that Bethlehem is little in *size*, but by no means the least in *significance*, since the Messiah was born there.

Finally, Matthew uses the phrase "who will shepherd My people Israel" and Micah does not. Micah 5:2 recognizes that there will be a ruler in Israel, and Matthew recognizes this as well. However, the phrase that is not mentioned in Micah is actually taken from 2 Samuel 5:2. The combining of verses does not take away what is being said, but it strengthens the point that the author is making. There are other instances where an author combines one Scripture with another. For example, Matthew 27:9–10 combines some of Zechariah 11:12–13 with Jeremiah 19:2, 11 and 32:6–9. Also, Mark 1:2–3 combines some of Isaiah 40:3 with Malachi 3:1. Only the first passage is mentioned, since it is the main passage being cited.

In brief, Matthew is not misrepresenting any information in his quotation of Micah 5:2 and 2 Samuel 5:2. Matthew's quote is still accurate even though he paraphrases part of it and combines another portion of Scripture with it.

## MATTHEW 2:23

### Didn't Matthew make a mistake by claiming a prophecy that is not found in the OT?

**Problem:** Matthew claims that Jesus moved to Nazareth to live, in order "that it might be fulfilled which was spoken by the prophets, He shall be called a Nazarene" (Matt. 2:23). However, no such prophecy is found in any OT prophet. Did Matthew make a mistake?

**Solution:** Matthew did not say that any particular OT "prophet" (singular) stated this. He simply affirmed that the OT "prophets" (plural) predicted that Jesus would be called a Nazarene. So we should not expect to find any given verse, but simply a general truth found in many prophets to correspond to His Nazarene-like character. There are several suggestions as to how Jesus could have "fulfilled" (brought to completion) this truth.

Some point to the fact that Jesus fulfilled the righteous require-
ments of the OT Law (Matt. 5:17–18; Rom. 8:3–4), one part of which
involved the holy commitment made in the vow of the "Nazarite." The
Nazarite took this vow "to separate himself to the Lord" (Num. 6:2),
and Jesus perfectly fulfilled this. However, the word is different both
in Hebrew and Greek, and Jesus never took this particular vow.

Others point to the fact that Nazareth comes from the basic
word *netzer* (branch). And many prophets spoke of the Messiah
as the "Branch" (cf. Isa. 11:1; Jer. 23:5; 33:15; Zech. 3:8; 6:12).

Still others note that the city of Nazareth, where Jesus lived,
was a despised place "on the other side of the tracks." This is evident in Nathaniel's response, "Can anything good come out of
Nazareth?" (John 1:46). In this sense, "Nazarene" was a term of
scorn appropriate to the Messiah, whom the prophets predicted
would be "despised and rejected of men" (Isa. 53:3; cf. Ps. 22:6;
Dan. 9:26; Zech. 12:10).

## MATTHEW 4:5–10 (cf. Luke 4:5–12)

*Is there a mistake in recording the wilderness temptation of Christ
by Matthew or Luke?*

**Problem:** According to both Matthew and Luke, the first temptation
was to turn stones into bread to satisfy Jesus's hunger. The second
temptation listed by Matthew took place at the pinnacle of the
temple. The third temptation listed by Matthew involved all the
kingdoms of the world. However, although Luke mentions these
same events, he lists them in reverse order—the kingdoms of the
world are mentioned second and the pinnacle of the temple is
mentioned third. Which is the correct order?

**Solution:** It may be that Matthew describes these temptations *chrono-
logically* while Luke lists them *climactically*, that is, topically. This
may be to express the climax he desired to emphasize. Matthew
4:5 begins with the word "then" while verse 8 begins with the
word "again." In Greek, these words suggest a more sequential
order of the events. In Luke's account, however, verses 5 and 9
each begin with a simple "and" (see NASB). The Greek in the case
of Luke's account does not necessarily indicate a sequential order

of events. Furthermore, there is no disagreement on the fact that these temptations actually happened.

## MATTHEW 5:43
### Why did the OT prescribe that one could hate his enemies?

**Problem:** Jesus said here of the OT, "You have heard that it was said, 'You shall love your neighbor and hate your enemy.'" How could a God of love (Exod. 20:2, 6; 1 John 4:16) command them to hate their enemies?

**Solution:** God never commanded His people at any time to hate their enemies (see comments on Mal. 1:3). God is an unchanging God of love (cf. 1 John 4:16; Mal. 3:6), and He cannot hate any person, nor can He command anyone else to do so. Jesus said the greatest commands were to love God and to love our neighbors as ourselves (Matt. 22:36–37, 39). In point of fact, this very command is taken by Jesus from the OT. Leviticus 19:18 declares: "you shall love your neighbor as yourself"!

Why then did Jesus say the OT taught that we should "hate our enemy" (Matt. 5:43)? He didn't, and for a very good reason. Nowhere in the OT can any such verse be found. In fact, Jesus is not quoting the OT here, but the pharisaical misinterpretation of the OT. Notice, Jesus does not say "it is *written*," as He often did when quoting the OT (cf. Matt. 4:4, 7, 10). Rather, He said, "you have *heard*," by which He meant the Jewish "tradition" that had grown up around the OT and by which they had made the commandment of God of no effect (cf. Matt. 15:3, 6). The truth is that the God of love commanded love both in the OT and NT and never at any time commanded that we hate other persons.

## MATTHEW 8:20 (cf. Matt. 20:18; 24:30; etc.)
### If Jesus was the Son of God, why did He call Himself the Son of Man?

**Problem:** Jesus referred to Himself most often as the Son of Man. This seems to point to His humanity more than His deity. If He was really the Messiah, the Son of God, why did He use the self-description "Son of Man"?

**Solution:** First of all, even if the phrase "Son of Man" were a reference to Jesus's humanity, it is not a denial of His deity. By becoming man, Jesus did not cease being God. The incarnation of Christ did not involve the subtraction of deity, but the addition of humanity. Jesus clearly claimed to be God on many occasions (Matt. 16:16–17; John 8:58; 10:30). But in addition to being divine, He was also human. He had two natures conjoined in one person.

Furthermore, Jesus was not denying His deity by referring to Himself as the Son of Man. The term "Son of Man" is used to describe Christ's deity. The Bible says that only God can forgive sins (Isa. 43:25; Mark 2:7). But, as the "Son of Man," Jesus had the power to forgive sins (Mark 2:10). Likewise, Christ will return to earth as the "Son of Man" in clouds of glory to reign on earth (Matt. 26:63–64). In this passage, Jesus is citing Daniel 7:13 where the Messiah is described as the "Ancient of Days," a phrase used to indicate His deity (cf. Dan. 7:9).

Further, when Jesus was asked by the high priest whether He was the "Son of God" (Matt. 26:63), He responded affirmatively, declaring that He was the "Son of Man" who would come in power and great glory (v. 64). This indicated that Jesus Himself used the phrase "Son of Man" to indicate His deity as the Son of God.

Finally, the phrase "Son of Man" emphasizes who Jesus is in relation to His incarnation and His work of salvation. In the OT (see Lev. 25:25–26, 48–49; Ruth 2:20), the kinsman redeemer was a close relative of someone who was in need of redemption. So Jesus, as our Kinsman Redeemer, was identifying Himself with humankind as its Savior and Redeemer. Those who knew the OT truth about Messiah being the Son of Man understood Jesus's implicit claims to deity. Those who did not would not recognize this. Jesus often said things in this way so as to test His audience and separate believers from unbelievers (cf. Matt. 13:10–17).

## MATTHEW 9:18

### Does Matthew falsely report the death of Jarius's daughter?

**Problem:** Matthew asserts that while Jesus was saying these things to them, a synagogue official named Jarius came and bowed down before Him, and said, "*My daughter has just died*; but come and lay Your hand on her, and she will live."

However, Mark 5:22–23 says, "One of the synagogue officials named Jarius came up, and on seeing Him, fell at His feet and implored Him earnestly, saying, '*My little daughter is at the point of death*; please come and lay Your hands on her, so that she will get well and live' "(NASB).[15] Later, "While He was still speaking, they came from the house of the synagogue official, saying, '*Your daughter has died*; why trouble the Teacher anymore?'" (Mark 5:35, NASB).

Likewise, Luke declares: "And there came a man named Jarius, and he was an official of the synagogue; and he fell at Jesus's feet, and began to implore Him to come to his house; for he had an only daughter, about twelve years old, and *she was dying*" (Luke 8:41–42, NASB). Later "While He was still speaking, someone came from the house of the synagogue official, saying, '*Your daughter has died*; do not trouble the Teacher anymore'" (Luke 8:49, NASB).

Clearly, Mark and Luke declare there were two stages: 1) An initial one where she was dying but not dead, and 2) a later one where she had died. But Matthew appears to say that she was dead (9:18) at the initial stage, when she was only dying according to Mark and Luke.

**Solution:** This apparent discrepancy can be explained by the fact that while Jesus was speaking to Jarius, someone came from his house to tell him the girl had died (Luke 8:49). Matthew did not mention that detail, but included the report of the girl's death in Jairus's request.[16] But Matthew does not record Jarius as saying anything that in fact he did not say. He merely merges the two events to stress the point that the girl actually died before Jesus got there. This is not an uncommon practice in Scripture. For example, Jesus once spoke to the contemporary "scribes and Pharisees" as the "you" who also killed the OT prophets, "whom you murdered" (Matt. 23:29, 35).

## MATTHEW 10:10 (cf. Mark 6:8)

*Did Jesus command that the disciples take a staff or not?*

**Problem:** In Matthew, Jesus seems to say that the disciples should not take a staff, but in Mark it appears that He allows them to have one.

**Solution:** A closer examination reveals that the account in Mark (6:8) declares that the disciples are to take nothing except a staff, which a traveler would normally have, whereas the account in Matthew states they are not to acquire another staff. There is no discrepancy between these texts. Mark's account is saying they may take the staff that they have, while Matthew is saying they should not take an *extra* staff or tunic. The text reads, "Provide neither . . . two tunics, nor sandals, nor staffs" (plural: vv. 9–10). It does not say they should not take a staff (singular). So there is no contradiction.

## MATTHEW 10:23

*Did Jesus promise to return to earth during the lifetime of the disciples?*

**Problem:** Jesus sent His disciples on a mission and promised them, "you will not have gone through the cities of Israel before the Son of Man comes." However, it is obvious that He never even went to heaven, to say nothing of returning again, before they had returned from their evangelistic tour.

**Solution:** There are many interpretations of this passage. Some take it to be a reference to the destruction of Jerusalem (AD 70) and the end of the Jewish economy. But this hardly suits as a fulfillment of the phrase "before the Son of Man comes," nor the other references to end-time events (vv. 26–32).

Others understand Jesus's statement to refer to an outpouring of the Holy Spirit or a great revival before the return of Christ to earth to set up His kingdom. They believe the preaching of the gospel will usher in the kingdom (cf. Matt. 24:14). But this, too, seems to go far beyond the literal meaning of the text here.

Another alternative is to take the promise literally and immediately and to interpret the phrase "before the Son of Man comes" as a reference to the fact that Jesus rejoined the disciples after their mission. They argue that the phrase "before the Son of Man comes" is never used by Matthew to describe the Second Coming. Further, they insist that it fits with a literal understanding of the first part of the verse. The disciples went literally and immediately into "the cities of Israel" to preach, and Jesus literally and immediately rejoined them after their itinerant ministry. Also, they assert that there is no indication here or anywhere else that the disciples believed that Jesus was going to go to heaven while they were gone on their preaching tour. This certainly would have startled them (cf. John 14:1–5). Indeed, He had already told them that He had to die and rise from the dead (John 2:19–22) before He could go to heaven and then return.

Finally, it is argued by some that this is a proleptic reference to Christ's second coming. Several arguments are offered in support of this view. First, the use of "truly" expresses a solemnity far greater than merely meeting up with them again after a short preaching tour. Second, "Son of Man" is a phrase used of Jesus in contexts of the Second Coming (cf. Dan. 7:13; Matt. 25:31). Third, Jesus referred here to enduring to the "the end," which is paralleled by His reference "to the end of the age" (Matt. 28:20). Fourth, the references to "hell" (v. 28), the final judgment (vv. 26–27), and "heaven" (v. 32) fit with the Second Coming. Fifth, the disciples would probably have not gone through all "the cities of Israel" in the short mission on which Jesus sent them. Finally, it is not uncommon in biblical prediction to use the "you" both of the immediate audience and then proleptically project into the future about a remote audience (viz., their descendants) in the future. Jesus even did this kind of projection backward from a "you" in His immediate audience to their Jewish ancestors when He said to His contemporaries, "Upon you [the immediate audience] may fall the guilt of all the righteous blood shed on the earth, from the blood of Abel to the blood of Merechiah, whom you [viz, your ancestors] murdered between the temple and the altar" (Matt. 23:35).

## MATTHEW 11:12

*How can God's sovereign and peaceful kingdom be entered by force?*

**Problem:** Paul declared that the kingdom (rule) of God is "peace and joy in the Holy Spirit" (Rom. 14:17). However, Matthew says "the kingdom of heaven suffers violence, and the violent take it by force." How can one enter God's kingdom by force?

**Solution:** This is a difficult passage, and it has been interpreted several ways. Some take it to mean that the kingdom is violently taken by its enemies. That is, the forceful religious leaders of Jesus's day were resisting the kingdom introduced by John. They wanted a kingdom, but not the kind that was being offered by John and Jesus (cf. Rom. 10:3). However, some object that this is opposed to the context, which is expressing the greatness of John the Baptist and the contrast between his day and Christ's.

Others see the "violence" as a figure of speech, meaning, first, that the kingdom breaks through or intrudes itself with great power and abruptness. Second, it refers to the intense endeavors of people who, on the preaching of John, were taking the kingdom by storm. On this view, it is speaking of the response to John's preaching as a great popular uprising, a storming of the kingdom of God by people rushing with eagerness to get in it with a violent zeal. This explains the use of the term "violence" and fits the overall context.

## MATTHEW 11:14

*Didn't Jesus say John the Baptist was Elijah reincarnated?*

**Problem:** Jesus refers here to John the Baptist as "Elijah who is to come" (cf. Matt. 17:12; Mark 9:11–13). But since Elijah had died many centuries before, John must have been a reincarnation of Elijah.

**Solution:** There are many reasons why this verse does not teach reincarnation. First, John and Elijah did not have the same *being*— they had the same *function*. Jesus was not teaching that John the Baptist was literally Elijah (cf. John 1:21), but simply that he came "in the spirit and power of Elijah" (Luke 1:17), namely, to continue his prophetic ministry.

Second, Jesus's disciples understood that He was speaking about John the Baptist, since Elijah appeared on the Mount of Transfiguration (Matt. 17:10–13). John had already lived and died by then, and Elijah still had the same name and self-consciousness.

Therefore, Elijah had obviously not been reincarnated as John the Baptist.

Third, Elijah does not fit the reincarnation model for another reason—he did not die. He was taken to heaven like Enoch, who did not "see death" (2 Kings 2:11; cf. Heb. 11:5). According to traditional reincarnation, one must first die before he or she can be reincarnated into another body.

Fourth, if there is any doubt about this passage, it should be understood in light of the clear teaching of Scripture opposing reincarnation. Hebrews, for example, declares, "it is appointed for men to die once, but after this the judgment" (Heb. 9:27; cf. John 9:2).

## MATTHEW 12:40 (cf. John 19:14)

### *If Jesus was crucified on Friday, how could He have been in the grave three days and nights?*

**Problem:** Christ rose on Sunday (Matt. 28:1), but He stated that He would be "three days and three nights in the heart of the earth." If Christ was crucified on Friday, how could He have been three days and three nights in the earth and rise on Sunday only two days later?

**Solution 1:** Some scholars believe Jesus was in the grave for three full days and nights (72 hours), being crucified on Wednesday. They offer the following in support of this contention.

First, they insist that this is the literal meaning of the phrase "three days and nights." Second, they point out that, on the view that Jesus was crucified on Friday, there is no explanation for what He did on Wednesday. All other days are accounted for. Third, they argue that the Passover was not a fixed day (Friday), but floated.

**Solution 2:** Most biblical scholars believe that Jesus was crucified on Friday. They take the phrase "three days and nights" to be a Hebrew figure of speech referring to any part of three days and nights. They offer the following in support of their position.

First, the phrase "day and night" does not necessarily mean a complete 24-hour period. The psalmist's reference to meditating "day and night" on God's Word does not mean one has to read the Bible all day and all night (Ps. 1:2).

Second, it is clear from the use of the phrase "three days and three nights" in the Book of Esther that it does not mean 72 hours. For, although they fasted three days and nights (4:16) between the time they started and the time Esther appeared before the king, the passage states that she appeared before the king "on the third day" (5:1). If they began on Friday, then the third day would be Sunday. Hence, "three days and nights" must mean any part of three days and nights.

Third, Jesus used the phrase "on the third day" to describe the time of His resurrection after His crucifixion (Matt. 16:21; 17:23; 20:19; cf. 26:61). But "*on* the third day" cannot mean "*after* three days," which 72 hours demands. On the other hand, the phrase "on the third day" or "three days and nights" can be understood to mean within three days and nights.

Fourth, this view fits best with the chronological order of events as given by Mark (cf. 14:1), as well as the fact that Jesus died on Passover day (Friday) to fulfill the conditions of being our Passover Lamb (1 Cor. 5:7; cf. Lev. 23:5–15).

The two views can be compared as follows on the chart on page 154.

## MATTHEW 13:31–32

*Did Jesus make a mistake when referring to the mustard seed as the smallest of all seeds?*

**Problem 1:** Jesus said that the mustard seed was "the least of all the seeds." However, today we know that the mustard seed is not the smallest seed of all. Some think Jesus was speaking of the black mustard seed. But even this is not the smallest of all seeds.

**Solution 1:** Jesus was not referring to all the seeds in the world, but only those that a Palestinian farmer sowed in his field. This is made clear by the qualifying phrase "which a man took and sowed in his field" (v. 31). And it is a fact that the mustard seed was the smallest of all seeds that the 1st century Jewish farmer *sowed in his field*. So there is no contradiction here between science

## THE LAST WEEK BEFORE THE CRUCIFIXION

| | Fri. | Sat. | Sun. | Mon. | Tue. | Wed. | Thur. | Fri. | Sat. | Sun. |
|---|---|---|---|---|---|---|---|---|---|---|
| **Wednesday Crucifixion "Reconstruction View"** | Arrived in Bethany; Feast in Bethany John 12:1 | Day the Passover Lamb Was Caught Exod. 12:3 | Triumphal Entry John 12:13 | Cursing of Fig Tree | Contest with Jewish leaders; Mt. of Olives Sermon | Jesus Died Exod. 12:6; Day of Preparation for Passover John 19:14 | A Sabbath John 19:31 | ◄ JESUS' BODY IN TOMB ► Thurs. – Day and Night / Fri. – Day and Night / Sat. – Day and Night MATT. 12:40 | | |
| **Jewish First Month (March/April)** | 9 Nisan | 10 Nisan | 11 Nisan | 12 Nisan | 13 Nisan | 14 Nisan | 15 Nisan | 16 Nisan | 17 Nisan | 18 Nisan |
| **Friday Crucifixion "Traditional View"** | | "6 Days before the Passover" | "The Nex Day" John 12:12 | "On the Morrow" Mark 11:12 | "The Following Day" Mark 11:20 | | "After Two Days" Mark 14:1 | "In the Morning" Mark 15:1 | | "The Sabbath Was Past" Mark 16:1 |
| | | Feast in Bethany; The Jews Plan Jesus's Death John 12:8–11 | Triumphal Entry into Jerusalem; He Wept over the City Luke 19:41 | Curse of Fig Tree Mark 11:14; Cleanse the Temple Mark 11:15–18; Receive Praise from Children Matt. 21:14–16 | Dead Fig Tree Mark 11:20; Contest with Jewish Leaders; Olivet Sermon Mark 13:1 | | Sends Peter into City Luke 22:7–13; Last Supper Mark 14:12 | Gethsemane Mark 14:32; Arrest Mark 14:48–52; Trial; Crucified; Buried John 19:38–42 | ◄ JESUS' BODY IN TOMB ► | Resurrection |

and Scripture. What Jesus said was literally true in the context in which He said it.

**Problem 2:** Some claim that the mustard seed cannot grow big enough to house birds, let alone grow to tree size.

**Solution 2:** This is not so; there is evidence that some mustard seeds grow into trees about ten feet tall. This would certainly provide enough branch space for a bird to build a nest (Matt. 13:32).

## MATTHEW 16:16

*Why does Peter's confession here differ from that recorded in Mark and Luke?*

**Problem:** Peter's confession of Christ in Caesarea Philippi is stated differently in the three Synoptic Gospels:

Matthew: "You are the Christ, the Son of the living God."
Mark: "You are the Christ" (8:29).
Luke: "The Christ of God" (9:20).

If the Bible is the inspired Word of God, why are there three different reports of what Peter said? What did he really say?

**Solution:** There are several reasons why the Gospel accounts of Peter's statements differ. First, Peter probably spoke Aramaic, while the Gospels are written in Greek. So, some changes come naturally as a result of translating the words differently. Second, the Gospel writers sometimes paraphrased the essence of what people said, much like journalists do today. Third, other writers selected and abbreviated what was said to fit the theme of their book or the emphasis they wished to make.

What is important to notice is that the Gospel writers never *created* these sayings, rather, they *reported* them. Further, their reports were in accordance with journalistic standards of the day (and even today for that matter). Also, whenever there are multiple reports, they all give the essence of what was said. For example, all three reports note that Peter confessed that Jesus is "the Christ of God." Sometimes, all the reports can be put together as a whole, giving what may have been the word-for-word original statement of Peter. For example, Peter may have said exactly what Matthew reported, and the others may have reported the important parts of Peter's confession, as illustrated in the following:

Matthew: "You are the Christ, the Son of the living God."
  Mark: "You are the Christ [the Son of the living God]."
  Luke: "[You are] the Christ [the Son] of [the living] God."

## MATTHEW 16:18

### Is Peter the rock on which the church is built?

**Problem:** Roman Catholics use this passage to support their belief in the primacy of Peter; that is, that he is the rock on which the church is built. But Paul said the church is built on Christ, not Peter (1 Cor. 3:11). Is Peter the "rock" in this passage?

**Solution:** There are different ways to understand this passage, but none of them support the Roman Catholic view that the church is built on St. Peter, who became the first pope—infallible in all his official pronouncements on faith and doctrine. This is evident for many reasons.

First of all, Peter was married (Matt. 8:14), and popes do not marry. If the first pope could marry, why later pronounce that no priest (or pope) could marry?

Second, Peter was not infallible in his views on the Christian life. Even Paul had to rebuke him for his hypocrisy, because he was not "straightforward about the truth of the gospel" (Gal. 2:14).

Third, the Bible clearly declares that Christ is the foundation of the Christian church, insisting that "no other foundation can anyone lay than that which is laid, which is Jesus Christ" (1 Cor. 3:11).

Fourth, the only sense in which Peter had a foundational role in the church was shared by all the other apostles in the same way. Peter was not unique in this respect. For Paul declared that in this sense the church is "built on the foundation of the apostles and prophets, Jesus Christ Himself being the chief cornerstone" (Eph. 2:20). Indeed, the early church "continued steadfastly in the apostles' doctrine [not just Peter's]" (Acts 2:42). Even "keys of the kingdom" given to Peter (Matt. 16:19) were also given to all the apostles (cf. Matt. 18:18).

Fifth, there is no indication that Peter was the head of the early church. When the first council was held at Jerusalem, Peter played only an introductory role (Acts 15:6–11). James seems to have a more significant position, summing up the conference and making the final pronouncement (cf. Acts 15:13–21). In any event, Peter is never referred to as *the* "pillar" in the church. Rather, Paul speaks of "pillars" (plural), such as, "James, Cephas, and John" (Gal. 2:9). Peter (Cephas) is not even listed first among the pillars.

Sixth, even some great Catholic scholars (like St. Augustine) argue that the "rock" does not refer to Peter but to his testimony about Christ.

Seventh, many Protestant interpreters believe that Jesus's mention of "this rock" (Matt. 16:18) upon which His church would be built referred to Peter's solid (rocklike) testimony that Jesus was "the Christ, the son of the living God" (Matt. 16:16). But even if "this rock" has reference to Peter (*Petros*, rock), which is certainly a possible interpretation, he was only *a* rock in the apostolic foundation of the church (Matt. 16:18), not *the* rock. Nor is he the *only* apostolic rock. Even Peter himself admitted that Christ is the chief rock ("cornerstone," 1 Peter 2:7). And Paul notes that the other apostles are all part of the "foundation" (Eph. 2:20).

## MATTHEW 16:20

*Why did Jesus instruct His disciples to tell no one He was the Christ?*

**Problem:** Jesus commissioned His disciples, "Go therefore and make disciples of all nations" (Matt. 28:19). Yet over and over again throughout His ministry, He insisted that His followers "tell no man" (cf. Matt. 8:4; 16:20; 17:9; Mark 7:36; 8:30; 9:9; Luke 5:14; 8:56; 9:21). Doesn't this contradict His Great Commission?

**Solution:** The problem is easily resolved if several things are remembered. First, there was often a stated or implied condition on this command to "tell no man." Jesus said clearly to His disciples on one occasion, "tell no one . . . till the Son of Man ha[s] risen from the dead" (Matt. 17:9; cf. Mark 9:9). There is no contradiction between this and His pronouncement to tell everyone after He rose from the dead (in Matt. 28:19).

Second, sometimes Jesus was simply trying to keep down the crowds so that He could continue His ministry. Mark writes, "He commanded them that they should tell no one; but the more He commanded them, the more widely they proclaimed it" (Mark 7:36). Likewise, Luke reports that immediately after Jesus instructed the cleansed leper to "tell no one" (Luke 5:14), "then the report went around concerning Him all the more. . . . So He Himself often withdrew into the wilderness and prayed" (vv. 15–16).

Finally, Jesus did not wish to parade His messianic claims, especially among the Jews, since they had a false expectation of a political redeemer who would deliver them from the yoke of Rome (see comments on John 4:26). On one occasion, they even wanted to make Him king by force because of the signs that He did (see John 6:14–15). Since that was not His purpose, He withdrew from them. His purpose was to die on the cross.

## MATTHEW 19:16–30 (cf. Mark 10:17–31; Luke 18:18–30)

*If Jesus was God, why did He seem to rebuke the rich young ruler for calling Him good?*

**Problem:** The rich young ruler called Jesus "Good Teacher," and Jesus rebuked him, saying, "Why do you call Me good? No one is good but One, that is, God." Yet on other occasions Jesus not only claimed to be God (Mark 2:8–10; John 8:58; 10:30), but He accepted the claim of others that He was God (John 20:28–29). Why did Jesus appear to deny that He was God to the young ruler?

**Solution:** Jesus did not deny He was God to the young ruler. He simply asked him to examine the implications of what he was saying. In effect, Jesus was saying to him, "Do you realize what you are saying when you call Me good? Are you saying I am God?"

The young man did not realize the implications of what he was saying. Thus Jesus was forcing him to a very uncomfortable dilemma. Either Jesus was good and God, or else He was bad and man. A good God or a bad man, but not merely a good man. Those are the real alternatives with regard to Christ. For no good man would claim to be God when he was not. The liberal Christ, who was only a good moral teacher but not God, is a figment of human imagination.

## MATTHEW 20:29–34 (cf. Mark 10:46–52; Luke 18:35–43)
*Did Jesus heal the blind man coming into or going out of Jericho?*

**Problem:** According to Luke, a blind man was healed as Jesus entered the city of Jericho (18:35), but Matthew and Mark declare that the healing took place as Jesus left the city of Jericho. Again, the accounts do not seem to be harmonious.

**Solution:** Some believe that the healing in Luke may have actually taken place as Jesus left Jericho, claiming that it was only the initial contact that took place as "He was coming near Jericho" (Luke 18:35) and the blind man may have followed Him through the city, since he was continually begging Jesus to heal him (vv. 38–39). But this seems unlikely, since even after the healing (v. 43) the very next verse (19:1) says, "then Jesus entered and passed through Jericho."

Others respond by noting there were two Jerichos, the old and the new, so that as He went out of one, He came into the other.

Still others suggest that these are two different events. Matthew and Mark clearly affirm the healing occurred as Jesus left the city (Matt. 20:29; Mark 10:46). But Luke speaks of healing one blind man as He entered the city. This is supported by the fact that Luke refers to only a "multitude" of people being present as Jesus entered the city (18:36), but both Matthew (20:29) and Mark (10:46) make a point to say there was a "great multitude" of people there by the time Jesus left the city. If the word spread of the miraculous healing on the way into the city, this would account for the swelling of the crowd. It might also explain why two blind men were waiting on the other side of the city to plead for Jesus to heal them. Perhaps the first blind man who was healed went quickly to tell his blind friends what happened to him. Or maybe the other blind men were already stationed at the other end of the city in their customary begging position. At any rate, there is no irresolvable difficulty in the passage. The two accounts can be understood in a completely compatible way.

## MATTHEW 21:2 (cf. Mark 11:2; Luke 19:30)

*Were there two donkeys involved in the triumphal entry or just one?*

**Problem:** Matthew's account records Jesus's request of two disciples to go into a village and get two donkeys. But in Mark and Luke, He requests that the two disciples get just the colt.

**Solution:** Both animals were involved in Jesus's triumphal entry into Jerusalem. There is no mistake in the accounts because Mark and Luke mention just the colt (*pōlos*), and Matthew refers to the colt (*pōlos*, 21:5) and its mother. The passage in Matthew is pointing out the literal fulfillment of the prophecy of Zechariah 9:9, which states, "Behold your king is coming to you . . . humble, and mounted on a donkey, even on a colt, the foal of a donkey." The Greek version of the OT uses the same word for colt (*pōlos*) as the NT passages. Matthew literally states that once the disciples placed their garments on the donkeys, Jesus sat on them, that is, on their garments. Matthew does not say that Jesus rode on both the mother and the colt. It merely states that Jesus sat on the garments that the disciples had placed on the donkeys. Perhaps they placed some garments on the mother and others on the colt, and Jesus sat on those garments that were placed on the colt. The fact is, the text of Matthew simply does not say on which donkey Jesus sat. Mark and Luke focus on the colt that Jesus rode, while Matthew mentions the presence of the colt's mother. Her presence may have been necessary because the colt was so young. Mark 11:12 states that no one had ridden on the colt, and that the colt would be taking a passenger through a noisy crowd (Mark 11:9). Perhaps the mother was brought along in order to be a calming influence upon her young.

## MATTHEW 21:12–19 (cf. Mark 11:12–14, 20–24)

*When was the fig tree cursed by Jesus, before or after the temple was cleansed?*

**Problem:** Matthew places the cursing of the fig tree after the cleansing of the temple. But Mark places the cursing before the temple was cleansed. But it cannot be both. Did one Gospel writer make a mistake?

**Solution:** Jesus actually cursed the fig tree on His way to the temple, as Mark said, but this does not mean that Matthew's account is mistaken. Christ made two trips to the temple, and He cursed the fig tree on His second trip.

Mark 11:11 says Christ entered the temple on the day of His triumphal entry. When Christ enters the temple, Mark does not mention Christ making any proclamations against any wrongdoing. Verse 12 says, "Now the next day," referring to the trip to the fig tree on the way to the temple on the second day. On this day, Christ threw out those who were buying and selling in the temple. Matthew, however, addresses the two trips of Christ to the temple as though they were one event. This gives the impression that the first day Christ entered the temple He also drove out the buyers and sellers. Mark's account, however, gives more detail to the events and reveals there were actually two trips to the temple. In view of this, we have no reason to believe there is a discrepancy in the accounts.

## MATTHEW 22:30

### Will we be like angels (spirits) in heaven, beings without physical bodies?

**Problem:** Jesus said that in the resurrection we will be "like the angels of God" (Matt. 22:30). But angels have no physical bodies—they are spirits (Heb. 1:14). Thus it is argued that we will have no physical bodies in the resurrection. This, however, is contradictory to those verses that claim there will be a resurrection of the physical body from the grave (John 5:28–29; Luke 24:39).

**Solution:** Jesus did not say we would be like angels in that they are spirits, but like them in that they *do not marry*. Two observations are relevant here.

First of all, the context is not talking about the nature of the resurrection body, but whether or not there will be marriage in heaven. The question Jesus answered with this statement was, "In the resurrection, whose wife of the seven [husbands she had] will she be, for they all had her?" (22:28). Jesus's reply was that, like angels, there will be no marriage in heaven. So the woman will not be married to any of these seven husbands in heaven. But Jesus said nothing here about having immaterial bodies in heaven. Such a conclusion is totally unwarranted by the context.

Second, when Jesus said "in the resurrection . . . [they] are like angels of God," He obviously meant like angels in that they will "neither marry nor [be] given in marriage" (v. 30). He did not say they would be like angels in that they would have no physical bodies. Rather, they would be like angels in that they would be *without sexual propagation.*

## MATTHEW 23:34–35

*Did Jesus make a mistake in referring to Zechariah the son of Berechiah rather than to Zechariah the son of Jehoiada?*

**Problem:** Jesus said to the scribes and Pharisees that the guilt of all the righteous blood from Abel to Zechariah would fall on them. Concerning Zechariah, Jesus said he was killed between the sanctuary and the altar. Some conclude that the Zechariah referred to by Christ is the son of Jehoiada (2 Chron. 24:20–22).

**Solution:** The Zechariah referred to has to be the son of Berechiah. This Zechariah is one of the minor prophets, and his father is listed as Berechiah (Zech. 1:1). He would be the most likely candidate because the other Zechariah (son of Jehoiada) died about 800 BC. If one thinks Christ referred to this Zechariah, then the time span from Abel to this Zechariah would not cover the OT period, which extended to 400 BC. Abel to Zechariah the son of Berechiah would make a much better sweep of the OT period than would the period from Abel to Zechariah the son of Jehoiada. Since many Zechariahs are mentioned in the OT, it would not be too difficult to imagine two Zechariahs dying from similar circumstances.

## MATTHEW 24:34

*Did Jesus err by affirming that the signs of the end time would be fulfilled in His era?*

**Problem:** Jesus spoke of signs and wonders regarding His second coming. But Jesus said "this generation" would not end before all these events took place. Did this mean that these events would occur in the lifetime of His hearers?

**Solution:** These events (e.g., the great tribulation, the sign of Christ's return, and the end of the age) did not occur in the lifetime of Christ's hearers. Therefore, it is reasonable to understand their fulfillment as something yet to come. This calls for a closer examination of the meaning of "generation" for meanings other than that of Jesus's contemporaries.

First, "generation" in Greek (*genea*) can mean "race." In this particular instance, Jesus's statement could mean that the Jewish race would not pass away until all things are fulfilled. Since there were many promises to Israel, including the eternal inheritance of the land of Palestine (Gen. 12; 14–15; 17) and the Davidic kingdom (2 Sam. 7), then Jesus could be referring to God's preservation of the nation of Israel in order to fulfill His promises to them. Indeed, Paul speaks of a future of the nation of Israel when they will be reinstated in God's covenantal promises (Rom. 11:11–26). And Jesus's response to His disciples' last question implied there would yet be a future kingdom for Israel, when they asked: "Lord, will You at this time restore the kingdom to Israel?" Rather than rebuking them for their misunderstanding, He replied that "It is not for you to know times or seasons which the Father has put in His own authority" (Acts 1:6–7). Indeed, Paul in Romans 11 speaks of the nation of Israel being restored to God's promised blessings (cf. vv. 25–26).

Second, "generation" could also refer to a generation in its commonly understood sense of the people alive at the time indicated. In this case, "generation" would refer to the group of people who are alive when these things come to pass in the future. In other words, the generation alive when these things (the abomination of desolation [v. 15], the great tribulation such as has never been seen before [v. 21], the sign of the Son of Man in heaven [v. 30], etc.) begin to come to pass will still be alive when these judgments are completed. Since it is commonly believed that the tribulation is a period of some seven years (Dan. 9:27; cf. Rev. 11:2) at the end of the age, then Jesus would be saying that "this generation" alive at the beginning of the tribulation will still be alive at the end of it. In any event, there is no reason to assume that Jesus made the obviously false assertion that the world would come to an end within the lifetime of His contemporaries.

## MATTHEW 26:34 (cf. Mark 14:30)

*When Peter denied Christ, did the rooster crow once or twice?*

**Problem:** Matthew and John (13:38) say before the rooster crows once, Peter will have denied the Lord three times. But Mark affirms that before the rooster crows *twice*, Peter will deny Christ three times. Which account is right?

**Solution:** There is no contradiction between the two accounts because, given the correctness of the text, Matthew and John do not expressly state how many times the rooster will crow. They simply say Peter will deny Christ three times "before the rooster crows," but they do not say how many times it will crow. Mark may simply be more specific, affirming exactly how many times the rooster would crow.

It is also possible that different accounts are due to an early copyist error in Mark, which resulted in the insertion of "two" in early manuscripts (at Mark 14:30 and 72). This would explain why some important manuscripts of Mark mention only one crowing, just like Matthew and John, and why "two" appears at different places in some manuscripts.

## MATTHEW 27:5 (cf. Acts 1:18)

*Did Judas die by hanging or by falling on rocks?*

**Problem:** Matthew declares that Judas hanged himself. However, the Book of Acts says that he fell and his body burst open.

**Solution:** These accounts are not contradictory, but mutually complementary. Judas hung himself exactly as Matthew affirms that he did. The account in Acts simply adds that Judas fell, and his body opened up at the middle and his intestines gushed out. This is the very thing one would expect of someone who hanged himself from a tree over a cliff and fell on sharp rocks below.

## MATTHEW 27:37 (cf. Mark 15:26; Luke 23:38; John 19:19)

*Why are all the Gospel accounts of the inscription on the cross different?*

**Problem:** The wording of the accusation above Christ's head on the cross is rendered differently in each Gospel account.

| | |
|---|---|
| Matthew 27:37 | "This is Jesus the king of the Jews" |
| Mark 15:26 | "The king of the Jews" |
| Luke 23:38 | "This is the king of the Jews" |
| John19:19 | "Jesus of Nazareth, the king of the Jews" |

**Solution:** All the statements together are perfectly compatible. While there is a difference in what is omitted, the important phrase, "the king of the Jews," is identical in all four Gospels. The differences can be accounted for in different ways.

First, John 19:20 says, "Then many of the Jews read this title, for the place where Jesus was crucified was near the city; and it was written in Hebrew, Greek, and Latin." So then, there are at least three different languages in which the sign above Christ's head was written. Some of the differences may come from it being rendered in different languages.

Further, it is possible that each Gospel only gives part of the complete statement as follows:

Matthew: "This is Jesus [of Nazareth] the king of the Jews."
Mark: "[This is Jesus of Nazareth] the king of the Jews."
Luke: "This is [Jesus of Nazareth] the king of the Jews."
John: "[This is] Jesus of Nazareth the king of the Jews."
Original: "This is Jesus of Nazareth, the king of the Jews."

In this case, each Gospel is giving the essential part ("the king of the Jews"), but no Gospel is giving the whole inscription. But neither is any Gospel contradicting what the other Gospels say. The accounts are divergent and mutually complementary, not contradictory.

## MATTHEW 27:48

*Did Jesus die on the cross or just swoon?*

**Problem:** Many skeptics, as well as Muslims, believe that Jesus did not die on the cross. Some say that He took a drug that put Him in a coma-like state and that He later revived in the tomb. Yet the Bible says repeatedly that Christ died on the cross (cf. Rom. 5:8; 1 Cor. 15:3; 1 Thess. 4:14).

**Solution:** Jesus never fainted or swooned, nor was He drugged on the cross. In fact, He refused the drug customarily offered to the victim before crucifixion to help deaden pain (Matt. 27:34), and He accepted only "vinegar" later (v. 48) to quench His thirst. Jesus's actual physical death on the cross is supported by overwhelming evidence.

First of all, the OT predicted that Christ would die (Isa. 53:5–10; Ps. 22:16; Dan. 9:26; Zech. 12:10). And Jesus fulfilled the OT prophecies about the Messiah (cf. Matt. 4:14–16; 5:17–18; 8:17; John 4:25–26; 5:39).

Second, Jesus announced many times during His ministry that He was going to die (John 2:19–21; 10:10–11; Matt. 12:40; Mark 8:31). Typical is Matthew 17:22–23 that says, "The Son of Man is about to be betrayed into the hands of men and they will kill Him, and the third day He will be raised up."

Third, all the predictions of His resurrection, both in the OT (cf. Ps. 16:10; Isa. 26:19; Dan. 12:2) and in the NT (cf. John 2:19–21; Matt. 12:40; 17:22–23), are based on the fact that He would die. Only a dead body can be resurrected.

Fourth, the nature and extent of Jesus's injuries indicate that He must have died. He had no sleep the night before He was crucified. He was beaten several times and whipped. And He collapsed on the way to His crucifixion while carrying His cross. This in itself, to say nothing of the crucifixion to follow, was totally exhausting and life-draining.

Fifth, the nature of the crucifixion assures death. Jesus was on the cross from 9:00 in the morning until just before sunset. He bled from wounded hands and feet plus from the thorns that pierced His head. There would be a tremendous loss of blood from doing this for more than six hours. Plus, crucifixion demands that a man constantly pull himself up in order to breathe, thus causing excruciating pain from the nails. Doing this all day would kill nearly anyone—even if they were previously in good health.

Sixth, the piercing of Jesus's side with the spear, from which came "blood and water" (John 19:34), is proof that He had physically died before the piercing. When this has happened, it is a medical proof that the person has already died (see point eleven below).

Seventh, Jesus said He was in the act of dying on the cross when He declared, "Father, into Your hands I commend My spirit" (Luke 23:46). And "having said this, He breathed His last" (v. 46). John renders this, "He gave up His spirit" (John 19:30). His death cry was heard by those who stood by (vv. 47–49).

Eighth, the Roman soldiers, accustomed to crucifixion and death, pronounced Jesus dead. Although it was a common practice to break the legs of the victim to speed death (so that the person can no longer lift himself and breathe), they did not even break Jesus's legs (John 19:33).

Ninth, Pilate double-checked to make sure Jesus was dead before he gave the corpse to Joseph to be buried. "Summoning the centurion, he asked him if He had been dead for some time. And when he found out from the centurion, he granted the body to Joseph" (Mark 15:44–45).

Tenth, Jesus was wrapped in about seventy-five pounds of cloth and spices and placed in a sealed tomb for three days (John 19:39–40; Matt. 27:60). If He was not dead by then, which He clearly was, He would have died from lack of food, water, and medical treatment.

Eleventh, medical authorities who have examined the circumstances and nature of Christ's death have concluded that He actually died on the cross. An article in the *Journal of the American Medical Society* concluded:

> Clearly, the weight of historical and medical evidence indicates that Jesus was dead before the wound to his side was inflicted and supports the traditional view that the spear, thrust between his right rib, probably perforated not only the right lung but also the pericardium and heart and thereby ensured his death. Accordingly, interpretations based on the assumption that Jesus did not die on the cross appear to be at odds with modern medical knowledge.[17]

## MATTHEW 27:54 (cf. Mark 15:39; Luke 23:47)

*What did the centurion really say about Christ on the cross?*

**Problem:** Matthew records the centurion saying, "Truly this was the Son of God," while Mark says substantially the same thing, adding only the word "man," rendering it, "Truly this Man was the Son of God." Luke records the words of the centurion as follows: "Certainly this was a righteous Man!" What did he really say?

**Solution:** He may have said both. The centurion's words need not be limited to one phrase or sentence. The centurion could have said both things. In accordance with his own emphasis on Christ as the perfect man, Luke may have chosen to use this phrase rather than the ones used by Matthew and Mark. There is no major difference between Matthew and Mark, for in Greek the word "man" is implied by the masculine singular use of the word "This." It is also possible that Luke may have been paraphrasing or drawing an implication from what was actually said.

Christian scholars do not claim to have the exact words of the speakers in every case, but only an accurate rendering of what they really said. First of all, it is generally agreed that they spoke in Aramaic, but the Gospels were written in Greek. So the words we have in the Greek text on which the English is based are already a translation. Second, the Gospel writers, like writers today, sometimes summarized or paraphrased what was said. In this way, it is understandable that the renderings will be slightly different. But in this case, as in all other cases, the essence of what was originally said is faithfully produced in the original text. While we do not have the *exact words*, we do have the *same meaning*. Finally, when the sentences are totally different (but not contradictory), then we may reasonably assume that both things were said on that occasion and that one writer uses one and another writer the other. This is a common literary practice even today.

## MATTHEW 28:5

*Why does Matthew say there was only angel at the tomb when John says there were two?*

**Problem:** Matthew 28:5 refers to the "angel" at the tomb after Jesus's resurrection, and yet John says there were "two angels" there (John 20:12).

**Solution:** Matthew does not say there was *only* one angel. John says there were two, and wherever there are two, there is always one; it never fails! The critic has to add the word "only" to Matthew's account in order to make it contradictory. But in this case, the problem is not with what the Bible actually says, but with what the critic adds to it.

Matthew probably focuses on the one who *spoke* and "said to the women, 'Do not be afraid' " (Matt. 28:5). John referred to how many angels they *saw*; "and she saw two angels" (John 20:12).

## MATTHEW 28:9

*To whom did Jesus appear first, the women or His disciples?*

**Problem:** Mark says, "He appeared first to Mary Magdalene" (16:9). But Paul lists Peter as the first one to whom Jesus appeared (1 Cor. 15:5).

**Solution:** Since Paul is giving an official list for apologetic purposes, only men are listed. A woman's testimony in that culture did not have the official weight as that of a man. The Gospels are giving an actual account of the events in which women are included. The failure to present a harmonized account of the postresurrection accounts supports the authenticity of the accounts. Putting all the accounts together, the following order of events emerges.

| Order of Resurrection Events | Evidence Provided |
|---|---|
| 1. Mary Magdalene and other women | Empty tomb |
| (Matt. 28:1; Mark 16:1–3; Luke 24:1–10; John 20:1) | |
| 2. The other women | Empty tomb, angel(s) |
| (Matt. 28:5–8; Mark 16:6–9; Luke 24:4–9) | |
| 3. Peter and John | Empty tomb, grave clothes |
| (John 20:3–10) | |
| 4. Mary Magdalene (#1) | Angels, heard, saw, touched |
| (Mark 16:9–10; John 20:11–18) | |
| 5. Other women (#2) | Saw, heard, touched |
| (Matt. 28:9–10) | |

| 6. | Peter (#3) | Saw, heard* |
|---|---|---|
| | (Luke 24:34; 1 Cor. 15:5) | |
| 7. | Two disciples (#4) | Saw, heard, ate |
| | (Luke 24:13–31; Mark 16:12) | |
| 8. | Ten disciples (#5) | Saw, scars, heard, touched,* ate |
| | (Mark 16:14; Luke 24:35–49; John 20:19–24; 1 Cor. 15:5) | |
| 9. | Eleven disciples (Thomas present) (#6) | Saw, scars, heard, touched* |
| | (John 20:26–29) | |
| 10. | Seven disciples by Sea of Galilee (#7) | Saw, heard, ate |
| | (John 21:1–23) | |
| 11. | Five hundred disciples in Galilee (#8) | Saw, heard |
| | (1 Cor. 15:6) | |
| 12. | All the apostles in Galilee (#9) | Saw, heard |
| | (Matt. 28:18–20). | |
| 13. | James (#10) | Saw, heard |
| | (1 Cor. 15:7) | |
| 14. | All the apostles in Jerusalem (#11) | Saw, heard, ate |
| | (1 Cor. 15:7; Mark 16:15–20; Luke 24:46–52; Acts 1:3–9) | |
| 15. | Paul (#12) | Saw, heard |
| | (Acts 9:1–8; 1 Cor. 9:1; 15:8) | |

*Implied

## Key Verses on Order of Events

First Corinthians 15:5–8 lists the order of separate appearances as to: Peter, the Twelve, five hundred brethren, James, all the apostles, and Paul. Luke 24:34 asserts that Jesus appeared to Peter before He appeared to the two disciples on the road to Emmaus and before He later appeared to the Eleven (Luke 24:33–36). John 21:1–13 declares that the appearance to the seven apostles at the Sea of Tiberias (Sea of Galilee, John 6:1) was the third appearance to His disciples as a group (John 21:14). Mark 16:9 affirms that Jesus appeared first to Mary Magdalene. Matthew, Mark, Luke, and John all say the women were at the empty tomb first. Mark 16:9 affirms that the first appearance was to Mary Magdalene. John 21:13–13 implies this also.

### Harmony of Postresurrection Order of Events

1. Early on Sunday morning after Jesus's crucifixion, Mary Magdalene, Mary the mother of James, Joanna, and Salome went to the tomb with spices to anoint Jesus (Matt. 28:1; Mark 16:1; Luke 24:1; John 20:1). Finding the tomb empty, Mary Magdalene ran to Peter and John to tell them someone had taken the body of Jesus (John 20:2).

2. The other women entered the tomb where an angel (Matt. 28:5) who had a companion (John 20:11; Luke 20:4) told them Jesus had risen and would meet the disciples in Galilee (Matt. 28:2–8; Mark 16:5–8; Luke 24:4–8). On their hurried return in trembling and astonishment (Mark 16:8), yet with great joy (Matt. 28:8), they said nothing to anyone along the way (Mark 16:8) but went back to the disciples and reported what they had seen and heard (Matt. 28:8; Mark 16:10; Luke 24:9–10; John 20:2).

3. Meanwhile, after hearing Mary Magdalene's report, Peter and John ran to the tomb (John 20:3) apparently by a different and more direct route. John arrived at the tomb first (John 20:4). He peered into the tomb and saw the grave clothes but did not enter (John 20:5). When Peter arrived he entered the tomb and saw the grave clothes (John 20:6). Then John entered, saw the grave clothes and the folded head cloth in a place by itself and believed (John 20:8). After this, they returned to the place the other disciples were staying by the same route (John 20:10) and so did not run into the women.

4. Arriving after Peter and John left, Mary Magdalene went into the tomb (for a second time) and saw the angels (John 20:13). **She also saw Jesus [#1]** and clung to Him and worshiped Him (John 20:11–17). She then returned to the disciples (John 20:18; Mark 16:10).

5. While the other women were on their way to the disciples, Jesus **appeared to them [#2]**. They took hold of His feet and worshiped Him (Matt. 28:9–10). Jesus asked them to tell His disciples that He would meet them in Galilee (Matt. 28:10). Meanwhile the guards were bribed and told to say the disciples stole His body (Matt. 28:11–15).

6. When Mary and the women found the disciples, they announced that they had seen Jesus (Mark 16:10–11; Luke 24:10; John 20:18). After hearing this, Peter probably rushed to find Jesus, and **Peter saw Him [#3]** that day (1 Cor. 15:5; cf Luke 24:10).

7. The same day Jesus **appeared to Cleopas and another unnamed disciple [#4]** (maybe Luke) on the road to Emmaus (Mark 16:12; Luke 24:13–31). He revealed Himself to them while eating with them, and He told them He had appeared to Peter (Luke 24:34; cf. 1 Cor. 15:5). (Luke 24:34 may mean either that the two told the Eleven that Jesus had appeared to Peter, or that when the two saw the Eleven, the latter were saying the Lord has appeared to Peter.)

8. After Jesus left them, they returned to Jerusalem where Jesus **appeared to the ten disciples [#5]** (Thomas being absent, John 20:24), showing His scars and eating fish (Mark 16:14; Luke 24:35–49; John 20:19–24).

9. After eight days, **Jesus appeared to the eleven disciples [#6]** (Thomas now present). He showed His wounds and challenged Thomas to believe. Thomas exclaimed, "My Lord and my God" (John 20:28).

10. **Jesus appeared to seven [#7]** of His disciples who had gone fishing in the Sea of Galilee (John 21:1). He ate breakfast with them (John 21:2–13) after which He restored Peter (21:15–19).

11. **Then He appeared to five hundred brethren** at one time **[#8]** (1 Cor. 15:6).

12. After this **He appeared to all the apostles [#9]** in Galilee and gave them the Great Commission (1 Cor. 15:7; Matt. 28:18–20).

13. Then, **He appeared to James [#10]** (1 Cor. 15:7), probably in Jerusalem.

14. Later in Jerusalem, **He appeared to all His apostles [#11]** (1 Cor. 15:7), presenting many convincing evidences to them (Acts 1:3), including eating with them (Acts 1:4). He answered their last question (Acts 1:6–8) and then ascended into heaven (Mark 16:15–20; Luke 24:46–52; Acts 1:9–11).

15. Several years later, on the road to Damascus, **Jesus appeared to Saul [#12]** of Tarsus (Acts 9:1–8; 1 Cor. 9:1; 15:8), later known as the Apostle Paul.

**An Apparent Conflict**

Luke 24:12 appears to conflict with John 20:3–10. Luke 24:12 mentions only that Peter ran to the tomb after all the women were there and came back and told the apostles. But John says it was both Peter and John who were there, and it was just after Mary Magdalene was there alone.

Assuming Luke 24:12 is reliable, Luke may have only mentioned Peter because he was the leader of the two. Likewise, Mary Magdalene may have been singled out because she was the one who spoke first. This seems to be the case when Matthew mentions only one angel at the tomb (Matt. 28:5) and John mentions two (John 20:12). The "we" (John 20:2) implies others were with Mary Magdalene. However, Luke 24:12 may be an early copyist error since it is not in some early manuscripts. The RSV omits it. The NASB brackets it and adds, "Some ancient manuscripts do not contain verse 12." The Nestle-Aland Greek New Testament lists many old Italian mss., some old Syriac mss., as well as Marcion, Tatian's *Diatessaron*, and Eusebius (2nd–4th century) as omitting verse 12.

## MATTHEW 28:18–20

*How can three persons be God when there is only one God?*

**Problem:** Matthew speaks of the "Father, Son, and Holy Spirit" all being part of one "name." But these are three distinct persons. How can there be three persons in the Godhead when there is only "one God" (Deut. 6:4; 1 Cor. 8:6)?

**Solution:** God is one in *essence*, but three in *persons*. God has one *nature*, but three *centers of consciousness*. That is, there is only one *What* in God, but there are three *Whos*. There is one *It*, but three *I's*. This is a mystery, but not a contradiction. It would be contradictory to say God was only one person, but also was three persons. Or that God is only one nature, but that He also had three natures. But to declare, as orthodox Christians do, that God is one essence, eternally revealed in three distinct persons, is not a contradiction.

# MARK

**Why does Mark omit giving any genealogy of Jesus like Matthew and Luke do?**

**Problem:** Both Matthew (chap. 1) and Luke (chap. 3) give an ancestry of Jesus (see Matt. 1:1). However, Mark provides no genealogy whatsoever. Why the omission?

**Solution:** Mark presents Christ as a servant, and servants need no genealogy. The Roman audience to whom Mark directed his Gospel was not interested in *where* a servant came from, but in *what* he could do. Unlike Mark's Roman audience, Matthew's Jewish audience looked for the Messiah, the King. Thus, Matthew traces Jesus back to His Jewish roots as the Son of David the king (Matt. 1:1). Likewise, Luke presents Christ as the perfect man. Hence, Christ's ancestry is traced back to the first man, Adam (Luke 3:38). John, on the other hand, presents Christ as the Son of God. Therefore, he traces Christ back to His eternal source with the Father.

Consider the following comparison of the four Gospels that explains why Mark needed no ancestry for Jesus.

|            | Matthew     | Mark         | Luke        | John     |
|------------|-------------|--------------|-------------|----------|
| Christ Presented | King  | Servant      | Man         | God      |
| Symbol     | Lion        | Ox           | Man         | Eagle    |
| Key        | Sovereignty | Ministry     | Humanity    | Deity    |
| Audience   | Jews        | Romans       | Greeks      | World    |
| Ancestry   | To royalty  | In anonymity | To humanity | To deity |

## MARK 1:2

### How can Mark's misquotation of this OT prophecy be justified?

**Problem:** Mark misquotes Malachi, as indicated by the italicized words:

| MALACHI 3:1 | MARK 1:2 |
|-------------|----------|
| Behold, I send *My* messenger, And he will prepare the way before *Me*. | Behold, I send *My* messenger before *Your face*, Who will prepare *Your way* before *You*. |

**Solution:** First, it should be pointed out that, in spite of the change in words, the *original sense* is retained. In view of one of the fundamental principles of understanding difficult texts (see introduction), a NT citation need not be an exact quotation. As long as the meaning is retained, the words can differ. Second, in this case, Mark simply draws out the meaning by adding "before Your face." This is implied in the original passage, but made explicit by Mark. Third, the change from "Me" (first person) to "You" is necessitated because God is speaking in the Malachi passage, whereas Mark is speaking about God. Had he not changed the words he would have changed the meaning.

## MARK 2:26

### Was Jesus wrong when He mentioned Abiathar as high priest instead of Ahimelech?

**Problem:** Jesus says that at the time David ate the consecrated bread, Abiathar was high priest. Yet 1 Samuel 21:1–6 mentions that the high priest at that time was Ahimelech.

**Solution:** First Samuel is correct in stating that the high priest was Ahimelech. On the other hand, neither was Jesus wrong. When we take a close look at Christ's words, we notice that He used the phrase "in the *days* of Abiathar" (v. 26), which does not necessarily imply that Abiathar was high priest at the time David ate the bread. After David met Ahimelech and ate the bread, King Saul had Ahimelech killed (1 Sam. 22:17–19). Abiathar escaped and went to David (v. 20) and later took the place of the high priest. So even though Abiathar was made high priest after David ate the bread, it is still correct to speak in this manner. After all, Abiathar was alive when David did this, and soon following he became the high priest after his father's death. Thus, it was during the *time* of Abiathar, but not during his *tenure* in office.

## MARK 6:5

### *If Jesus is God, why couldn't He do mighty works here?*

**Problem:** First of all, the Bible describes Jesus as God (John 1:1) who has, with the Father, "all authority in heaven and earth" (Matt. 28:18). However, on this occasion Jesus "could do no mighty work there" (v. 5). Why couldn't He, if He is all-powerful?

**Solution:** Jesus is almighty as God, but not almighty as man. As the God-man, Jesus has both a divine nature and a human nature. What He can do in one nature, He cannot necessarily do in the other. For example, as God, Jesus never got tired (Ps. 121:4), but as man He did (cf. John 4:6).

Furthermore, just because Jesus *possessed* all power does not mean that He always chose to *exercise* it. The "could not" in Mark 6:5 is a moral "could not," not an actual "could not." It is akin to a Christian saying to a boss who asks them to lie, "I just can't do that." They could, but they choose not to do so because it is against their morals. Similarly, Jesus could not have done more miracles there because it was contrary to His convictions to perform miracles "because of their unbelief" (6:6). Jesus was not an entertainer, nor did He cast pearls before swine. So the necessity here is moral not metaphysical. He had the ability to do miracles there and in fact did some (v. 5), only He refused to do more because He deemed it a wasted effort.

## MARK 8:11–12

*Did Jesus contradict Himself by saying there would be no sign given (cf. Matt. 12:38–39)?*

**Problem:** In Mark, the Pharisees ask for a sign from Jesus, but He says that no sign shall be given to that generation. But Matthew's account says that Christ responded that the sign of the prophet Jonah would be given (namely, Jesus's resurrection).

**Solution:** First, the main point here is that Christ was not willing to grant their *immediate* request for a sign. Jesus does not say in Matthew that the sign of the prophet Jonah will be immediately given. This sign (of His death and resurrection) occurred *later*. So, even in Matthew He did not grant the requests of the Pharisees. Jesus refused to do miracles just to entertain (Luke 23:8). He did not "cast pearls before swine." However He did perform miracles to confirm His identity as Messiah (John 20:31), and the resurrection was the crowning miracle of that nature (cf. Acts 2:22–32).

Second, it is evident that on more than one occasion Jesus was asked to give a sign. Luke 11:16, 29–30 states that others sought for a sign. Here in Luke, Jesus responds very similar to the way He does in Matthew 12. Also, again in Matthew 16:1–4 the Pharisees ask for a sign from Jesus, to which He responds that none will be given except the sign of Jonah, just as He had said in chapter 12. It is clear that on other occasions Jesus was asked to give a sign, and each time Jesus refused to agree to their immediate demands. Miracles are performed according to God's will, not according to human want (cf. Heb. 2:4; 1 Cor. 12:11).

## MARK 11:13

*Was Jesus unwise in cursing the fig tree?*

**Problem:** Jesus cursed a fig tree for not having fruit in the springtime before fig trees bear fruit. Is this a sign that He was not very wise?

**Solution:** Jesus did not make an unwise decision in cursing the fig tree for not having fruit, since it was the time of year (Passover) that early figs do appear on fig trees. This is why the text says: "and seeing from afar a fig tree having leaves, He went to find out if it had any fruit" (v. 13).

The fruit of the fig tree appears along with the leaves and sometimes even before leaves appear. The presence of leaves offered the promise of fruit, even though this was ahead of the season. It was the foliage that drew Jesus to the tree in hope of finding fruit. The lack of fruit on a fig tree that already had an abundance of foliage signified that the tree would have no fruit during that season. This outward appearance of fruitfulness without any real fruit was a spiritually significant lesson about Israel for the disciples.

Furthermore, if Jesus is the Creator, then He can curse a fig tree for reasons unknown to us. After all, simply because a finite being does not see a reason for some event does not mean that an infinite Mind does not have one. After all, the fig tree is going to eventually wither and die. Jesus simply sped up the process.

Finally, Jesus's wise purpose is manifest in the text. The fig tree was used to illustrate that Israel's rejection of their Messiah would lead to their downfall. And immediately after the tree was cursed, Jesus was accosted in the temple by the Jewish authorities (v. 23), who would soon call for His crucifixion.

## MARK 13:32

### Was Jesus ignorant of the time of His second coming?

**Problem:** The Bible teaches that Jesus is God (John 1:1) and that He knows all things (John 2:24; Col. 2:3). On the other hand, He "increased in wisdom" (Luke 2:52) and sometimes did not seem to know certain things (cf. John 11:34). Indeed, He denied knowing the time of His own second coming here, saying, "but of that day and hour no one knows, neither the angels in heaven, nor the Son, but only the Father."

**Solution:** We must distinguish between what Jesus knew *as God* (everything) and what He knew *as man*. As God, Jesus was omniscient (all-knowing), but as man He was limited in His knowledge. The situation can be schematized as follows:

| JESUS AS GOD | JESUS AS MAN |
|---|---|
| Unlimited in knowledge | Limited in knowledge |
| No growth in knowledge | Growth in knowledge |
| Knew the time of His second coming | Did not know the time of His second coming |

## MARK 15:25 (cf. John 19:14)

*Was Jesus crucified in the third hour or the sixth hour?*

**Problem:** Mark's Gospel account says that it was the third hour (9 a.m. Jewish time) when Christ was crucified (15:25). John's Gospel says that it was about the sixth hour (which would be 6 a.m.) when Jesus was still on trial (19:14). This would make His crucifixion much later than specified by Mark. Which Gospel is correct? One would be an error.

**Solution:** Both Gospel writers are correct in their assertions. The difficulty is answered when we realize that each Gospel writer used a different time system. John follows the *Roman* time system while Mark follows the *Jewish* time system (see A. T. Robertson, *Harmony of the Gospels*, 224).

According to Roman time, the day ran from midnight to midnight. The Jewish 24-hour period began in the evening at 6 p.m. and the morning of that day began at 6 a.m. Therefore, when Mark asserts that at the third hour Christ was crucified, this was about 9 a.m. John stated that Christ's trial was about the sixth hour. This would place the trial *before* the crucifixion and would not negate any testimony of the Gospel writers. This fits with John's other references to time. For example, he speaks about Jesus being weary from His journey on His trip from Judea to Samaria at the "sixth hour" and asking for water from the woman at the well. Considering the length of His trip, His weariness, and the normal evening time when people come to the well to drink and to water their animals, this fits better with 6 p.m., which is "the sixth hour" of the night by Roman time reckoning. The same is true of John's reference to the tenth hour in John 1:39, which would be 10 a.m., a more likely time to be out preaching than 4 a.m.

## MARK 16:9–20

*Why is this passage of Scripture omitted in some Bibles?*

**Problem:** Most modern Bibles contain this ending of the Gospel of Mark, including the KJV, ASV, NASB, and the NKJV. However, both the RSV and the NIV set it off from the rest of the text. A note in the NIV says, "Most reliable early manuscripts and other ancient witnesses do not have Mark 16:9–20." Were these verses in the original Gospel of Mark?

**Solution:** Scholars are divided over the canonicity of these verses. Those who follow the received text tradition point to the fact that this text is found in the majority of biblical manuscripts down through the centuries. Thus, they believe it was in the original manuscript of Mark.

On the other hand, those who follow the critical text tradition insist that we should not *add* evidence, but *weigh* it. Truth is not determined, they say, by majority vote, but by the most qualified witnesses. They point to the following arguments for rejecting these verses: (1) These verses are lacking in many of the oldest and most reliable Greek manuscripts, as well as in important Old Latin, Syriac, Armenian, and Ethiopic manuscripts. (2) Many of the ancient church fathers reveal no knowledge of these verses, including Clement, Origen, and Eusebius. Jerome admitted that almost all Greek copies do not have it. (3) Many manuscripts that do have this section place a mark by it indicating it is a spurious addition to the text. (4) There is another (shorter) ending to Mark that is found in some manuscripts. (5) Others point to the fact that the style and vocabulary are not the same as the rest of the Gospel of Mark.

Whether or not this piece of *text* belongs in the original, the *truth* it contains certainly accords with it. So, the bottom line is that it does not make any difference, since if it does belong here, there is nothing in it contrary to the rest of Scripture. And if it does not belong, there is no truth missing in the Bible, since everything taught here is found elsewhere in Scripture. This includes tongues (see Acts 2:1ff), baptism (Acts 2:38), and God's first-century super-natural protection of His messengers who were unwittingly bitten by poisonous snakes (cf. Acts 28:3–5). So, in the final analysis, it is simply a debate about whether this particular *text* belongs in the Bible, not over whether any *truth* is missing.

# LUKE

*Did Luke make a mistake when he mentioned a worldwide census under Caesar Augustus?*

**Problem:** Luke refers to a worldwide census under Caesar Augustus when Quirinius was governor of Syria. However, according to the annals of ancient history, no such census took place.

**Solution:** Until recently, it has been widely held by critics that Luke made an error in his assertion about a registration under Caesar Augustus, and that the census actually took place in AD 6 or 7 (which is mentioned by Luke in Gamaliel's speech recorded in Acts 5:37). The lack of any extrabiblical support has led some to claim this is an error. However, recent scholarship has reversed this trend, and it is now widely admitted that there was in fact an earlier registration as Luke records. This has been asserted on the basis of several factors.

First of all, since the people of a subjugated land were compelled to take an oath of allegiance to the emperor, it was not unusual for the emperor to require an imperial census as an expression of this allegiance and as a means of enlisting men for military service, or, as was probably true in this case, in preparation to levy taxes. Because of the strained relations between Herod and Augustus in the later years of Herod's reign, as the

Jewish historian Josephus reports, it is understandable that Augustus would begin to treat Herod's domain as a subject land, and consequently would impose such a census to maintain control of Herod and the people.

Second, periodic registrations of this sort took place on a regular basis every fourteen years. According to the very papers that recorded the censuses (see Sir William M. Ramsay, *Was Christ Born in Bethlehem?*, 1898), there was in fact a census taken in about 8 or 7 BC. Because of this regular pattern of census taking, any such action would naturally be regarded as a result of the general policy of Augustus, even though a local census may have been instigated by a local governor. Therefore, Luke recognizes the census as stemming from the decree of Augustus.

Third, a census was a massive project that probably took several years to complete. Such a census for the purpose of taxation was begun in Gaul between 10–9 BC that took a period of forty years to complete. It is quite likely that the decree to begin the census, in about 8 or 7 BC, may not have actually begun in Palestine until some time later. Problems of organization and preparation may have delayed the actual census until 5 BC or even later.

Fourth, it was not an unusual requirement that people return to the place of their origin, or to the place where they owned property. A decree of C. Vibius Mazimius in AD 104 required all those who were away from their hometowns to return there for the purpose of the census. For the Jews, such travel would not have been unusual at all since they were quite used to the annual pilgrimage to Jerusalem. There is simply no reason to suspect Luke's statement regarding the census at the time of Jesus's birth. Luke's account fits the regular pattern of census taking, and its date would not be an unreasonable one. Also, this may have been simply a local census that was taken as a result of the general policy of Augustus. Luke simply provides us with a reliable historical record of an event not otherwise recorded. Since Dr. Luke has proven himself to be a reliable historian in other matters (see Sir William M. Ramsay, *St. Paul the Traveler and Roman Citizen*, 1896), there is no reason to doubt him here (see also comments on Luke 2:2).

## LUKE 2:2

*Why does Luke say the census was during Quirinius's governorship, since Quirinius was not governor until AD 6?*

**Problem:** Luke states that the census decreed by Augustus was the first one taken while Quirinius was governor of Syria. However, Quirinius did not become governor of Syria until after the death of Herod in about AD 6. Is this an error in Luke's historical record?

**Solution:** Luke has not made an error. There are reasonable solutions to this difficulty.

First, Quintilius Varus was governor of Syria from about 7 BC to about 4 BC. Varus was not a trustworthy leader, a fact that was disastrously demonstrated in AD 9 when he lost three legions of soldiers in the Teutoburger forest in Germany. To the contrary, Quirinius was a notable military leader who was responsible for squelching the rebellion of the Homonadensians in Asia Minor. When it came time to begin the census, in about 8 or 7 BC, Augustus entrusted Quirinius with the delicate problem in the volatile area of Palestine, effectively superseding the authority and governorship of Varus by appointing Quirinius to a place of special authority in this matter.

It has also been proposed that Quirinius was governor of Syria on two separate occasions, once while prosecuting the military action against the Homonadensians between 12 and 2 BC, and later beginning about AD 6. A Latin inscription discovered in 1764 has been interpreted to refer to Quirinius as having served as governor of Syria on two occasions.

It is possible that Luke 2:2 reads, "This census took place *before* Quirinius was governing Syria." In this case, the Greek word translated "first" (*prōtos*) is translated as a comparative, "before." Because of the awkward construction of the sentence, this is not an unlikely reading.

Regardless of which solution is accepted, it is not necessary to conclude that Luke has made an error in recording the historical events surrounding the birth of Jesus. Luke has proven himself to be a reliable historian even in the details. Sir William M. Ramsay has shown that in making reference to 32 countries, 54 cities, and 9 islands he made no mistakes.

## LUKE 3:23

*Why does Luke present a different ancestral tree for Jesus than the one in Matthew?*

**Problem:** Jesus has a different grandfather here in Luke 3:23 (Heli) than He does in Matthew 1:16 (Jacob). Which one is the right one?

**Solution:** This should be expected, since they are two different lines of ancestors, one traced through His *legal* father, Joseph, and the other through His *actual* mother, Mary. Matthew gives the *official* line, since he addresses Jesus's genealogy to Jewish concerns for the Jewish Messiah's credentials that required that Messiah come from the seed of Abraham and the line of David (cf. Matt. 1:1). Luke, with a broader *Greek* audience in view, addresses himself to their interest in Jesus as the *Perfect Man* (which was the quest of Greek thought). Thus, he traces Jesus back to the first man, Adam (Luke 3:38).

That Matthew gives Jesus's paternal genealogy and Luke his maternal genealogy is further supported by several facts. First of all, while both lines trace Christ to David, each is through a different son of David. Matthew traces Jesus through Joseph (His *legal father*) to David's son *Solomon* the king, by whom Christ rightfully inherited the throne of David (cf. 2 Sam. 7:12ff). Luke's purpose, on the other hand, is to show Christ as an actual human. So he traces Christ to David's son *Nathan*, through His *actual mother*, Mary, through whom He can rightfully claim to be fully human, the redeemer of humanity.

Further, Luke does not say that he is giving Jesus's genealogy through Joseph. Rather, he notes that Jesus was "as was supposed" (Luke 3:23) the son of Joseph, while He was actually the son of Mary. Also, that Luke would record Mary's genealogy fits with his interest as a doctor in mothers and birth and with his emphasis on women in his Gospel, which has been called "the Gospel for Women."

Finally, the fact that the two genealogies have some names in common (such as Shealtiel and Zerubbabel, Matt. 1:12; cf. Luke 3:27) does not prove they are the same genealogy for two reasons. One, these are not uncommon names. Further, even the same genealogy (Luke's) has a repeat of the names Joseph and Judah (3:26, 30).

The two genealogies can be summarized as follows:

| MATTHEW | LUKE |
|---|---|
| David | David |
| Solomon | Nathan |
| Rehoboam | Mattathah |
| Abijah | Menan |
| Asa | Melea |
| Jehoshaphat | Eliakim |
| . . . . . | . . . . . |
| Jacob | Heli |
| Joseph—Mary—legal wife (legal father) | Joseph—Mary—actual mother (legal husband) |
| Jesus | Jesus |

## LUKE 24:23

### *Were Jesus's resurrection appearances physical or mere visions?*

**Problem:** Jesus spoke of His resurrection body having "flesh and bones" (Luke 24:39). He ate physical food (v. 42) and was touched by human hands (Matt. 28:9). But Luke calls it a "vision" in this passage, which implies that it was not a real physical appearance. In addition, some point to the fact that those who were with Paul during his Damascus road experience did not see Christ (see Acts 9:7).

**Solution:** The resurrection appearances were literal, physical appearances. This is evident for several reasons. First of all, the passage cited above from Luke (24:23) does not refer to seeing Christ. It refers only to the women seeing angels at the tomb, not to any appearance of Christ. The Gospels never speak of a resurrection appearance of Christ as a vision, nor does Paul in his list in 1 Corinthians 15.

Second, the postresurrection encounters with Christ are described by Paul as literal "appearances" (1 Cor. 15:5–8), not as visions. The difference between a mere vision and a physical appearance is significant. Visions are of invisible, spiritual realities, such as God and angels. Appearances, on the other hand, are of physical objects that can be seen with the naked eye. Visions have no physical manifestations associated with them, but appearances do.

People sometimes "see" or "hear" things in their visions (Luke 1:1ff; Acts 10:9ff), but not with their naked physical senses. When someone saw angels with the naked eye, or had some physical contact with them (Gen. 18:8; 32:24; Dan. 8:18), it was not a vision but an actual appearance of an angel in the physical world. During these appearances, the angels temporarily assumed a visible form, after which they returned to their normal invisible state. However, the resurrection appearances of Christ were experiences of seeing Christ with the naked eye in His continued visible, physical form. In any event, there is a significant difference between a mere vision and a physical appearance.

| VISION | APPEARANCE |
|---|---|
| Of a spiritual reality | Of a physical object |
| No physical manifestations | Physical manifestations |
| Daniel 2; 7 | 1 Corinthians 15 |
| 2 Corinthians 12 | Acts 9 |

Third, certainly the most common way to describe an encounter with the resurrected Christ is as an "appearance." These appearances were accompanied by physical manifestations, such as the audible voice of Jesus, His physical body and crucifixion scars, physical sensations (such as touch), and eating on three occasions. These phenomena are not purely subjective or internal—they involve a physical, external reality.

Finally, the contention that Paul's experience must have been a vision because those with him did not see Christ is unfounded, since they both heard the physical sound and saw the physical light, just as Paul did. Only Paul looked into the light, and so only he saw Jesus.

## LUKE 24:31

*If Jesus had the same physical body after His resurrection, why did His disciples not recognize Him?*

**Problem:** These two disciples walked with Jesus, talked with Him, and ate with Him and still did not recognize Him. Other disciples had the same experience (see verses below). If He rose in the same physical body (cf. Luke 24:39; John 20:27), then why didn't they recognize Him?

**Solution:** Jesus did rise in the numerically same body of flesh and bones in which He died (see comments on 1 Cor. 15:37). There were many reasons why He was not immediately recognized by His disciples:

1. Dullness—Luke 24:25–26
2. Disbelief—John 20:24–25
3. Disappointment—John 20:11–15
4. Dread—Luke 24:36–37
5. Dimness—John 20:1, 14–15
6. Distance—John 21:4
7. Different clothes—John 19:23–24; cf. 20:6–8

Notice, however, two important things: the problem was only *temporary*, and before the appearance was over, they were absolutely convinced that it was the same Jesus in the same physical body of flesh, bones, and scars that He had before the resurrection! And they went out of His presence to turn the world upside down, fearlessly facing death, because they had not the slightest doubt that He had conquered death in the same physical body in which He had experienced it.

# JOHN

## JOHN 1:1

*Is Jesus the true God or just a god?*

**Problem:** Orthodox Christians believe Jesus is God and often appeal to this passage to prove it. However, Jehovah's Witnesses translate this verse "and the Word (Christ) was a god" because there is no definite article ("the") in the Greek of this verse.

**Solution:** In Greek, when the definite article is used, it often stresses the *individual*, and, when it is not present, it refers to the *nature* of the one denoted. Thus, the verse can be rendered, "and the Word was of the nature of God." The full deity of Christ is supported not only by general usage of the same construction, but by other references in John to Jesus being God (cf. 8:58; 10:30; 20:28) and the rest of the NT (cf. Col. 1:15–16; 2:9; Titus 2:13).

Furthermore, some NT texts use the definite article and speak of Christ as "the God." So it does not matter whether John did or did not use the definite article here—the Bible clearly teaches that Jesus is God, not just a god (cf. Heb. 1:8).

That Jesus is Jehovah (Yahweh) is clear from the fact that the NT attributes characteristics to Jesus that in the OT apply only to God (cf. John 19:37 and Zech. 12:10).

## JOHN 1:18

### *Was Jesus alone the Son of God?*

**Problem:** Jesus is called "the only begotten Son" in this verse. Yet only a few verses earlier, John informs us that we can by faith "become children of God" (1:12). If then we are sons of God, how can Jesus be the only Son of God?

**Solution:** There is a gigantic difference between the senses in which Jesus is the "Son of God" and we are "sons of God." First, He is the unique Son of God; I am only a son of God. He is the Son of God with a capital "S"; human beings can become sons of God only with a small "s." Jesus was the Son of God by eternal right of inheritance (Col. 1:15); we are the sons of God only by adoption (Rom. 8:14). He is the Son of God because He is God by His very nature (John 1:1), whereas we are only made in the image of God (Gen. 1:27) and remade in "the image of Him" by redemption (Col. 3:10). Jesus is *of* God by His very nature; we are only *from* God. He *is* divine in nature, but we only participate in it by salvation (2 Peter 1:4). And we can participate only in God's moral attributes (like holiness and love), not in His nonmoral attributes (like infinity and eternity). To summarize the differences:

| JESUS AS THE SON OF GOD | HUMANS AS SONS OF GOD |
|---|---|
| Natural Son | Adopted sons |
| No beginning | Beginning |
| Creator | Creature |
| God by nature | Not God by nature |

## JOHN 3:5

### *Does this verse teach baptismal regeneration?*

**Problem:** Jesus told Nicodemus that "unless one is born of water and the Spirit, he cannot enter the kingdom of God." Does this mean a person has to be baptized to be saved?

**Solution:** Baptism is not necessary for salvation (see comments on Acts 2:38). Salvation is by grace through faith and not by works of righteousness (Eph. 2:8–9; Titus 3:5–6). But baptism is a work of righteousness (cf. Matt. 3:15). What then did Jesus mean when He referred to being "born of water"? There are three basic ways to understand this, none of which involve baptismal regeneration.

Some believe Jesus is speaking of the *water of the womb*, since He had just mentioned one's "mother's womb" in the preceding verse. If so, then He was saying "unless you are born once by water (at your physical birth) and then again by the 'Spirit' at your spiritual birth, you cannot be saved."

Others take "born of water" to refer to the "washing of *water by the word*" (Eph. 5:26). They note that Peter refers to being "born again . . . through the word of God" (1 Peter 1:23), the very thing John is speaking about in these verses (cf. John 3:3, 7).

Still others think that "born of water" refers to the *baptism of John* (John 1:26). John said he baptized by water, but Jesus would baptize by the Spirit (Matt. 3:11), saying, "repent for the kingdom of heaven is at hand" (Matt. 3:2). If this is what is meant, then when Jesus said they must be "born of water and the Spirit" (John 3:5), He meant that the Jews of His day had to undergo the baptism of repentance by John and also later the baptism of the Holy Spirit before they could "enter the kingdom of God."

## JOHN 4:26

*Why did Jesus confess He was the Messiah here, but avoid doing it elsewhere?*

**Problem:** In the Synoptic Gospels (Matthew, Mark, and Luke), Jesus seemed to go out of His way to avoid claiming He was the Jewish Messiah. He would ask His disciples in private (Matt. 16:13) and would sometimes exhort people who discovered it "to tell no man" (see comments on Matt. 16:20). Yet here in John the woman of Samaria said, "I know that Messiah is coming who is called Christ" (John 4:25). Jesus forthrightly volunteered, "I who speak to you am He" (v. 26).

**Solution:** Here Jesus was in Samaria, not Judea. The Jews of Jesus's day had a distorted concept of the Messiah, namely, as one who would deliver them from the political oppression of Rome. In this context, Jesus was more careful to make His claims more covert, so as to elicit from His disciples a more spiritual concept of the one who came to redeem His people (cf. Luke 19:10; John 10:10).

Indeed, this is why Jesus so often spoke in parables, so that those who were truly seeking would understand, but those who had a false concept would be confused (see Matt. 13:13). This is why, when Jesus performed miracles, He would sometimes exhort the person to tell no one, since He did not want to be thronged by the curious. Indeed, Jesus rebuked those who, having seen Him multiply the loaves, wanted to make Him king (John 6:15), declaring that they followed Him "because you ate of the loaves and were filled" (v. 26). However, in Samaria, where this false Jewish concept of a political deliverer from Rome who could feed the masses did not prevail, Jesus did not hesitate to claim that He indeed was the true Messiah. Furthermore, Jesus said this to only one Samaritan woman in private, not to the masses of Jews in Judea.

Nonetheless, Jesus did claim to be the Messiah in public, in Judea, and to the Jews. Usually, however, His claim was more covert, trying to get them to discover for themselves who He was. However, when the chips were down and it became necessary to declare Himself before the high priest, Jesus explicitly answered the question "Are You the Christ, the Son of the Blessed?" by declaring, "I am [the Christ]" (Mark 14:61–62; cf. Matt. 26:64; cf. Luke 22:70).

## JOHN 6:35
### Why are the "I AM" statements of Jesus only mentioned in John?

**Problem:** John mentions numerous times that Jesus said "I am" (e.g., John 6:35; 8:58; 10:9; 14:6). Yet not one of these statements is mentioned in any other Gospel. Did John make these up, or did Jesus actually say them?

**Solution:** John reported accurately what he heard and saw. First of all, he was an eyewitness of the events (John 21:24; cf. 1 John 1:1). His Gospel is filled with details of geography (3:23), topography

(6:10), and private conversations that betray a firsthand, first-century knowledge of the events (cf. John 3; 4; 13–17).

Further, when John records events and/or conversation found in the other Gospels, he does so in substantially the same way they do. This includes the preaching of John the Baptist (1:19–28), the feeding of the five thousand (6:1–14), Jesus's walking on the water (6:15–21), eating the Passover with His disciples (13:1–2), Peter's denial (13:36–38; 18:15–27), Judas's betrayal (18:1–11), His trials (18–19), His crucifixion (19), and His resurrection (20–21).

In addition, the other Gospels record some of the same types of conversation recorded in John. Matthew 11:25–30 sounds like something right out of the Gospel of John. Even Jesus's characteristic use of "verily" (KJV; "truly," NASB; "assuredly," NKJV) in John (cf. 1:51; 3:3, 11; 5:19, 24, etc.) is found in other Gospels (cf. Matt. 5:18, 26; Mark 3:28; 9:1; Luke 4:24; 18:17), though John alone doubles it, perhaps for emphasis.

Finally, John's differences from the Synoptic Gospels can be accounted for in several ways. First of all, John writes primarily about Jesus's Judean ministry, whereas the other Gospels speak largely about His Galilean ministry. Second, John records many of Jesus's private conversations (cf. chaps. 3–4; 13–17), whereas the other Gospels speak mostly about His public ministry. Third, clear "I Am" statements come usually after Jesus has been challenged and He declares His point simply and emphatically. Even so, they are not without parallel in the other Gospels, where Jesus says "I am [the Christ]" (Mark 14:62).

## JOHN 6:53–54

*What did Jesus mean when He said we should eat His flesh?*

**Problem:** Evangelical Christians believe in taking the Bible literally. But Jesus said, "unless you eat the flesh of the Son of Man and drink His blood, you have no life in you" (John 6:53). Should this be taken literally too?

**Solution:** The literal (i.e., actual) meaning of a text is the correct one, but the literal meaning does not mean that everything should be taken literally. For example, the literal meaning of Jesus's statement "I am the true vine" (John 15:1) is that He is the real source of our spiritual life. But it does not mean that Jesus is a literal vine with leaves growing out of His arms and ears! Literal meaning can be communicated by means of figures of speech. Christ is the actual foundation of the church (1 Cor. 3:11; Eph. 2:20), but He is not literally a granite cornerstone with engraving on it.

There are many indications in John 6 that Jesus literally meant that the command to "eat His flesh" should be taken in a figurative way. First, Jesus indicated that His statement should not be taken in a materialistic sense when He said, "The words that I speak to you are spirit, and they are life" (John 6:63). Second, it is absurd and cannibalistic to take it in a physical way. Third, He was not speaking of physical life, but "eternal life" (John 6:54). Fourth, He called Himself the "bread of life" (John 6:48) and contrasted this with the physical bread the Jews ate in the wilderness (John 6:58). Fifth, He used the figure of "eating" His flesh in parallel with the idea of "abiding" in Him (cf. John 15:4–5), which is another figure of speech. Neither figure is to be taken literally. Sixth, if eating His flesh and drinking His blood is to be taken in a literalistic way, this would contradict other commands of Scripture not to eat human flesh and blood (cf. Acts 15:20). Finally, in view of the figurative meaning here, this verse cannot be used to support the Roman Catholic concept of transubstantiation—that is, eating Jesus's actual body in the Communion.

## JOHN 10:34

### Did Jesus advocate that man could become God?

**Problem:** Jesus answered a group of Jews and said, "Is it not written in your law, 'I said, you are gods'?" Does this mean that humans can become God, as pantheistic religions and New Age advocates claim?

**Solution:** The context of this passage reveals that Christ had just pronounced Himself one with the Father, saying, "I and My Father are one" (10:30). The Jews wanted to stone Him because they thought Christ was blaspheming since He was making Himself out to be equal with God (vv. 31–33).

Jesus responded by quoting Psalm 82:6, which says, "I said, you are gods." This psalm addresses judges who are judging unjustly. The title of "gods" is not addressed to everyone, but only to those judges about whom Jesus said were those to "whom the word of God came" (v. 35). Jesus was showing that if the OT Scriptures could give some divine status to divinely appointed judges, why should they find it incredible that He should call Himself the Son of God? Thus, Jesus was giving a defense for His own deity, not for the deification of man.

## JOHN 14:28

*Did Jesus think of Himself as less than God?*

**Problem:** Orthodox Christianity confesses Jesus is both fully man and fully God. Yet Jesus said in John 14:28, "My Father is greater than I." How can the Father be greater if Jesus is equal to God?

**Solution:** The Father is greater than the Son by *office*, but not by *nature*, since both are God (see John 1:1; 8:58; 10:30). Just as an earthly father is equally human with, but holds a higher office than, his son, even so the Father and the Son in the Trinity are equal in *essence*, but different in *function*. In like manner, we speak of the president of our country as being a greater man, not by virtue of his *character*, but by virtue of his *position*. Therefore, Jesus cannot ever be said to say that He considered Himself anything less than God by nature. The following summary helps to crystalize the differences:

| JESUS IS EQUAL TO THE FATHER | THE FATHER IS GREATER THAN JESUS |
|---|---|
| In essence | In function |
| In nature | In office |
| In character | In position |

## JOHN 20:19

*How could Jesus walk through a closed door with a physical body?*

**Problem:** It is inferred by some critics that, since the resurrected Christ could appear in a room with closed doors (John 20:19), this proves that His body must have dematerialized to do so, showing that His resurrection body was not essentially or continuously material. However, many other Scriptures indicate that Jesus's resurrection body was literal "flesh and bones" (Luke 24:39) that could eat physical food and even had the crucifixion scars in it (Luke 24:40–43).

**Solution:** Jesus's resurrection body was essentially and continuously material. The fact that Jesus could get into a room with a closed door in no way proves that He had to dematerialize in order to do so. This is clear for several reasons.

First, the text does not actually say Jesus passed through a closed door. It simply says that "when the doors were shut where the disciples were assembled, for fear of the Jews, Jesus came and stood in the midst" (John 20:19). The Bible does not say *how* He got into the room.

Second, if He chose to do so, Jesus could have performed this same miracle before His death in His preresurrection material body. As the Son of God, His miraculous powers were just as great before the resurrection.

Third, even before His resurrection, Jesus performed miracles with His physical body that transcended natural laws, such as walking on water (John 6:16–20). But walking on water did not prove that His preresurrection body was immaterial. Otherwise, Peter's preresurrection walk on water (Matt. 14:29) would mean his body dematerialized for a moment and then quickly rematerialized!

Fourth, although physical, the resurrection body is by its very nature a supernatural body (see comments on 1 Cor. 15:44). Hence, it should be expected that it can do supernatural things, such as appearing in a room with closed doors.

Fifth, according to modern physics, it is not an impossibility for a material object to pass through a door. It is only statistically improbable. Physical objects are mostly empty space. All that is necessary for one physical object to pass through another is for the right alignment of the particles in the two physical objects. This is no problem for the One who created the body in the first place.

# ACTS

*Did Peter declare that baptism was necessary for salvation?*

**Problem:** Peter seems to be saying that those who responded had to repent and be baptized before they could receive the Holy Spirit. But this is contrary to Paul's teaching that baptism is not part of the gospel (1 Cor. 1:17) and that we are saved by faith alone, not by any work of righteousness (Rom. 4:4; Eph. 2:8–9), which baptism is (Matt. 3:15).

**Solution:** This is resolved when we consider the possible meaning of being baptized "for" the remission of sins in the light of its usage, the whole context, and the rest of Scripture. Consider the following:

First, the word "for" (*eis*) can mean "with a view to" or even "because of." In this case, water baptism would be *because* they had been saved, not *in order to* be saved.

Second, people are saved by receiving God's Word, and Peter's audience "gladly received his word" before they were baptized (Acts 2:41).

Third, verse 44 speaks of "all who believed" as constituting the early church, not all who were baptized.

Fourth, Peter later describes this event as God giving the Spirit to those who "believed in the Lord Jesus" (Acts 11:17).

Fifth, later, those who believed Peter's message clearly received the Holy Spirit *before* they were baptized. Peter said, "Can anyone forbid water, that these should not be baptized who have received the Holy Spirit just as we have?" (Acts 10:47).

Sixth, Paul separates baptism from the gospel, saying, "Christ did not send me to baptize, but to preach the gospel" (1 Cor. 1:17). But it is the gospel that saves us (Rom. 1:16). Therefore, baptism is not part of what saves us.

Seventh, Jesus referred to baptism as a work of righteousness (Matt. 3:15). But the Bible declares clearly it is "not by works of righteousness which we have done, but according to His mercy He saved us" (Titus 3:5).

Eighth, not once in the entire Gospel of John—written explicitly so that people could believe and be saved (John 20:31)—does it give baptism as part of the condition of salvation. It simply says over and over that people should "believe" and be saved (cf. John 3:16, 18, 36).

In view of all these factors, it seems best to understand Peter's statement like this: "Repent and be baptized with a view to the forgiveness of sins." That this view looked backward (to their sins being forgiven after they were saved) is made clear by the context and the rest of Scripture. Believing (or repenting) and being baptized are placed together, since baptism should follow belief. But nowhere does it say, "He who is not *baptized* will be condemned" (cf. Mark 16:16). Yet Jesus said emphatically that "he who does not *believe* is condemned already" (John 3:18). So neither Peter nor the rest of Scripture makes baptism a condition of salvation.

## ACTS 4:12

### *Is Christ the only way of salvation?*

**Problem:** Peter declares that "there is no other name under heaven given among men by which we must be saved." But isn't this a narrow exclusivism? What about the sincere pagan or Buddhist? Is God going to send them to hell?

**Solution:** Several observations are relevant to this question. First of all, sincerity is not a good test of truth. Many people can and have been sincerely wrong about many things (Prov. 14:12).

Second, all *truth* is exclusive. The truth that "two plus three equals five" is very exclusive too. It does not allow for any other conclusion. The same is true of value statements, such as "Racism is wrong" and "People should not be cruel." These views do not tolerate any alternatives.

Third, all truth *claims* are exclusive. For example, if humanism is true, then all nonhumanisms are false. If atheism is true, then all who believe in God are wrong. Every truth claim excludes its opposite. Hence, if Jesus is the only way to God, then there are no other ways. This is no more exclusive than any other truth claim. The question is whether the claim is true.

Fourth, Jesus and the NT clearly and repeatedly emphasize that Jesus is the only way of salvation. (1) Jesus said, "I am the way, the truth, and the life. No one comes to the Father except through Me" (John 14:6). (2) Jesus also claimed He was the door (John 10:9), insisting that "he who does not enter the sheepfold by the door . . . the same is a thief and a robber" (v. 1). (3) The Apostle Peter added, "Nor is there salvation in any other, for there is no other name under heaven given among men by which we must be saved" (Acts 4:12). (4) And Paul contended that "there is one God and one Mediator between God and men, the Man Christ Jesus" (1 Tim. 2:5).

## ACTS 7:14

*Why does this text say "seventy-five people" when Exodus 1:5 says there were "seventy persons"?*

**Problem:** According to Exodus 1:5, there were only seventy descendants who went down into Egypt with Jacob. But, when Stephen relates this same incident in Acts 7:14, he gives the number as 75. This appears to be a flat contradiction.

**Solutions:** There are several possible ways to explain the difference between these accounts. First, some scholars suggest that Acts 7:14 is correct in stating 75. They note that both the Greek translation of the OT (Septuagint) and a Hebrew manuscript found in the Dead Sea area use the number 75 just as Stephen said.

Others suggest that while Luke accurately records Stephen's sermon, Stephen nevertheless made a mistake. Thus Acts is an inerrant record of the speech in which Stephen made this error. The parallel account in Genesis 46:27 also gives the number as seventy. The main objection to this view is the fact that Luke's inclusion of this speech carries with it the implication that what he said is correct. Further, the text states that Stephen was "full of the Holy Spirit" when he gave the addresses (7:55).

Another explanation points out that the discrepancies can be explained by the fact that Stephen was probably quoting from the Septuagint (the Greek version of the OT), which states, "And all the souls from Jacob were seventy-five" (Exod. 1:5), rather than the Hebrew, which states, "And all the persons who came from the loins of Jacob were seventy in number, but Joseph was already in Egypt" (Exod. 1:5, NASB). The difference arises from the difference in the way the totals are calculated.

Jacob has twelve sons. Adding Jacob's grandsons and great-grandsons, the total was 66. Adding Ephraim and Manasseh who were born to Joseph in Egypt, the total is 68. When you add Jacob and his wife, the total is seventy, as the Hebrew records. The Septuagint, however, starting with Jacob's twelve sons, added Jacob's grandsons and great-grandsons for a total of 66. Then, it added the seven additional descendants of Joseph who were probably sons of Ephraim and Manasseh, born to Joseph's sons sometime after the migration of Jacob to Egypt but before Jacob died. The Septuagint also omitted Jacob and his wife. This makes a total of 75, as Stephen mentions in the Acts passage.

| | HEBREW TEXT | GREEK TEXT |
|---|---|---|
| Jacob and his wife | 2 | not counted |
| Jacob's sons | 12 | 12 |
| Jacob's grandsons and great grandsons | 54 | 54 |
| Joseph's sons Ephraim and Manasseh | 2 | 2 |
| Joseph's additional descendants in Egypt | not counted | 7 |
| **TOTAL** | 70 | 75 |

## ACTS 9:7 (cf. 22:9)

### Did Paul's companions hear the voice?

**Problem:** According to Acts 9:7, "the men which journeyed with him stood speechless, hearing a voice, but seeing no man" (KJV). But Acts 22:9 declares that "they that were with me saw indeed the light, and were afraid; but they heard not the voice of them that spake to me" (KJV). This appears to be an outright contradiction.

**Solution:** The contradiction is only verbal, not real. The word "hear" (*akouo*) can have different meanings in Greek, just as it does in English. It can mean hear a voice (as in Acts 9:7), or it can mean understand the meaning of what was said. Thus, the NIV correctly translates the two passages (emphasis added):

> Acts 9:7: "The men travelling with Saul stood there speechless; they *heard the sound* but did not see anyone."

> Acts 22:9: "My companions saw the light, but they *did not understand the voice* of him who was speaking to me."

This resolves the apparent contradiction. A number of considerations support these translations.

First, the same word "hear" (*akouo*) can mean different things. It can mean hear a voice without understanding the words. It can also mean hear a voice with understanding of the words. It can also mean to hear in the sense of "to obey" (see Matt. 17:5).

Second, though the usual meaning of "hear" (*akouo*) is simply audio without understanding *(suniami)*, there are examples in the New Testament where "hear" (*akouo*) means "understand." For example, 1 Corinthians 14:2 reads: "For anyone who speaks in a tongue does not speak to men but to God. Indeed, no one understands [*akouo*] him; he utters mysteries with his spirit."

Third, there are even times when "hear" (*akouo*) and "understand" *(suniami)* are used interchangeably. In Matthew 13:13, Jesus said, "This is why I speak to them in parables: 'Though seeing they do not see; though hearing [*akouo*], they do not hear [*akouo*] or understand [*suniami*].'"

Fourth, the word "voice" (*phona*) is used in a different form in Acts 9:7 (*phonas*, the genitive) from that in Acts 22:9 (*phonan*, the accusative). This may signal a different sense of the word in each context. Since the basic significance of the genitive is to stress quality, its use here may indicate that even though they heard the voice, its quality was such that it was not understood by them. This would reconcile it with Acts 22:9, which says they did not "hear" (understand) the voice.

Fifth, "voice" (*phona*) is sometimes translated as "sound" or "noise" that is not in intelligible words (cf. Rev. 4:5; 6:1; 8:5). In John 12:38 it is even used of the voice of God, which some heard only as thunder. In 1 Corinthians 14:11, Paul refers to not knowing the meaning of the voice (*phona*) that is being heard.

Sixth, there is another example in Scripture of the same voice of God being heard only by some in an audio way, but also understood by others. The voice of God spoke from heaven (John 12:28) about glorifying the Father's name, declaring, "I have both glorified it and will glorify it again." When this happened, some heard only the noise but did not understand the meaning, affirming that it had merely thundered (v. 29). But others heard the message (vv. 28, 30).

## ACTS 16:1-3

*Why did Paul have Timothy circumcised when he himself spoke so strongly against it?*

**Problem:** Paul's main point in Galatians can be summarized in his words, "If you become circumcised, Christ will profit you nothing" (Gal. 5:2). Yet Paul admits that he had Timothy circumcised "because of the Jews who were in that region" (Acts 16:3). Wasn't this a contradiction to his own teaching?

**Solution:** Even if Paul were wrong here in his action, it would not prove that the Bible erred in its teaching, but simply that it is a true record of Paul's error. Paul, like any other human being, was capable of error. Since the Bible is the Word of God (see introduction), it is not capable of erring in anything it teaches.

Furthermore, Paul's action in having Timothy circumcised is not necessarily inconsistent with what he taught in Galatians, since the two cases are different. Paul was violently opposed to any who made circumcision *necessary for salvation*. But he never opposed it as *helpful for evangelism*. Indeed, Paul said elsewhere, "to the Jews I became as a Jew, that I might win Jews" (1 Cor. 9:20). However, when Judaizers insisted that "unless you are circumcised according to the custom of Moses, you cannot be saved" (Acts 15:1), then Paul took an intractable stand against circumcision.

# ROMANS

*Are the heathen lost?*

**Problem:** Jesus said, "I am the way, the truth, and the life. No one comes to the Father, except through Me" (John 14:6). Also, Acts 4:12 says of Christ, "And there is salvation in no one else; for there is no other name under heaven that has been given among men, by which we must be saved" (NASB). But what if someone has never heard the gospel of Christ, will he be eternally lost? Paul seems to answer this in the affirmative. But is it fair to condemn people who have never even heard about Christ?

**Solution:** Paul's answer is clear. He said that the heathen are "without excuse" (1:20) because "what may be known of God *is manifest in them*, for *God has shown it to them*. For since the creation of the world His invisible attributes *are clearly seen, being understood* by the things that are made" (1:19–20). So, the heathen are justly condemned for several reasons. First, Romans 2:12 states, "For as many as have sinned without Law will also perish without Law, and as many as have sinned in the Law will be judged by the Law." This passage teaches that the Jew is judged by the Law, the Hebrew Scriptures, but the Gentile is condemned by "the Law written in their hearts."

"For when Gentiles who do not have the Law do instinctively the things of the Law, these, not having the Law, are a law to themselves, in that they show the work of the Law written in their hearts, their conscience bearing witness, and their thoughts alternately accusing or else defending them" (Rom. 2:14–15, NASB).

Second, the question assumes innocence on the part of the man who hasn't heard the gospel. But the Bible tells us that "all have sinned and fall short of the glory of God" (Rom. 3:23). In addition, Romans 1:18–20 says that God clearly reveals Himself through natural revelation "so that they are without excuse." Human beings are not innocent regarding God's natural revelation.

Third, if a person who has not heard the gospel lives his life to the best of his ability, he is simply doing works for salvation. But salvation is by grace: "For by grace you have been saved through faith, and that not of yourselves; it is the gift of God" (Eph. 2:8). Not in any way, shape, or form can anybody do anything to gain access into heaven. If there was such a way, then the work of Christ on the cross was a futile act.

Finally, the Bible says in essence, "seek and you will find." That is, those who seek the light they have through nature, which is not sufficient for salvation, will get the light they need for salvation. Hebrews 11:6 says, "But without faith it is impossible to please Him, for he who comes to God must believe that He is, and that He is a rewarder of those who diligently seek Him." Acts 10:35 adds, "But in every nation whoever fears Him and works righteousness is accepted by Him." God has many ways to get the truth about salvation through Christ to those who seek Him. He can send a missionary (Acts 10), or a Bible (Ps. 119:130), give them a vision (Dan. 2; 7), or send an angel (Rev. 14). But those who turn their back on the light they have (through nature) and find themselves lost in darkness have no one to blame but themselves. For "men loved darkness rather than light, because their deeds were evil" (John 3:19).

## ROMANS 5:14

### Is it fair to judge all people because of Adam's sin?

**Problem:** Death came to all people because of the sin of Adam (Rom. 5:12), but Romans 5:14 says, "Nevertheless death reigned from Adam to Moses, *even over those who had not sinned according to* *the likeness of the transgression of Adam.*" But if they did not sin like Adam, why are they held accountable?

**Solution:** There are two types of people who may fall into this category: (1) infants, and (2) those who do not deliberately disobey God's dictate.

First, many Bible scholars believe that infants and small children who die before the age of moral accountability will go to heaven. This is based on the following verses. (1) In 2 Samuel 12:23, when David's baby died, he said, "I shall go to him, but he shall not return to me." This implies that the baby was with the Lord. (2) In Psalm 139, David speaks of even an unborn baby as written in God's book in heaven (v. 16). (3) Further, Isaiah distinguishes between those who are not yet old enough to "know to refuse the evil and choose the good" (7:15; cf. Deut. 1:39), which implies they are not yet morally accountable. (4) Jesus added, "if you were blind, you would have no sin" (John 9:41). (5) And Paul speaks of Christ's sacrifice making all righteous (Rom. 5:19), which would cover even little children who are born in sin (Ps. 51:5). (See also comments on 2 Sam. 12:23.)

Second, we "all sinned [in Adam]" as our representative, and as a consequence the guilt of Adam's sin was imputed to all of us. But Christ's death cancelled this and released the human race from this judicial guilt (Rom. 5:18–19). Even so, those who attain the age of accountability are responsible for their personal sin and therefore are justly condemned.

So those who did not sin in the likeness of Adam nevertheless still sinned in Adam (Rom. 5:12). That is why death still reigned from the time of Adam and Moses. Romans 2:14–15 affirms that the Gentiles, even if they have not the Mosaic Law, still were a law to themselves. They have the Law written in their hearts and their conscience bears witness to their actions. Humans after Adam are still sinful and responsible for their actions.

Just because people do not sin in the likeness of Adam does not mean that they are not sinful. In other words, it doesn't mean that humans are not held accountable by God for their actions. Man dies because man sins (Rom. 6:23). God is just in condemning sin, and He is merciful in providing salvation for those who will receive it.

## ROMANS 5:19
### If all are made righteous by Christ, why aren't all saved?

**Problem:** It is agreed by scholars that in Paul's contrast between the "one" and the "many" here, that "many" means all. For the "many" were "made sinners" by the "one" (Adam's) sin, and Paul had already concluded that "all have sinned [in Adam]" a few verses earlier (Rom. 5:12). But if all were "made sinners" means all actually became sinners, then why doesn't all "will be made righteous" in the same verse mean that all will be saved? (Rom. 5:19).

**Solution:** There are two broad answers to this question—universalism and particularism. That is, those who claim this verse as proof that all people will eventually be saved and those who believe only some will be saved. Since the Bible clearly rejects universalism (see comments on Col. 1:20), we will focus here on the two general responses of particularists.

*The Potential View*: Some scholars believe Paul is simply referring to being "made righteous" by Christ's death in a *potential* sense. That is to say, by the cross all people are made *savable*, but not all people will be saved. Those who hold this position point to the fact that the parallel is not perfect, for we were "made sinners" in Adam without our personal free choice. Nevertheless, we cannot be "made righteous" in Christ without freely receiving the "gift" (5:16–17).

*The Judicial View*: According to this position, all persons were "made sinners" and "made righteous" in the same sense—*judicially*. That is, both Christ and Adam were our *legal* representatives. And while in Adam all his race were before God made sinners *officially*, nonetheless, in Christ all are officially made righteous, though not actually and personally. And just as every person, when they come to the age of accountability (see comments on 2 Sam. 12:23 and Rom. 5:14), must personally sin to be personally guilty, even so everyone must personally accept Christ to be personally saved. Christ removed the official and judicial guilt that was imputed to the race because of Adam's sin. This does not mean that everyone is *actually* saved, but only that they are no longer *legally* condemned.

## ROMANS 8:30

*Are all the called ones saved, or only some?*

**Problem:** Paul indicates here that all who are "called" by God are eventually "justified" and "glorified" (Rom. 8:30). But Jesus said that "many are called, but few chosen" (Matt. 20:16).

**Solution:** The word "called" is being used in different senses. This is not uncommon in languages. Take, for example, the following sentence: "The dog would *bark* by the tree but did not scratch the *bark* from the tree." Clearly the word "bark" is used in two different senses. Likewise, Paul and Jesus are using different senses of the word "called," which can be contrasted as follows:

| GENERAL CALL | SPECIFIC CALL |
|---|---|
| Call for salvation | Call of salvation |
| For all men | Only for believers |
| Not effectual | Effectual for salvation |

In brief, when Jesus referred to a "call," He was speaking of a general invitation for all to believe. Paul, however, has reference to the specific "call" of God by which God brings believers to salvation. The first is the call for salvation to all; the last is the call of salvation to some.

## ROMANS 9:17

*How can Pharaoh be free if God hardened his heart?*

**Problem:** God said to Pharaoh, "For this very purpose I raised you up, to demonstrate My power in you, and that My name might be proclaimed throughout the whole earth" (Rom. 9:17, NASB). In fulfillment of this, it says that God hardened Pharaoh's heart (Exod. 4:21; cf. Exod. 7:3). But if God raised up Pharaoh and even hardened his heart to accomplish His divine purposes, then isn't Pharaoh exempt from responsibility for his actions?

**Solution:** First, God in His omniscience foreknew exactly how Pharaoh would respond, and He used it to accomplish His purposes. God ordained the means of Pharaoh's free but stubborn action as well as the end of Israel's deliverance. In Exodus 3:19,

God told Moses, "But I am sure that the king of Egypt will not let you go, no, not even by a mighty hand." Pharaoh rejected the request of Moses and only after ten plagues did Pharaoh finally let the people go.

Second, it is important to note that Pharaoh first hardened his own heart many times. When Moses initially approached Pharaoh concerning the release of the Israelites (Exod. 5:1), Pharaoh responded, "Who is the Lord that I should obey His voice to let Israel go? I do not know the Lord, nor will I let Israel go" (Exod. 5:2). The passage Paul quotes (in Rom. 9:17) is Exodus 9:16, which, in context, is the plague of the boils, the sixth plague. But Pharaoh hardened his own heart before God made this statement. Just because God raised up Pharaoh does not mean that Pharaoh is not responsible for his actions.

Third, God uses the unrighteousness of humans to show His glory. God still holds Pharaoh accountable, but in the process of his hardened heart, God used Pharaoh to display His greatness and glory. God sometimes uses evil acts to bring about good results. The story of Joseph is a good example of this point. Joseph is sold by his brothers and later becomes a ruler in Egypt. In Egypt, Joseph saves many lives during a famine. When he later reveals himself to his brothers and forgives them, he says, "But as for you, you meant evil against me; but God meant it for good, in order to bring it about as it is this day, to save many people alive" (Gen. 50:20). God can use bad actions to bring about His glory.

## ROMANS 11:26-27

*How can there be a future for the nation of Israel since they rejected the Messiah?*

**Problem:** The nation of Israel clearly rejected Christ as their Messiah (Rom. 9–10; cf. John 1:10–11). And the Bible says that the promises of Abraham go to his spiritual seed, not his descendants according to the flesh (Rom. 4; Gal. 3). Why then does Romans 11 speak of a future for the nation of Israel?

**Solution:** Abraham has both a spiritual seed (descendants) and literal descendants. Anyone who believes in Christ can become a *spiritual* heir of the promise for justification (Rom. 4; cf. Gen. 15), because Christ came of the seed of Abraham (Gal. 3:16).

However, there are also promises to Abraham's *literal* descendants, the Jews, that have never yet been completely fulfilled. For example, God unconditionally promised that Abraham's literal descendants would inherit the land of Palestine forever (Gen. 12:1–3; 13:15–17; 15:7–21; 17:8). Only one short time in Israel's history did they inherit this land (Josh. 11:23), but God gave it to them by an unconditional oath (cf. Gen. 15:7–21) "forever" (Gen. 13:15), as an "everlasting possession" (17:8). Since God cannot break an unconditional promise (Heb. 6:17–18; 2 Tim. 2:13), this promise is yet to be fulfilled for the nation of Israel.

Paul is speaking of the literal descendants of Abraham, the children of Israel in Romans 9–11. He calls them "my kinsmen according to the flesh, who are Israelites" (Rom. 9:3–4) and "Israel" (Rom. 10:1). This same national group (Israel) that was temporarily cut off will be grafted again into the tree, and "all Israel will be saved" (Rom. 11:26). Jesus spoke of this time in Acts 1 when asked by His disciples, "Will You at this time restore the kingdom to Israel?" (Acts 1:6). His answer was not a stern rebuke for misunderstanding the Scriptures, but an assurance that only the Father knows the "times or seasons" in which this will occur (v. 7). Earlier Jesus spoke of "the regeneration, when the Son of Man sits on the throne of His glory, [and] you who have followed Me will also sit on twelve thrones, judging the twelve tribes of Israel" (Matt. 19:28). Indeed, in the final book of the Bible, the Apostle John spoke of God redeeming out of the tribulation "one hundred and forty-four thousand of all the tribes of the children of Israel" (Rev. 7:4). So there is every reason to believe that God will honor His unconditional covenant to Israel to give them the land of Palestine forever.

# 1 CORINTHIANS

*Did Paul oppose water baptism?*

**Problem:** Paul declares that Christ did not send him to baptize. Yet Christ commissioned His disciples to "make disciples of all the nations, baptizing them in the name of the Father, and of the Son, and of the Holy Spirit" (Matt. 28:19). Does Paul contradict Christ?

**Solution:** Paul was not opposed to baptism, but neither did he believe it was a condition of salvation (see comments on Acts 2:38). Paul himself was baptized by water (Acts 9:18; 22:16), and he taught water baptism in his epistles (cf. Rom. 6:3–4; Col. 2:12). Indeed, in this very passage (1 Cor. 1), Paul admits that he baptized several people (vv. 14, 16) as he did the Philippian jailor after he was saved (Acts 16:31–33). While Paul believed water baptism was a symbol of salvation, he did not believe it was part of the gospel or essential to salvation.

*Does this passage support the Roman Catholic view of purgatory?*

**Problem:** Roman Catholics appeal to this passage in support of the doctrine of temporary punishment for those not good enough

212

to go directly to heaven. They point to the fact that it speaks of people who "suffer loss" when their works are "burned" by fire and yet are eventually "saved" (1 Cor. 3:15). Does the Bible teach that there is a temporary hell (purgatory) where people suffer for their sins before they are let into heaven?

**Solution:** Nowhere does the Bible teach the doctrine of purgatory. This doctrine is contrary to many facts of Scripture. First, God has only one place of punishment and it is called hell. And it is a permanent place of "everlasting fire" (Matt. 25:41). It entails "everlasting destruction from the presence of the Lord" (2 Thess. 1:9; see comments on that passage). Jesus declared it is a place where the fire "shall never be quenched" and where the body "does not die" (Mark 9:45, 48).

Second, once one goes to hell, he can never get out. Jesus said there is "a great gulf fixed, so that those who want to pass" from one side to the other cannot do so (Luke 16:26). This is true even if they regret being there (Luke 16:23, 38).

Third, the doctrine of purgatory is an insult to the all-sufficiency of the death of Christ on the cross for our sins and all their consequences. When Jesus died for our sins (1 Cor. 15:3), He announced, "It is finished" (John 19:30). Looking forward to the cross, He prayed to the Father, "I have finished the work which You have given Me to do" (John 17:4). Hebrews informs us that "after He [Jesus] had offered one sacrifice for sins forever, [He] sat down at the right hand of God" (Heb. 10:12). "For by one offering He has perfected forever those who are being sanctified" (Heb. 10:14). Isaiah 53:4–5 makes it clear that this included the consequences of our sins.

Fourth, the only purgatory ever to be experienced was experienced by Christ on the cross when He purged sins. Hebrews declares that "when He had by Himself purged our sins, [He] sat down at the right hand of the Majesty on high" (Heb. 1:3).

Fifth, the doctrine of purgatory is based on the apocryphal book of 2 Maccabees (12:46, Douay), which says it is a holy and wholesome thought to pray for the dead that they may be loosed from their sins. But this second-century BC book never claimed to be inspired, nor did any of the apocryphal books. First Maccabees even disclaims inspiration (1 Macc. 9:27). These apocryphal books were never accepted by Judaism as inspired. Neither Jesus nor the NT writers ever cite them as inspired. Even Jerome, the Roman Catholic translator of the great Latin Vulgate Bible, rejected 2 Maccabees along with the other apocryphal books. Furthermore, 2 Maccabees was not officially added to the Bible by the Roman Catholic Church until AD 1546, some 29 years after Martin Luther started his reformation, during which he spoke out against purgatory and prayers for the dead. Finally, even when 2 Maccabees was added by Rome to the Bible (along with other apocryphal books), it rejected another apocryphal book that spoke against prayers for the dead. Second Esdras (called 4 Esdras by Roman Catholics), speaking of the day of death, declares, "no one shall ever pray for another on that day" (2 Esdras 7:105). Rejecting this book and accepting Maccabees manifests the arbitrariness of the decision to choose books to support doctrines that had been added to the Bible.

Finally, in 1 Corinthians, Paul is not speaking of purgatory, but of the "judgment seat of Christ," before which all believers must come to receive their rewards "for the things done in the body" (2 Cor. 5:10). All our "work" will be "revealed by fire." And "if anyone's work . . . endures, he will receive a reward" (1 Cor. 3:13–14). And "if anyone's work is burned, he will suffer loss [of reward]; but he himself will be saved, yet so as through the fire" (1 Cor. 3:14–15). Since salvation from hell is by grace, not by works (Rom. 4:5; Eph. 2:8–9; Titus 3:5–7), it is clear that this passage is speaking about the "work" and "reward" of the believer for serving Christ, not about any alleged purgatory where they (instead of Christ) suffer for their sins.

## 1 Corinthians 7:12 (cf. 7:40)

*How can Paul's words be inspired if he says he is merely giving his own opinion?*

**Problem:** In two places in 1 Corinthians (7:12, 40), the Apostle Paul seems to imply that he is writing on his own authority, not the Lord's. First, in 7:12 Paul says, "But to the rest I, not the Lord." And in 7:40 he says, "and I think I also have the Spirit of God," which seems to imply that Paul is not sure if he has the Holy Spirit. How can these verses be harmonized with the divine authority claimed by Paul in his epistles (cf. Gal. 1:11–17; 2 Tim. 3:16–17)?

**Solution:** First, concerning 1 Corinthians 7:12, Paul is referring to the fact that the Lord did not directly address this issue when He spoke about divorce and marriage (Matt. 5:31–32; 19:4–12). So Paul does speak to it here, giving his authoritative view on whether a believing wife should stay with an unbelieving husband.

Second, Paul was not uncertain of his possession of the Holy Spirit on this matter, since he said clearly, "I also have the Spirit of God" (1 Cor. 7:40). So this passage cannot be used to show that Paul disclaimed divine authority.

Finally, Paul clearly affirmed his divine authority in this very book, declaring what he wrote as "words . . . the Holy Spirit teaches" (1 Cor. 2:13). Indeed, he concludes the book by saying, "the things which I write to you are the commandments of the Lord" (14:37). So his words in chapter 7 should be taken in harmony with these emphatic claims.

## 1 Corinthians 15:5–8

### Did Jesus only appear to believers?

**Problem:** Some critics have attempted to cast doubt on the validity of Christ's resurrection by insisting that He appeared only to believers, but never to unbelievers. Is this so?

**Solution:** It is incorrect to claim that Jesus did not appear to unbelievers. This is clear for several reasons. First, He appeared to the most hostile unbeliever of all, Saul of Tarsus (Acts 9:2ff). The Bible devotes much of several chapters to relate this story (Acts 9; 22; 26).

Second, even Jesus's disciples were unbelievers in the resurrection when He first appeared to them. When Mary Magdalene and others reported that Jesus was resurrected, "their words seemed to them like idle tales, and they did not believe them" (Luke 24:11). Later, Jesus had to chide the two disciples on the road to Emmaus about disbelief in His resurrection: "O foolish ones, and slow of heart to believe in all that the prophets have spoken!" (Luke 24:25). Even after Jesus had appeared to the women, to Peter, to the two disciples, and to the ten apostles, still Thomas said, "Unless I see the nail marks in his hands and put my finger where the nails were, and put my hand into his side, I will not believe it" (John 20:25, NIV). He was hardly a believer in the resurrection.

Finally, in addition to appearing to His unbelieving disciples, Jesus also appeared to some who were not His disciples at all. He appeared to His brother James (1 Cor. 15:7), who, with His other brothers, was not a believer before the resurrection (John 7:5). So, it is simply false to claim that Jesus did not appear to unbelievers.

## 1 Corinthians 15:44
### Is the resurrection body material or immaterial?

**Problem:** Paul declares that the resurrection body is a "spiritual body" (1 Cor. 15:44), but a spiritual body is an immaterial body. However, elsewhere the Bible says Jesus's resurrection body was made of "flesh and bones" (Luke 24:39).

**Solution:** A "spiritual" body denotes an immortal body, not an immaterial body. A "spiritual" body is one dominated by the spirit, not one devoid of matter. The Greek word *pneumatikos* (translated "spiritual" here) means a body directed by the spirit, as opposed to one under the dominion of the flesh. It is not ruled by flesh that perishes, but by the spirit that endures (1 Cor. 15:50–58). So "spiritual body" does not mean immaterial and invisible, but immortal and imperishable. This is clear from several facts:

First, notice the parallelism mentioned by Paul:

| PRERESURRECTION BODY | POSTRESURRECTION BODY |
|---|---|
| Earthly (v. 40) | Heavenly |
| Perishable (v. 42) | Imperishable |
| Weak (v. 43) | Powerful |
| Mortal (v. 53) | Immortal |
| Natural (v. 44) | [Supernatural] |

The complete context indicates that "spiritual" (*pneumatikos*) could be translated "supernatural" in contrast to "natural." This is made clear by the parallels of perishable and imperishable and corruptible and incorruptible. In fact, this same Greek word (*pneumatikos*) is translated "supernatural" in 1 Corinthians 10:4 when it speaks of the "supernatural rock that followed them in the wilderness" (RSV).

Second, the word "spiritual" (*pneumatikos*) in 1 Corinthians refers to material objects. Paul spoke of the "spiritual rock" that followed Israel in the wilderness from which they got "spiritual drink" (1 Cor. 10:4). But the OT story (Exod. 17; Num. 20) reveals that it was a physical rock from which they got literal water to drink. But the actual water they drank from that material rock was produced supernaturally. When Jesus supernaturally made bread for the five thousand (John 6), He made literal bread. However, this literal, material bread could have been called "spiritual" bread (because of its supernatural source) in the same way that the literal manna given to Israel is called "spiritual food" (1 Cor. 10:3).

Further, when Paul spoke about a "spiritual food" (1 Cor. 2:15), he obviously did not mean an invisible, immaterial man with no corporeal body. He was, as a matter of fact, speaking of a flesh and blood human being whose life was lived by the supernatural power of God. He was referring to a literal person whose life was Spirit directed. A spiritual man is one who is taught by the Spirit and who receives the things that come from the Spirit of God (1 Cor. 2:13–14). The resurrection body can be called a "spiritual body" in much the same way we speak of the Bible as a "spiritual book." Regardless of their spiritual source and power, both the resurrection body and the Bible are material objects.

## 1 Corinthians 15:50

*If flesh and blood cannot enter heaven, then how can there be a physical resurrection?*

**Problem:** The Bible speaks of the resurrection of the physical body from the grave (John 5:28–29), which is composed of "flesh and bones" (Luke 24:39) and leaves an empty tomb behind (Matt.

28:6). However, according to this verse, "flesh and blood cannot inherit the kingdom of God."

**Solution:** To conclude from this phrase that the resurrection body will not be a body of physical flesh is without biblical justification. First of all, the very next phrase omitted from the above quotation clearly indicates that Paul is speaking not of flesh as such, but of *corruptible* flesh. For he adds, "nor does corruption inherit incorruption" (v. 50). So, Paul is not affirming that the resurrection body will not have flesh, but that it will not have *perishable* flesh.

Second, to convince the frightened disciples that He was not an immaterial spirit (Luke 24:37), Jesus emphatically told them, "Look at my hands and my feet. It is I myself! Touch me and see; a ghost does not have *flesh and bones*, as you see I have" (Luke 24:39, NIV, emphasis added). Peter declared that the resurrection body would be the same body of *flesh* that went into the tomb and never saw corruption (Acts 2:31). Paul also reaffirmed this truth in a parallel passage (Acts 13:35). And John implies that it is against Christ to deny that He remains "in the *flesh*" even after His resurrection (1 John 4:2; 2 John 7).

Third, this conclusion cannot be avoided by claiming that Jesus's resurrection body had flesh and bones, but not flesh and blood. For if it had flesh and bones, then it was a literal, material body, whether or not it had blood. "Flesh and bones" stresses the solidity of Jesus's physical postresurrection body. They are more obvious signs of tangibility than blood, which cannot be as easily seen or touched.

Fourth, the phrase "flesh and blood" in this context apparently means *mortal* flesh and blood, that is, a mere human being. This is supported by parallel uses in the NT. When Jesus said to Peter, "Flesh and blood has not revealed this to you" (Matt. 16:17), He could not have been referring to the mere substance of the body as such, which obviously could not reveal that He was the Son of God. Rather, the most natural interpretation of 1 Corinthians 15:50 seems to be that *humans, as they are now, earth-bound and perishable creatures*, cannot have a place in God's glorious, heavenly kingdom.

# 2 CORINTHIANS

*How could Jesus be made sin when He was sinless?*

**Problem:** Paul asserts here that Jesus was "made to be sin." However, many other Scriptures insist that Jesus was "without sin" (Heb. 4:15; cf. 1 Peter 3:18). But how could Jesus be without sin if He was made sin for us?

**Solution:** Jesus was always without sin *actually*, but He was made to be sin for us *judicially*. That is, by His death on the cross, He paid the penalty for our sins and thereby cancelled the debt of sin against us. So, while Jesus never committed a sin personally, He was made to be sin for us substitutionally. The issue can be summarized as follows:

| CHRIST WAS NOT SINFUL | CHRIST WAS MADE TO BE SIN |
|:---:|:---:|
| In Himself | For us |
| Personally | Substitutionally |
| Actually | Judicially |

# GALATIANS

## GALATIANS 3:17
*Does Paul err in the amount of time between Abraham and the time the Law was given?*

**Problem:** In Galatians 3:17, the apostle states that a period of 430 years elapsed between the time of God's promises to Abraham (Gen. 12:1–3), which was about 2000 BC, and the giving of the Law to Moses, which was around 1450 BC. This would be a mistake of over one hundred years.

**Solution:** The time that Paul refers to is not the initial *giving* of the Abrahamic covenant (Gen. 12–15), but the later *confirmation* of the covenant to Jacob (Gen. 46), which was about 1877 BC. Since the Exodus occurred around 1447 BC (cf. 1 Kings 6:1), this would be exactly 430. There is good indication that Paul is referring to the confirmation to Jacob, not to the initiation of the covenant to Abraham. The text clearly dates the 430 years from "the covenant that was *confirmed*" (Gal. 3:17). Thus, the time period is the final reaffirmation of the Abrahamic promises to the descendants (seed) of Abraham that takes place in Genesis 46:2–4 to Jacob, a descendent of Abraham, which was 430 years before the children of Israel came out of Egypt.

# EPHESIANS

*How could the mystery of Christ be hidden in previous ages and yet known by the OT prophets?*

**Problem:** According to this passage, the mystery of the church, the body of Christ, was not known in other ages. Yet the apostle goes on to say that it was revealed to the "apostles and prophets." But the prophets lived prior to the time of Paul. How could the prophets have known if people in the OT did not know the mystery?

**Solution:** There are several reasons for believing that Paul is referring to NT prophets, not OT ones. First, the order in which he mentions them is not prophets and then apostles, but "apostles and prophets."

Second, this same phrase is used to describe the foundation of the NT church that is built on the "foundation of the apostles and prophets" (Eph. 2:20). The NT church did not begin in the OT, but only after Christ announced it in Matthew 16:18.

Third, the text says clearly that the mystery of the spiritual body of Christ "was not made known" to the sons of men "in other ages" but only now to "the apostles and prophets" (Eph. 3:5).

Finally, the parallel passage in Colossians says emphatically, "the mystery . . . has been hidden from ages and from generations, but now has been revealed to His saints" (1:26). Thus, the "prophets" to whom it was made known were NT prophets (cf. 1 Cor. 12:28; Eph. 4:11).

## EPHESIANS 4:9

### Did Jesus descend into hell?

**Problem:** Paul claims here that Jesus "descended into the lower parts of the earth." And the Apostles' Creed declares that after Jesus died, He "descended into hell." However, when Jesus was dying, He committed His spirit into His Father's hand (Luke 23:46) and told the thief that He would be with Him in "Paradise" (Luke 23:43), which is in the "third heaven" (2 Cor. 12:2, 4). Where did Jesus go when He died—to heaven or to hell?

**Solution:** There are two views as to where Jesus went the three days His body was in the grave before His resurrection.

*The Hades View:* One position claims that Christ's spirit went to the spirit world, while His body was in the grave. Here He spoke to the "spirits in prison" (1 Peter 3:19) who were in a temporary holding place until He would come and "lead captivity captive," that is, take them to heaven. According to this view, there were two compartments in Hades (or *Sheol*), one for the saved and another for the unsaved. They were separated by a "great gulf" (Luke 16:26) that no person could pass. The section for the saved was called "Abraham's bosom" (Luke 16:23). When Christ, as the "firstfruits" of the resurrection (1 Cor. 15:20), ascended, He led these OT saints into heaven with Him for the first time.

*The Heaven View:* This teaching, which we believe is the correct one, holds that the souls of OT believers went directly to heaven the moment they died. It offers the following arguments in support of its teaching. First, Jesus affirmed that His spirit was going directly to heaven, declaring, "Father, into Your hands I commit My spirit" (Luke 23:46).

Second, Jesus promised the thief on the cross, "Today you will be with Me in Paradise" (Luke 23:43). But "Paradise" is defined as "the third heaven" in 2 Corinthians 12:2, 4.

Third, when OT saints departed this life, they went directly to heaven. God took Enoch to be with Himself (Gen. 5:24; cf. Heb.

11:5), and Elijah was caught up into "heaven" when he departed (2 Kings 2:1).

Fourth, "Abraham's bosom" (Luke 16:23) is a description of heaven. At no time is it ever described as hell. It is the place that Abraham went, which is the "kingdom of heaven" (Matt. 8:11).

Fifth, when OT saints appear before the cross, they appear from heaven, as Moses and Elijah did on the Mount of Transfiguration (Matt. 17:3).

Sixth, OT saints had to await Christ's resurrection before their *bodies* could be resurrected (1 Cor. 15:20; cf. Matt. 27:53), but their *souls* went directly to heaven. Christ was the Lamb slain "from the foundation of the world" (Rev. 13:8), and they were there on the merits of what God knew Christ would accomplish.

Seventh, "descending into the lower parts of the earth" is not a reference to hell, but to the grave. Even a woman's womb is described as "lowest parts of the earth" (Ps. 139:15). The phrase simply means caves, graves, or enclosures on the earth, as opposed to higher parts such as mountains. Besides, hell is not in the lower parts of the earth—it is "under the earth" (Phil. 2:10).

Eighth, the phrase "descended into hell" was not in the earliest Apostles' Creed. It was not added until the 4th century. Further, as a creed it is not inspired—it is only a human confession of faith.

Ninth, the "spirits in prison" were not saved, but unsaved beings. Indeed, they may refer to angels, not to human beings (see comments on 1 Peter 3:19).

Finally, when Christ "led captivity captive," He was not leading friends into heaven but bringing foes into bondage. It is a reference to His conquering the forces of evil. Christians are not "captives" in heaven. We are not forced to go there against our own free choice (see Matt. 23:37; 2 Peter 3:9).

# PHILIPPIANS

*If Christ emptied Himself of deity while on earth, then how could He be God?*

**Problem:** Paul seems to say that Jesus "emptied Himself" of His deity or "equality with God" (vv. 6–7), becoming "a man" (v. 8). But elsewhere Jesus claimed to be God on earth (John 8:58; 20:28). But how could Jesus be God while on earth if He left His deity aside to become man?

**Solution:** Jesus did not cease being God while on earth. Rather, in addition to being God, He also became man. His incarnation was not the subtraction of deity, but the addition of humanity. Several things in this text support this position. First, it does not say Christ gave up or emptied Himself of His deity, but merely of His *rights* as deity, assuming the "form of a servant" (v. 7) so as to be an example for us (v. 5). Second, the text declares that He was in the "form of God" or "in very nature God" (v. 6, NIV). Just as the "form of a servant" (v. 7) is a servant by nature, so the "form of God" (v. 6) is God by nature. Third, this very passage declares that every knee will one day confess Jesus is "Lord," a citation from Isaiah 45:23 that refers to *Yahweh*, a name used exclusively of God.

# COLOSSIANS

## COLOSSIANS 1:18

*If Christ is only the firstborn in creation, then how can He be God?*

**Problem:** John declared Christ to be eternal and equal with God (John 1:1; 8:58; 20:28). But here Paul seems to say that Christ was only a creature, the first one born (created) in the universe.

**Solution:** Paul clearly declares Christ to be God in this very letter by saying He "created all things" (1:16) and has "the fullness of the Godhead" (2:9). The reference to "firstborn" does not mean He is the firstborn *in* creation, but the firstborn *over* creation (v. 15), since "He is before all things" (v. 17). "Firstborn" in this context does not mean the first one to be born, but the heir of all, the Creator and owner of all things. As Creator of "all things," He could not have been a created thing.

## COLOSSIANS 4:16

*What happened to the lost epistle of the Laodiceans?*

**Problem:** Paul refers to the "epistle from Laodicea" as a book he wrote that should be read by the church at Colosse, just as the inspired Book of Colossians was to be read by the Laodiceans. However, no such 1st century epistle to the Laodiceans exists (though there is a 4th century fraud). But it is very strange that an inspired book would perish. Why would God inspire it for the faith and practice of the church (2 Tim. 3:16–17) and then allow it to be destroyed?

**Solution:** There are two possibilities. First, it is possible that not all divinely authoritative or inspired books were intended by God to be in the Bible. Luke refers to other gospels (Luke 1:1), and John affirmed that there were many other things Jesus did that are not recorded in his Gospel (John 20:30; 21:25). So, it is possible that only those inspired books that God preserved by His providence were intended to be in the canon of Scripture.

Second, there are some good reasons to believe that "the epistle from Laodicea" is not really lost, but is really the Book of Ephesians. First of all, the text does not call it the epistle *of* the Laodiceans, but the "epistle [coming] *from* Laodicea" (Col. 4:16), whatever name it may have had. Second, it is known that Paul wrote Ephesians at the same time he wrote Colossians and sent it to another church in the same general area. Third, there is evidence that the Book of Ephesians did not originally bear that title, but was a kind of cyclical letter sent to the churches of Asia Minor. As a matter of fact, some early manuscripts do not have the phrase "in Ephesus" in Ephesians 1:1. It is certainly strange that Paul, who spent three years ministering to the Ephesians (Acts 20:31), sent no personal greetings to them, if the book known as "Ephesians" was intended for them alone. By contrast, Paul had never visited Rome, but he greeted numerous people in his letter to them (Rom. 16:1–16). Fourth, no epistle of the Laodiceans is cited by any early church father, though they make over 36,000 NT citations, including every book and almost every verse of the NT. A fraudulent epistle of the Laodiceans appeared in the 4th century, but scholars do not believe it is the one referred to by Paul. Indeed, it is largely a collection of quotations from Ephesians and Colossians that the church Council of Nicea (AD 787) called a "forged epistle."

# —— 1 THESSALONIANS ——

## Did Paul teach the doctrine of soul-sleep?

**Problem:** Several times the Bible refers to the dead as being asleep. Does this mean that the soul is not conscious between death and resurrection?

**Solution:** The souls of both believers and unbelievers are conscious between death and the resurrection. Unbelievers are in conscious woe (see Luke 16:23; Mark 9:48; Matt. 25:41) and believers are in conscious bliss. "Sleep" is a reference to the body, not the soul. Sleep is an appropriate figure of speech for death of the body, since death is temporary until the resurrection when the body will "awake" from it.

The evidence that the soul (spirit) is conscious between death and resurrection is very strong:

1. Enoch was taken to be with God (Gen. 5:24; Heb. 11:5).
2. David spoke of bliss in God's presence after death (Ps. 16:10–11).
3. Elijah was taken up into heaven (2 Kings 2:1).
4. Moses and Elijah were conscious on the Mount of Transfiguration (Matt. 17:3) long after their time on earth.

5. Jesus said He went to the Father the day He died (Luke 23:56).
6. Jesus promised the repentant thief that he would be with Him in Paradise the very day he died (Luke 23:43).
7. Paul said it was far better to die and be with Christ (Phil. 1:23).
8. Paul affirmed that when we are "absent from the body" then "we are present with the Lord" (2 Cor. 5:8).
9. The writer of Hebrews refers to heaven as a place where "the spirits of just men [are] made perfect" (Heb. 12:23).
10. The "souls" of those martyred during the tribulation were conscious in heaven, singing and praying to God (Rev. 6:9).

# —— 2 THESSALONIANS ——

## 2 Thessalonians 1:9
### *Will the wicked be annihilated or suffer conscious punishment forever?*

**Problem:** In some passages of Scripture, like this one, it speaks of the wicked being "destroyed" by God, suffering "the second death" (Rev. 20:14), or going to "perdition" (2 Peter 3:7). Yet in other places, it speaks of them suffering conscious torment (e.g., Luke 16:22–28). Will unsaved persons be annihilated, or will they consciously suffer forever?

**Solution:** "Destruction" does not mean annihilation here, otherwise it would not be "everlasting" destruction. Annihilation only takes an instant, and it is over. If people undergo everlasting destruction, then they have to have everlasting existence.

Furthermore, "death" does not mean annihilation, but separation. Adam and Eve died spiritually the moment they sinned, yet they still existed and could hear God's voice (Gen. 2:17; cf. 3:10). Likewise, before someone is saved, he or she is "dead in trespasses and sins" (Eph. 2:1), and yet is still in God's image (Gen. 1:27; cf. 9:6; James 3:9) and is called on to believe (Acts 16:31), to repent (Acts 17:30), and be saved.

Likewise, when the wicked are said to go into "perdition" (2 Peter 3:7), and Judas is called the "son of perdition" (John 17:12), it does not mean they will be annihilated. The word "perdition" (*apōleia*) simply means to perish or to come to ruin. Junk cars have perished, in the sense of having been ruined. But they are still cars, ruined as they may be, and they are still in the junkyard. In this connection, Jesus spoke of hell as a junkyard or dump where the fire would not cease and where a person's resurrected body would not be consumed (see comments on Mark 9:48).

Finally, there are several lines of evidence that support the everlasting consciousness of the lost. First, the rich man who died and went to hell was in conscious torment (Luke 16:22–28), and there is absolutely no indication in the text that it was ever going to cease.

Second, Jesus spoke repeatedly of the people in hell as "weeping and gnashing [their] teeth" (Matt. 8:12; 22:13; 24:51; 25:30), which indicates they were conscious.

Third, hell is said to be of the same duration as heaven, namely, "everlasting" (Matt. 25:41).

Fourth, the fact that their punishment is everlasting indicates that they too must be everlasting. A person cannot suffer punishment, unless he or she exists to be punished (2 Thess. 1:9).

Fifth, the beast and the false prophet were thrown "alive" into the lake of fire at the beginning of the one thousand years (Rev. 19:20), and they were still there, conscious and alive, after the one thousand years (Rev. 20:10).

Sixth, the Scriptures affirm that the devil, the beast, and the false prophet "will be tormented day and night forever and ever" (Rev. 20:10). But there is no way to experience torment forever and ever without being conscious forever and ever.

Seventh, Jesus repeatedly referred to hell as a place where "the fire is not quenched" (Mark 9:48), where the very bodies of the wicked will never die (cf. Luke 12:4–5). But it would make no sense to have everlasting flames and bodies without any souls in them to experience the torment.

Eighth, the same word used to describe the wicked perishing in the OT (*abad*) is used to describe the righteous perishing (see Isa. 57:1; Mic. 7:2). The same word is used to describe things that are merely lost but then later found (Deut. 22:3), which proves that "lost" does not here mean to go out of existence. So, if perish means to annihilate, then the saved would have to be annihilated too. But we know they are not.

Ninth, it would be contrary to the created nature of human beings to annihilate them, since they are made in God's image and likeness, which is everlasting (Gen. 1:27). For God to annihilate His image in man would be to attack the reflection of Himself.

Tenth, annihilation would be demeaning both to the love of God and to the nature of human beings as free moral creatures. It would be as if God said to them, *I will allow you to be free only if you do what I say! If you don't, then I will snuff out your very freedom and existence!* This would be like a father telling his son he wanted him to be a doctor, and, when he chose instead to be a park ranger, the father shot him! Eternal suffering is an eternal testimony to the freedom and dignity of humans, even unrepentant humans.

# 1 TIMOTHY

*Does the Bible limit the ministry of women?*

**Problem:** Paul said here that he did not "permit a woman to teach or to have authority over a man, but to be in silence." Likewise, in 1 Corinthians 14:34 he added, "Let your women keep silent in the churches, for they are not permitted to speak" (cf. 1 Peter 3:5–6). Doesn't this deny women a ministry and degrade their personality?

**Solution:** Not at all. When properly understood in context, these and many other passages in the Bible exalt the role of women and give them a tremendous ministry in the body of Christ. Several things should be kept in mind on the topic of the role of women in the church.

First, the Bible declares that women, like men, are in the image of God (Gen. 1:27). That is, they are equal with men by nature. There is no essential difference—both male and female are *equally human by creation.*

Second, both women and men are *equal by redemption.* They both have the same Lord and both share equally in exactly the same salvation. For in Christ "there is neither male nor female; for you are all one in Christ Jesus" (Gal. 3:28).

Third, men and women are *equal by gifts*. There are no sex symbols on the ministry gifts listed in the Bible. It does not say, "gift of teaching—male; gift of helps—female." In other words, women have the same gifts for ministry to the body of Christ that men do.

Fourth, throughout the Bible, God gifted, blessed, and greatly used women in the ministry. This includes Miriam the first minister of music (Exod. 15:20), Deborah (Judg. 4:4), Huldah the prophetess (2 Chron. 34:22), Anna the prophetess (Luke 2:36), Priscilla the Bible teacher (Acts 18:26), and Phoebe the deaconess (Rom. 16:1).

Fifth, Jesus had many women who assisted Him in the ministry (cf. Luke 23:49; John 11). Indeed, it is very significant that in a patriarchal culture Jesus chose women for His first *two* resurrection appearances (Matt. 28:1–10; John 20:10–18). St. Peter did not make it until the third round (1 Cor. 15:5)!

Sixth, whatever Paul may have meant by the "women be silent" passages, he certainly did *not* mean that they should have no ministry in the church. This is clear for several reasons. For one thing, in the same book (1 Cor.), Paul instructed women on *how they should pray and prophesy* in the church, namely, in a decent and orderly way (cf. 11:5). Further, there were also times when all the men were to be "silent" as well, namely, when someone else was giving an utterance from God (cf. 14:28). Finally, Paul did not hesitate to use women to assist him in the ministry, as is indicated by the crucial role he gave to Phoebe in delivering the great epistle to the Romans to its destination (Rom. 16:1).

Seventh, when understood in context, the "silence" passages are not negating the *ministry* of women, but are limiting the *authority* of women. Paul asserts that women were not permitted "to have authority over a man" (1 Tim. 2:12). Likewise, he follows his exhortation to "keep silent" by reminding them to be "submissive" (1 Cor. 14:34). Of course, men too were under authority and needed to submit to the headship of Christ over them (1 Cor. 11:3). Indeed, the ultimate proof that there is nothing degrading about being submissive is that Christ, who was God in human flesh, is always submissive to the Father, both on earth (Phil. 2:5–8) and even in heaven (1 Cor. 15:28). That male headship and leadership is not simply a cultural matter is evident by the fact that it is based on the very order of creation (1 Cor. 11:9; 1 Tim. 2:13). Thus, elders are to be men, "the husband of one wife" (1 Tim. 3:2). This, however, in no way demeans or diminishes the role of women, either in the family or in the church. The fact that men cannot have babies is not demeaning to their humanity or their role in the family. It is simply that God has not granted them this function, but rather a different one.

Eighth, God has given women an exalted role both by order of creation and redemption. First of all, Eve was not created from Adam's feet to be walked on by him, nor from his head to rule over him, but from his side to be equal to him and companion of him (cf. Gen. 2:19–25). Furthermore, every man ever born was carried in a woman's womb (1 Cor. 11:12) and then the vast majority were nurtured by her through infancy, childhood, and youth until they grew up. In addition, when God chose the vessel by which He Himself would become manifest in human flesh (John 1:14), it was not by direct creation of a body (as Adam), or in assuming a visible form (as the angel of the Lord), nor was it by cloning a male human being. Rather, it was by being miraculously conceived and carried to full term in a woman's womb, that of the blessed virgin Mary (Matt. 1:20–21; Gal. 4:4). What is more, God has, through the birth and nurturing process, endowed woman with the most marvelous role in forming all human beings, including every man, at the most tender and impressionable time in their lives, both prenatal (cf. Ps. 139:13–18) and postnatal. Finally, in the church, God has made women "one in Christ Jesus" (Gal. 3:28) and bestowed upon them the gifts of the spirit (1 Cor. 12; 14; Rom. 12) whereby they can edify the body of Christ, including prophecy (cf. Acts 2:17–18; 21:9) and teaching (Acts 18:26; Titus 2:4).

## 1 Timothy 5:23

### Was Paul recommending wine drinking for Christians?

**Problem:** The Bible repeatedly warns against abuse of strong drink and drunkenness (Prov. 20:1; 31:4–5; Isa. 24:9; 1 Cor. 6:9–10;

Eph. 5:18). However, here Paul tells Timothy to "no longer drink only water, but use a little wine for your stomach's sake and your frequent infirmities." Doesn't this commend wine drinking?

**Solution:** Once the entire context is understood, there is no basis here for Christians to engage in the social drinking of wine (or other alcoholic beverages). First, Paul says "a little," not a lot. Paul elsewhere urges Christian leaders to be temperate (1 Tim. 3:3, 8).

Second, it was "for his frequent infirmities," not for pleasure. In other words, it was recommended for medicinal purposes, not for social purposes.

Third, the Bible speaks often of the evil of wine drinking. It pronounces woes on those who drink in excess (Isa. 5:11; Amos 6:6; Mic. 2:11). All are warned that too much alcohol will lead to disgrace and judgment (Amos 6:6–7).

Finally, the wine used in biblical times was mixed: three parts water to one part wine, thus diluting it to a relatively harmless amount of alcohol. When this minimal amount was taken in conjunction with a meal, there was little chance in a nonalcoholic society for it to be personally or socially harmful. The same is not true today, since the wine, beer, and liquor being imbibed is, by biblical standards, "strong drink." And this is even more problematic in an alcoholic culture where one out of every ten persons who begin to drink becomes a problem drinker. In this context it is better to follow the advice of Paul elsewhere when he said, "it is good neither to eat meat nor drink wine nor do anything by which your brother stumbles or is offended or is made weak" (Rom. 14:21).

## 1 Timothy 6:16
### Does only God have immortality or do humans also have it?

**Problem:** According to Paul, in this passage, God "alone has immortality, dwelling in unapproachable light." However, in other places, Paul speaks of Christians being raised in "immortal" physical bodies (1 Cor. 15:53) and partaking of "immortality" through the gospel (2 Tim. 1:10). But if God alone has immortality, then how can anyone else have it?

**Solution:** God is the only one who has *intrinsic* immortality, by virtue of His very nature. All believers receive it as a gift from God, but it is not inherent to their very nature as creatures. Or, to put it another way, only God *is* immortal—human beings simply *have* immortality. Likewise, God alone *is* existence (cf. Exod. 3:14)—creatures only *have* existence (cf. Acts 17:28). Further, God's immortality is *without beginning or end*. Our immortality has *a beginning with no end*. In summary:

| GOD'S IMMORTALITY | HUMAN IMMORTALITY |
| --- | --- |
| Intrinsic to His nature | Not intrinsic to our nature |
| Something God *is* | Something humans *have* |
| Possesses by His essence | Possess by participation |
| Inherent | Derived |
| No beginning or end | A beginning but no end |

# 2 TIMOTHY

## 2 Timothy 1:10

*If Jesus abolished death, why do we still die?*

**Problem:** Paul affirms in this text that Christ "has abolished death and brought life and immortality to light through the gospel." But death is not abolished, since "death spread to all men" (Rom. 5:12), and "it is appointed for men to die once" (Heb. 9:27).

**Solution:** First of all, Christ did not abolish physical death *immediately*, but by His death and resurrection it will be abolished *eventually*. Christ is the first one to experience resurrection in an immortal body (1 Cor. 15:20)—the rest of the human race will experience this later, at His second coming (1 Cor. 15:50–56). Second, Christ abolished death *officially* when He personally defeated it by His resurrection. However, physical death will not be completely destroyed *actually* until He returns again and "death is swallowed up in victory" (1 Cor. 15:54). For Paul tells us that "the last enemy that will be destroyed is death" (1 Cor. 15:26).

## 2 Timothy 2:25

*Is repentance a gift of God or an act of man?*

**Problem:** Paul speaks here of God "granting them repentance, so that they may know the truth" (cf. Acts 5:31). Yet in other places, repentance is considered a person's own act. Jesus, for example, calls on people to "Repent, and believe in the gospel" (Mark 1:15). Paul tells us that God "commands all men everywhere to repent" (Acts 17:30). But doesn't it have to be either an act of God or else an act of the individual believer?

**Solution:** There are two possible answers here, neither of which negates a person's God-given responsibility to exercise free choice. First, repentance could be an actual gift of God, but like other gifts, it must be received to be enjoyed. On this view, God offers all who are willing the gift of repentance unto eternal life. Those who are not willing do not get repentance. In this way, God is impartial in His offer, but man is still responsible to accept or reject the gift of repentance necessary for salvation.

A second view simply notes the two different senses in which repentance is used in these seemingly opposed verses. One set of verses is speaking of repentance as an *opportunity* and the other as an *act*. The former is simply a *disposition* given by God, leaving the actual *action* of repenting to human beings. The former is a God-given *provision*, while the latter is a man-made *decision*. This view can be summarized as follows:

**TWO DIFFERENT SENSES OF REPENTANCE**

| | |
|---|---|
| As a God-given opportunity | As a free human act |
| As a disposition from God | As an action of man |
| As a provision of God | As a decision of man |

Understood like this, there is no contradiction in the diverse texts on repentance. Whichever interpretation is taken, one thing is certain: there is no verse saying God repents *for* us. Each free moral creature is responsible to repent for him- or herself. The same can be said about whether faith is a gift of God or not.

## 2 Timothy 3:16

*Does this passage prove the inspiration of all Scripture, or just some?*

**Problem:** Paul says in this passage that "All Scripture is given by inspiration of God." Some think that the word "all" should be replaced by the word "every." Plus, some believe that the copula "is" should be placed after the remark concerning the inspiration of the Scriptures, not before. In doing so this can lead to the conclusion that some Scripture is not inspired.

**Solution:** First, most versions translate this verse "All Scripture is God-breathed," except those that translate this verse with copula "is" after the word "God." This makes it sound like there are some Scriptures that are not inspired of God (e.g., RSV, ASV), although the marginal notes in these translations give a more accurate rendering. But most Bibles see the verse as reading "All Scripture is inspired of God."

Second, concerning whether the word "all" should be translated "every," some argue that it should, because if the definite article is missing in reference to this word, the verse should be translated "every." However, whenever the word "Scripture" (*graphē*) is used in the NT, it always refers to authoritative and inspired writings—never the opposite—with or without the definite article in Greek. This word is used of the Hebrew Scriptures (as in our present verse) or NT writings (2 Peter 3:16).

Third, the word for "inspired of God" suggests that God so guided the NT authors as to write the very Word of God. As we notice in 2 Peter 1:20–21, no prophecy of Scripture came about by the will of man but by the Holy Spirit moving (carrying along) the writers of Scripture to speak from God. The word for "moved" (*pherō*) in 2 Peter is the same word used in Acts 27:15 where the ship that carried Paul was so caught up in a storm they could not face the wind. They gave way to it, and let themselves be "driven along" by the storm. This is true of the Holy Spirit inspiring the authors of Holy Scripture to write the Word of God. But if all the authors of Scripture were moved by God, then the words of Scripture were breathed out by God and are without error, since God cannot err (Heb. 6:18; Titus 1:2; John 17:17).

Finally, even if it could be argued from the NT that not every use of "the Scriptures" refers to an inspired writing, nonetheless, it would not undermine Paul's teaching here that the entire OT is inspired of God. For the context makes it clear that the "Scripture" to which he refers is "the Holy Scriptures" (1:15) that Timothy's Jewish mother and grandmother had taught him (cf. 2 Tim. 1:5), and this could be none other than the whole Jewish OT.

# TITUS

*Doesn't Paul pronounce this pagan poet inspired by making him part of Scripture?*

**Problem:** Christians believe that only the Bible is the Word of God (2 Tim. 3:16). Yet the Apostle Paul quotes pagan poets on at least three occasions. But in so doing he seems to give assent to the sources he quotes as inspired, just as when he quotes OT Scripture as the Word of God (cf. Matt. 4:4, 7, 10).

**Solution:** Paul is not quoting this non-Christian source as *inspired*, but simply as *true*. All truth is God's truth, no matter who said it. Caiaphas the Jewish high priest uttered a truth about Christ (John 11:49). The Bible often uses noninspired sources (cf. Num. 21:14; Josh. 10:13; 1 Kings 15:31). Three times Paul cites non-Christian thinkers (Acts 17:28; 1 Cor. 15:33; Titus 1:12). Jude alludes to truths found in two noncanonical books (Jude 9, 14). But never does the Bible cite them as divinely authoritative, but simply as containing the truth quoted. The usual phrases, such as "thus saith the Lord" (cf. Isa. 7:7; Jer. 2:5, KJV) or "it is written" (cf. Matt. 4:4, 7, 10), are never found when these noninspired sources are cited. Nonetheless, truth is truth wherever it is found. And there is no reason, therefore, that a biblical author, by direction of the Holy Spirit, cannot utilize truth from whatever source he may find it.

# PHILEMON

*Doesn't Paul approve of the institution of slavery?*

**Problem:** The Apostle Paul seems to favor the institution of human slavery by sending a runaway slave, Onesimus, back to his owner. But slavery is unethical. It is a violation of the principles of human freedom and dignity.

**Solution:** Slavery is unethical and unbiblical and neither Paul's actions nor his writings approve of this debasing form of treatment. In fact, it was the application of biblical principles that ultimately led to the overthrow of slavery. Several important facts should be noted in this connection.

First, from the very beginning, God declared that all humans participate in the image of God (Gen. 1:27). The apostle reaffirmed this, declaring, "we are the offspring of God" (Acts 17:29), and He "has made from one blood every nation of men to dwell on all the face of the earth" (Acts 17:26).

Second, in spite of the fact that slavery was countenanced in the Semitic cultures of the day, the Law demanded that slaves eventually be set free (Exod. 21:2; Lev. 25:40). Likewise, servants had to be treated with respect (Exod. 21:20, 26).

Third, Israel, itself in slavery in Egypt, was constantly reminded by God of this (Deut. 5:15), and their emancipation became the model for the liberation of all slaves (cf. Lev. 25:40).

Fourth, in the NT, Paul declared that in Christianity "there is neither Jew nor Greek, there is neither slave nor free, there is neither male nor female; for you are alone in Christ Jesus" (Gal. 3:28). All social classes are broken down in Christ; we are all equal before God.

Fifth, the NT explicitly forbids the evil system of this world that traded the "bodies and souls of men" (Rev. 18:13). Slave trade is so repugnant to God that He pronounces His final judgment on the evil system that perpetrated it (Rev. 17–18).

Sixth, when Paul urges, "Servants, be obedient to those who are your masters" (Eph. 6:5; cf. Col. 3:22), he is not thereby approving of the institution of slavery, but simply alluding to the de facto situation in his day. Rather, he is instructing them to be good employees, just as believers should be today, but he was not thereby commending slavery.

Seventh, a closer look at Philemon reveals that Paul did not perpetuate slavery but actually undermined it, for he urged Philemon, Onesimus's owner, to treat him as "a beloved brother" (v. 16). So, by emphasizing the inherent equality of all human beings, both by creation and redemption, the Bible laid down the very moral principles that were used to overthrow slavery and to help restore the dignity and freedom of all persons of whatever color or ethnic group.

# HEBREWS

*Does the devil have the power of death or does God?*

**Problem:** The writer of Hebrews speaks here about Christ's coming so "that through death He might destroy him who had the power of death, that is, the devil." But in other places the Bible asserts that only God has the power over life and death: "I kill and I make alive" (Deut. 32:39; cf. Job 1:21).

**Solution:** God is sovereign over all life. Only He can create it, and only He has determined the number of our days (Ps. 90:10–12) and has "appointed" the day of our death (Heb. 9:27). But by tempting Adam and Eve, the devil succeeded in bringing on the human race God's pronounced judgment of death for disobedience (Gen. 2:27; Rom. 5:12). So, in this sense, the devil may be said to have had the power of death (Heb. 2:14). However, by tasting death for every man (Heb. 2:9) and rising triumphantly from the grave (Rom. 4:25), Christ now holds "the keys of Hades and of Death" (Rev. 1:18), having "abolished death and brought life and immortality to light through the gospel" (2 Tim. 1:10).

## HEBREWS 2:17–18

### Was it possible for Christ to have sinned?

**Problem:** The writer of Hebrews says that Christ "had to be made like His brethren in all things. . . . For since He Himself was tempted in that which He has suffered, He is able to come to the aid of those who are tempted" (2:17–18, NASB). Does this mean that Christ could have sinned?

**Solution:** Some argue that Christ *could not* have sinned. They believe that our Lord was tempted like we are and that He can sympathize with our weaknesses, but that He was incapable of sinning. In support of this view they argue, first, that since Christ was God, and since God cannot sin (Heb. 6:17; James 1:13), it follows that Christ could not sin either. Second, since Christ had no fallen human nature, as we do, He had no propensity to sin. Finally, they observe that His temptation was only from without, not from within. Hence, He could be tempted without having the real possibility of sinning.

Other orthodox scholars believe that Christ had the ability to sin (since He had the power of free choice), but did not sin. In short, sin was possible, but not actual in Jesus's life. To deny this possibility, they believe, would deny His full humanity, His ability to "sympathize with our weaknesses" (Heb. 4:15), and would make His temptation into a charade. They note that while Jesus could not sin *as God*, nonetheless, He could have sinned (but didn't) *as man*. Since Jesus had two natures, one divine and one human, a distinction must be made in what He could do in each nature. For example, He could not get tired, hungry, or sleepy as God. But He did all of these as man. His divine nature could not die. Yet He died as man. Likewise, they argue, Christ could not have sinned as God but could have sinned as man.

## HEBREWS 10:11

### Did OT sacrifices make atonement for sins?

**Problem:** Leviticus 17:11 affirmed that God gave blood sacrifices "to make atonement" for our souls. But Hebrews seems to contradict that, insisting that the Aaronic priest "stands ministering daily and offering repeatedly the same sacrifices, which can never take away sins" (10:11).

**Solution:** The sacrifices in the OT were not intended to *take away* sin, but only to *cover over* sin until Christ came to do away with it. Each blood sacrifice before Christ looked forward to Christ. The Passover lamb was a type that anticipated fulfillment in "Christ, our Passover, [who] was sacrificed for us" (1 Cor. 5:7). They provided only a *temporary* covering for sins until Christ could bring in the *permanent* solution to the sin question. Old Testament offerings had, as it were, an IOU attached to them, awaiting the price to be paid by the "Lamb of God who takes away the sin of the world" (John 1:29).

# JAMES

*If God doesn't tempt anyone, then why did He tempt Abraham?*

**Problem:** The Bible says, "God tempted Abraham" (Gen. 22:1, KJV), and Jesus taught His disciples to pray to God, "do not lead us into temptation" (Matt. 6:13). How then can James say of God, "nor does He Himself tempt anyone" (James 1:13)?

**Solution:** God did not *tempt* Abraham (nor anyone) to sin. Rather, He *tested* Abraham to see if he would sin or be faithful to Him. God allows Satan to tempt us (cf. Matt. 4:1–10; James 4:7; 1 Peter 5:8–9), but James is correct in saying that never does God "Himself tempt anyone." God cannot be tempted by sin, since He is absolutely and unchangeably perfect (Matt. 5:48; Heb. 6:18), nor can He tempt anyone else to sin (James 1:13). When we sinful human beings are tempted, it is because we allow ourselves to be drawn away by our own lustful desires (James 1:14–15). The source of temptation comes from within, not from without. It comes from sinful man, not from a sinless God.

While God does not and cannot actually tempt anyone to sin, He can and does allow us to be tempted by Satan and our own lustful desires. Of course, His purpose in permitting (but not producing or promoting) evil is to make us more perfect. God allowed Satan to tempt Job so that Job could say "When He has tested me, I shall come forth as gold" (Job 23:10). God allowed evil to befall Joseph at the hands of his brothers. But in the end Joseph was able to say to them, "you meant evil against me; but God meant it for good" (Gen. 50:20).

## JAMES 2:19

### If the demons believe in God, then why are they not saved?

**Problem:** According to the Bible, all that is necessary to be saved is to "believe on the Lord Jesus Christ" (Acts 16:31), for "whoever believes in Him should not perish but have everlasting life" (John 3:16). Paul said salvation comes "to him who does not work but believes on Him" (Rom. 4:5). If this is so, then why are not the demons saved, since the Bible admits that "even the demons believe" (v. 19).

**Solution:** The demons are not saved because they do not exercise a saving kind of faith. This is James's very point, namely, not any kind of faith can save a person. Only the kind of faith that produces good works can save (James 2:17). While we are saved by faith alone, nevertheless, the faith that saves is not alone. It is always accompanied by good works. We are not saved *by* works (Eph. 2:8–9), but we are saved *for* works (Eph. 2:10).

The difference between saving faith and nonsaving faith is that the former is only belief *that* God exists. The latter is faith *in* God. No one can be saved by believing *that* God exists and *that* Christ died for their sins and rose again. They must believe in Him (i.e., trust Him). In like manner, no one can get to the top floor by an elevator if she simply believes *that* elevators can get her there. She must believe *in* the elevator (i.e., trust it) enough to step in it and allow it to get her there. The demons do not believe *in* God (trust God) for their salvation—they simply believe *that* God exists, but they continue in their rebellion against Him (Jude 6; Rev. 12:4).

## JAMES 2:21

### If Abraham was saved by works, why does the Bible say he was justified by faith?

**Problem:** Paul clearly teaches that we are justified by faith and not by works (Rom. 1:17). He declared, "But to him who does not work but believes on Him who justifies the ungodly, his faith is accounted for righteousness" (Rom. 4:5). It is "not by works of righteousness which we have done, but according to His mercy He saved us" (Titus 3:5). For "by grace you have been saved through faith, and that not of yourselves; it is the gift of God, not of works, lest anyone should boast" (Eph. 2:8–9).

But James seems to flatly contradict this by declaring, "a man is justified by works and not by faith only" (2:24), for "faith without works is dead" (2:26). Indeed, while Paul said Abraham was justified by faith (Rom. 4:1–4), James declares, "Was not Abraham our father justified by works" (2:21). Are these not flatly contradictory?

**Solution:** James and Paul would be contradictory if they were speaking about the same thing, but there are many indications in the text that they are not. Paul is speaking about justification *before God*, while James is talking about justification *before humans*. This is indicated by the fact that James stressed that we should "show" (2:18) our faith. It must be something that can be seen by others in "works" (2:18–20). Further, James acknowledged that Abraham was justified before God by faith, not works, when he said, "Abraham believed God, and it was accounted to him for righteousness" (2:23). When he adds that Abraham was "justified by works" (v. 21), he is speaking of what Abraham *did that could be seen by people*, namely, offer his son Isaac on the altar (2:21–22).

Further, while Paul is stressing the *root* of justification (faith), James is stressing the *fruit* of justification (works). But each man acknowledges both. Immediately after affirming that we are "saved by grace through faith" (Eph. 2:8–9), Paul quickly adds, "we are His workmanship, created in Christ Jesus for good works, which God prepared beforehand that we should walk in them" (Eph. 2:10). Likewise, right after declaring that it is "not by works of righteousness which we have done, but according to His mercy He saved us" (Titus 3:5–7), Paul urges that "those who have believed in God should be careful to maintain good works" (Eph. 2:8). The relation between Paul and James can be summarized this way:

| PAUL | JAMES |
|------|-------|
| Justification *before God* | Justification *before humans* |
| The *root* of justification | The *fruit* of justification |
| Justification *by* faith | Justification *for* works |
| Faith as *producer of works* | Works as the *proof of faith* |

# 1 PETER

*Was Jesus raised in the Spirit or in a physical body?*

**Problem:** Peter declares that Christ was "put to death in the flesh but made alive in the spirit" (NASB). This seems to imply that Jesus did not rise in the flesh, but only in His spirit, which conflicts with Jesus's statement that His resurrection body was "flesh and bones" (Luke 24:39).

**Solution:** To interpret this as proof of a spiritual rather than a physical resurrection is neither necessary nor consistent with the context of this passage and the rest of Scripture. Several reasons support this conclusion.

First, the passage can be translated, "he was put to death in the body but made alive by the [Holy] Spirit" (NIV). The passage is translated with this same understanding by the NKJV and others.

Second, the parallel between death and being made alive normally refers to the resurrection of the body in the NT. For example, Paul declared that "Christ died and rose and lived again" (Rom. 14:9), and "He was crucified in weakness, yet He lives by the power of God" (2 Cor. 13:4).

Third, the context refers to the event as "the resurrection of Jesus Christ" (3:21). But this is everywhere understood as a bodily resurrection in the NT (cf. Acts 4:33; Rom. 1:4; 1 Cor. 15:21; 1 Peter 1:3; Rev. 20:5).

Fourth, even if "spirit" refers to Jesus's human spirit (not to the Holy Spirit), it cannot mean He had no resurrection body. Otherwise, the reference to His "body" (flesh) before the resurrection would mean He had no human spirit then. It seems better to take "flesh" in this context as a reference to His whole condition of humiliation before the resurrection and "spirit" as a reference to His unlimited power and imperishable life after the resurrection.

## 1 Peter 3:19

*Does Peter support the view that a person can be saved after he dies?*

**Problem:** First Peter 3:19 says that, after His death, Christ "went and preached to the spirits in prison." But the Bible also says that "it is appointed for men to die once, but after this the judgment" (Heb. 9:27). These two verses appear to teach mutually opposing positions.

**Solution:** The Bible is clear that there is no second chance after death (cf. Heb. 9:27). The Book of Revelation records the Great White Throne of Judgment in which those who are not found in the Book of Life are sent to the lake of fire (Rev. 20:11–15). Luke informs us that once a person dies he goes either to heaven (Abraham's bosom) or to hell, and that there is a great gulf fixed "so that those who want to pass" from one to the other cannot (Luke 16:26). The whole urgency of responding to God in this life, before we die, gives further support to the fact that there is no hope beyond the grave (cf. John 3:36; 5:24).

There are other ways to understand this passage without involving a second chance at salvation after death. Some claim that it is not clear that the phrase "spirits in prison" even refers to human beings, arguing that nowhere else is such a phrase used of human beings in hell. They claim these spirits are fallen angels, since the "Sons of God" (fallen angels, see Job 1:6; 2:1; 38:7) were "disobedient . . . in the days of Noah" (1 Peter 3:20; cf. Gen. 6:1–4). Peter may be referring to this in 2 Peter 2:4, where he mentions the angels sinning immediately before he refers to the flood (v. 5). In response, it is argued that angels cannot marry (Matt. 22:30), and they certainly could not intermarry with human beings, since angels, being spirits, have no reproductive organs.

Another interpretation is that this refers to Christ's announcement to departed spirits of the triumph of His resurrection, declaring to them the victory He had achieved by His death and resurrection, as pointed out in the previous verse (see 1 Peter 3:18). Some suggest that Jesus offered no hope of salvation to these "spirits in prison." They point to the fact that the text does not say Christ *evangelized* them, but simply that He *proclaimed* the victory of His resurrection to them. They insist that there is nothing stated in this passage about preaching the gospel to people in hell. In response to this view, others note that in the very next chapter, Peter, apparently extending this subject, does say "the gospel was preached also to those who are dead" (see comments on 1 Peter 4:6). This view fits the context here, is in accord with the teaching of other verses (cf. Eph. 4:8; Col. 2:15), and avoids the major problems of the other view.

# 2 PETER

## 2 Peter 1:1

*Did the Apostle Peter really write this book?*

**Problem:** The style of writing in 1 Peter is different than 2 Peter. Also the tone used in the fist epistle is different than that of the second epistle. How can evangelicals claim that Peter wrote this epistle?

**Solution:** First, in his earlier epistle, Peter had Silas as a secretary (5:12, NIV), but in the second epistle Peter seems to have written it himself. This could account for the lack of smoothness and style between the two epistles.

Second, different styles and tones should be expected in two different letters written for two different purposes at different times. First Peter is written to encourage believers who are suffering, while 2 Peter contains warnings against false teachers. Some of the difference in style and tone can be accounted for in light of the different circumstances. After all, a man would not write to his girlfriend the same way he would write to his congressman.

Third, there is good internal evidence that the letter is from Peter. Verse 1 claims it is from the Apostle Peter. Peter remembers the words of Jesus concerning His death, as recorded in John 21:18–19 (cf. 2 Peter 1:14). The author of this letter was an eyewitness to the Mount of Transfiguration, which is recorded in

Matthew 17:1–8 (cf. 1:16–18). Peter even calls this his "second letter" (3:1, NIV), which presupposes a first. And he is aware of the writings of the Apostle Paul and calls him "our beloved brother Paul" (3:15–16).

Fourth, there are not only some differences between epistles, but also some likenesses. Both place emphasis on Christ, 1 Peter on His suffering and 2 Peter on His glory. And in both epistles Peter refers to Noah and the flood (1 Peter 3:20; 2 Peter 2:5; 3:5–6).

Fifth, there is good external evidence that it was written in the first century by someone like Peter who was a contemporary of the events. The noted archaeologist William F. Albright dated 2 Peter before AD 80. The discovery of the Bodmer papyri (P72, ca. AD 250) reveals that it was highly respected in Egypt at an early date. The book was cited as authentic by numerous early church fathers, including Origen, Eusebius, Jerome, and Augustine.

Finally, if it was not written by Peter, then it is a biblical forgery, because the letter is said to be written by him. If it has not been written by Peter, then it is deceiving us and cannot be trusted in what it purports to tell us (i.e., his testimony to be a witness of the Transfiguration). Consideration of all the above factors provides strong evidence that the Apostle Peter is the writer of this epistle and not someone else. Therefore, we have no reason to distrust its content.

# 1 JOHN

## 1 John 3:9

### Doesn't John contradict himself when he asserts that Christians are without sin?

**Problem:** John affirms here that "Whoever has been born of God does not sin." But in the first chapter he insisted that "If we say that we have no sin, we deceive ourselves, and the truth is not in us" (1:8).

**Solution:** John nowhere claims that believers are without sin or never commit a sin. First John 3:9 is in the present continuous tense and should be translated "Whoever is born of God does not continually practice sin." Conversely, if a person habitually practices sin, he is not born of God. As James argued, true faith will produce good works (James 2:14ff). If a pig and a lamb fall into the mud, the pig wants to stay there, but the lamb wants to get out. Both a believer and an unbeliever can *fall* into the same sin, but a believer cannot *stay* in it and feel comfortable.

## 1 John 4:18

### If love casts out all fear, why are we told to fear God?

**Problem:** John affirms here that "perfect love casts out all fear." Yet we are told that the "fear of the Lord is the beginning of knowledge" (Prov. 1:7) and that we should "serve the Lord with fear" (Ps. 2:11). Indeed, Paul said, "knowing . . . the terror [fear] of the Lord, we persuade men" (2 Cor. 5:11).

**Solution:** Fear is being used in different senses. Fear in the good sense is a *reverential trust* in God. In the bad sense it is a sense of *recoiling torment* in the face of God. While proper fear brings a healthy respect for God, unwholesome fear engenders an unhealthy sense that He is out to get us. Perfect love casts out this kind of "torment." When one properly understands that "God is love" (1 John 4:16), he can no longer fear Him in this unhealthy sense. For "he who fears has not been made perfect in love" (1 John 4:18). Nonetheless, at no time does proper love for God ever show disrespect for Him. Rather, it is perfectly compatible with a reverential awe for Him, which is what the Bible means by "fearing God" in the good sense (cf. 2 Cor. 7:1; 1 Peter 2:17).

# 2 JOHN

*Who was the "elect lady"?*

**Problem:** John addresses his second letter to "the elect lady." Some have argued that because this was strictly a personal letter addressed to a particular lady, that it does not belong in the canon of Scripture. Was the "elect lady" a person or not?

**Solution:** First of all, if the "elect lady" were a particular person, this would not exclude it from the canon of Scripture. Several of the epistles of Paul were personal letters to particular individuals (e.g., Timothy, Titus, Philemon).

Second, it is possible that the elect lady was not a particular person. The proposals of commentators basically fall into two categories, the literal and the figurative. Those who understand this address to be *literal* hold that this was indeed a certain individual whom John knew. It seems to be more natural to take the words as an address to an actual lady and her children. Further, this view fits with the references to the children of the elect lady, her sister (v. 13), and her sister's children (v. 13). Also the basic structure of the greeting in verse 1 fits with the basic structure of the greeting of 3 John 1 ("To the . . . whom I love in truth"), which itself was an address to a certain individual. Finally, if the term "lady" refers to the church, then to whom does the word "children" refer? Are the "children" not included in the church? Are they somehow different from the church?

Third, those who hold the view that this is a *figure of speech* maintain that this is a reference to the church as a whole, or to a particular local church. The following points are made in support of this view. First, John states that the lady is loved not only by him, but by "all those who have known the truth" (v. 1). This would mean that she was known by everyone. However, this kind of observation would fit better with reference to a local church than an individual. Second, although John uses the singular pronoun "you," he does switch to the plural in verse 8 where he seems to be warning the lady to "Look to yourselves." But, if this was a literal woman, why would he use a plural at all? Third, the appeal to "love one another" (v. 5) makes more sense when directed to a community of believers than to a woman and her children. Fourth, the personification of the church in feminine terms is a common use in the Bible (e.g., Eph. 5:29ff where Paul develops the idea that the church is the bride of Christ; 1 Peter 5:13 where Peter uses the feminine expression of the church).

Although we may not be able to decide the issue definitively on the basis of our current information, it is clear that if this was a personal letter to a literal woman, this fact would not exclude it from the canon of Scripture. Also, it is not clear that it is a reference to an individual lady.

# 3 JOHN

*Should money be taken from unbelievers to do God's work?*

**Problem:** John claims here that the brethren took no support for their ministry from unbelievers. Yet when Solomon built the temple, he accepted gifts from Gentiles (1 Kings 5:10; 2 Chron. 2:13–16). Is it always wrong to take money from unbelievers for God's work?

**Solution:** As a rule, God's work should be supported by God's people. Those who benefit spiritually should share materially with their teachers (1 Cor. 9:1–14). On the other hand, it may offend unbelievers to turn down their gifts and place an obstacle in the way of their becoming believers. Moses did not reject gifts from Egypt (Exod. 12:25–36). Nor did Solomon reject the gifts and help of the Gentile King Hiram (2 Chron. 2:13–16) or the Queen of Sheba (1 Kings 10:10). So, while money should not be sought from unbelievers, neither should it be rejected—unless of course there are strings attached. Under no conditions should spiritual or other favors be bought by anyone.

Furthermore, it should be noted that this passage in 3 John is not prescriptive, but descriptive. It does not say "Never take money from unbelievers." It simply notes that these believers on this journey did not accept help from the heathen. No doubt they wanted to refrain from any appearance of selling the truth (cf. 2 Cor. 11:7; 1 Thess. 2:9). Rather, as it should have been, they depended on other believers to "send them forward on their journey in a manner worthy of God" (v. 6). We should not expect unbelievers to support the cause of faith.

# JUDE

*Isn't the dispute between Michael the archangel and the devil based on an apocryphal story?*

**Problem:** Jude records an account in which Michael the archangel and the devil have a dispute over the body of Moses, saying, "Yet Michael the archangel, in contending with the devil, when he disputed about the body of Moses, dared not bring against him a reviling accusation, but said, 'The Lord rebuke you!'" (v. 9). This account is not found in the OT but is considered to be found in a pseudepigraphal book (false writing) titled *The Assumption of Moses.*

**Solution:** Just because the account is not found in any OT passages of Scripture doesn't mean that the event did not occur. The Bible often cites truths from books that are not inspired but that nevertheless contain some true statements. A biblical author is not limited to citing only Scripture. All truth is God's truth, wherever it is found.

# REVELATION

*How can the Holy Spirit be seven spirits if He is one person?*

**Problem:** According to the orthodox doctrine of the Trinity, the Holy Spirit is one person, the third person of the triune Godhead. Jesus referred to the Holy Spirit as "He" (singular). But John referred to "the seven Spirits who are before His [God's] throne" (Rev. 1:4), which many commentators see as a reference to the Holy Spirit. But how can the Holy Spirit be seven spirits?

**Solution:** The Book of Revelation contains a good bit of symbolism, and this is only one example. There is similar symbolism in other portions of this book. For instance, most agree that Revelation 12:3 speaks about Satan, but he is called a "great red dragon" with "seven heads and ten horns." Here, the seven heads and ten horns are attributed to one individual, Satan. Also, speaking of the beast from the sea, Revelation 13:1 says that he has "seven heads and ten horns." The number seven symbolizes completeness, as there are seven days in a complete week.

Other symbols are used of the Holy Spirit in Scripture. For instance, He is spoken of as a dove in Mark 1:10 and is likened to the wind in John 3:8 and water in John 4:14. He is also portrayed as "tongues as of fire" in Acts 2:3. And Ephesians 1:13 says we are "sealed" by the Holy Spirit, signifying God's ownership of us and the security of our salvation.

Many Bible students believe the sevenfold nature of the Holy Spirit may derive from the reference in Isaiah 11:2, where He is called the Spirit of the *Lord*, the Spirit of *wisdom*, of *understanding*, of *counsel*, of *might*, of *knowledge*, and of the *fear of the Lord*—seven different characteristics of one and the same Spirit.

## REVELATION 16:14

### Can demons perform miracles?

**Problem:** The Bible sometimes uses the same words (sign, wonders, power) to describe the power of demons as those used to describe miracles of God (Rev. 16:14; 2 Thess. 2:9). However, a miracle is a supernatural act of God, and only God can perform such acts. The devil is a created being and has only limited power.

**Solution:** Although Satan has great spiritual powers, there is a gigantic difference between the power of the devil and the power of God. First, God is infinite in power (omnipotent); the devil (and demons) is only finite and limited. Second, only God can create life (Gen. 1:1, 21; Deut. 32:39); the devil cannot (cf. Exod. 8:19). Only God can raise the dead (John 10:18; Rev. 1:18); the devil cannot, for he merely gave "breath" (animation) to the idolatrous *image* of the Antichrist (Rev. 13:15).

The devil has great power to deceive people (Rev. 12:9), to oppress those who yield to him, and even to possess them (Acts 16:16). He is a master magician and superscientist. And with his vast knowledge of God, man, and the universe, he is able to perform "lying wonders" (2 Thess. 2:9; cf. Rev. 13:13–14). But true miracles can be performed only by God. The devil can do the supernormal but not the supernatural. Only God can control the natural laws He has established, though on one occasion He granted Satan the power to bring a whirlwind on Job's family (Job 1:19). Further, all the power the devil has is given him by God and is carefully limited and monitored (cf. Job 1:10–12).

Christ had defeated the devil and triumphed over him and all his host (Heb. 2:14–15; Col. 2:15), thus giving power to His people to be victorious over demonic forces (Eph. 4:4–11). Thus, John informed believers: "He who is in you is greater than he who is in the world" (1 John 4:4).

# Notes

1. For a more complete discussion, see Norman L. Geisler and William E. Nix, *A General Introduction to the Bible: Revised and Expanded* (Chicago: Moody, 1986), chapters 3–6.

2. See ibid., chapters 1–11.

3. For a defense of the inerrancy of the Bible by a coalition of evangelical scholars, see Norman L. Geisler, ed., *Inerrancy* (Grand Rapids: Zondervan, 1979).

4. For further discussion of this, see Norman L. Geisler, "The Concept of Truth in the Inerrancy Debate" in *Bibliotheca Sacra* (Oct–Dec 1980).

5. This is the mistake of G. C. Berkouwer, *Holy Scripture* (Grand Rapids: Eerdmans, 1975) and Jack Rogers, *Biblical Authority* (Waco: Word, 1978). Defining error as what misleads, rather than what is mistaken, they make all sincere errors unfalsifiable.

6. St. Augustine, "Reply to Faustus the Manichaean," 11.5 in Philip Schaff, *A Select Library of the Nicene and Ante-Nicene Fathers of the Christian Church* (Grand Rapids: Eerdmans, 1956), vol. 4.

7. For a proponent of verbal dictation, see John R. Rice, *Our God-Breathed Book— The Bible* (Murfeesboro, Tenn: Sword of the Lord, 1969).

8. The biblical authors include a lawgiver (Moses), a general (Joshua), prophets (Samuel, Isaiah et al.), kings (David and Solomon), a musician (Asaph), a herdsman (Amos), a prince and statesman (Daniel), a priest (Ezra), a tax collector (Matthew), a physician (Luke), a scholar (Paul), and fishermen (Peter and John). With such a variety of occupations represented by biblical writers, it is only natural that their personal interests and differences should be reflected in their writings.

9. Lennart Moller, *The Exodus Case: New Discoveries of the Historical Exodus* (Denmark: Scandinavia, 2008), 215.

10. Ibid., 216.

11. Umberto Cassuto, *Commentary on the Book of Exodus* (Jerusalem: Magnes Press, 1967).

12. See chapter 6 of Geisler and Brooks, *When Skeptics Ask* (Ontario: Victor Books, 1990).

13. See Geisler and Nix, *General Introduction to the Bible*, 241–42.

14. The "y" in the word *rbym* is normally represented by the long "i" vowel. However, since the consonant *yod* was written to represent long vowels before the vowel points were added, it is inserted here as a transliteration of the letter that would have appeared in the unpointed text.

15. Literally, "be saved."

16. John F. Walvoord and Roy B. Zuck, *The Bible Knowledge Commentary*, NT Edition (Ontario: Victor Books, 1983), 40.

17. William D. Edwards et al. "On the Physical Death of Jesus Christ," *Journal of the American Medical Society* (March 21, 1986), 1463.